VANUATU

Simon Proudman

FARFLUNGPLACES

The Far Flung Places Travel Guide to Vanuatu

© Simon Proudman.

1st Edition. 2016. All rights reserved.

1 – 2 – 5

ISBN 978-1534864313

Keep in Touch - Follow Far Flung Places on Social Media

 Blog: www.farflungplaces.net

 Twitter: www.twitter.com/farflungplaces

 Facebook: www.facebook.com/farflungplaces.net

 Pinterest: www.pinterest.com/farflungplaces

Keeping the book up to date

Things change in Vanuatu. Even if the changes are small and occur at a relaxed place, in typical island time fashion. New hotels and bungalows are built, and restaurants open and close.

Please help me in keeping this guide as up-to-date as possible. If you discover new places to eat, to stay, to visit, or find that the ones mentioned in this book have either vanished, or changed in some way, please drop me a line.

The book will be updated regulary to keep it current.

I will acknowledge all contributors, and the best updates will get a copy of the next edition of this book.

Many thanks,

Simon

simon@farflungplaces.net

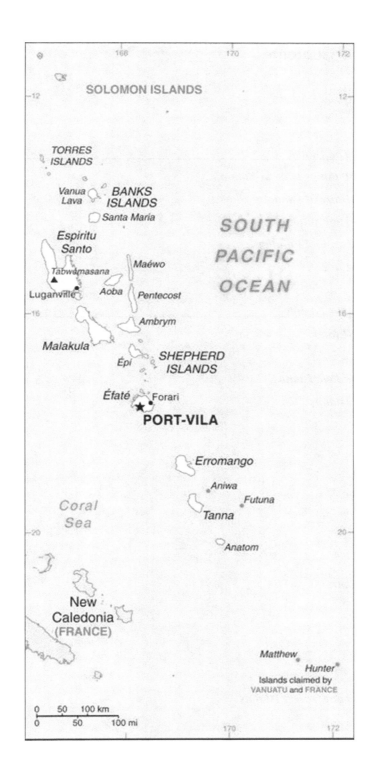

Table of Contents

Foreword

Vanuatu is one of the least visited Islands in the Pacific. Around 150,000 tourists come each year and they mainly visit Efate, Tanna and Espiritu Santo.

In a nutshell: Vanuatu is 83 Islands, 260,000 inhabitants, 120+ languages, and a democratically elected Parliament, with a mainly Melanesian population. Beautiful proud and dear people.

On our very first journey, one of the first things we noticed in Port Vila was that every person you meet in the street will look you in the eye, greet you and smile at you. As European city people, we found this amazing.

On later journeys when we travelled to the outer islands, we experienced even more warm encounters. People there would walk up and start talking to you, shake your hand and want to know where you are from.

The best encounter was on the island of Rah. I was walking along the beach when I saw two women in the sea on the reef with baskets gathering shellfish. I walked up to them to say hello and they both kissed me on the cheek.

We travelled to the Banks and Torres islands in a Twin Otter of Air Vanuatu, a tiny plane that takes only about 20 passengers. The landing strips are covered with grass and the lobby is usually as small as my living room at home.

We were usually the only tourists on the plane and on an island. The accommodation is often basic: bamboo huts with braided palm leaf roof, low beds with a thin mattress and mosquito net. Rainwater to drink, and, at the most, two hours of electricity per day (if any), no stores, no restaurants, with the food prepared by our hosts.

On the Torres Islands we were the first Dutch visitors ever according to our host. There were no cars, no electricity, no running water, and no telephone coverage. The only contact with the outside world is via the radio telephone of Air Vanuatu, for the Twin Otter plane lands there twice a week, if there are passengers.

It was also on our travels to the outer islands, that I realized in full the remoteness of Vanuatu and of the people who live there. We have met quite a few young people who have never been away from their home island. There is no TV broadcasting, hardly any radio, no newspapers and often no mobile phone coverage.

In Port Vila you can find the first signs of urbanization. Women have jobs and can join their spouse in the nakamal for a shell of kava. On the outer islands the kastom is much more part of everyday life, and this would be impossible.

There are nine active volcanoes. And when I say active, I mean very active: Mount Yasur on Tanna island is a strombolic volcano that erupts every three minutes, which you can watch from the crater. I could not leave until my throat got sore from the smoke and ash.

Beautiful and wild Malekula is mysterious and has large uninhabitable mountains. We had planned a tour to the Big Nambas tribe. We were the only visitors. The people of the village performed an impressive kastom dance for us.

The chief told us that the village is pleased when there are visitors, because it gives the young boys the opportunity to practice the kastom ceremonies that they would not have otherwise. So tourism is being appreciated.

We have visited Espiritu Santo many times. One time we decided to do the Millennium Cave Tour. We were told that is was a fine tour for people with an average condition. We considered ourselves as healthy with an average condition. We learnt that the Ni-Van have a somewhat different perception of "average condition".

In Vanuatu elderly people are strong and sturdy, they walk many miles through the bush every day, work hard in the gardens, and build their own houses. It was much harder for a European middle-aged couple, like ourselves. We finished the Cave Tour, but it took us two more hours more than planned. And we had a lot of sore muscles the next day. No need to say that this was a memorable experience that we enjoyed very much.

We have been to Pentecost to see the famous land diving. That was exciting and impressive. Most tourists returned to Port Vila right after the ceremony. But we stayed for a few days in a small village near the waterfall on the south coast. On our first evening there was a moonless crystal clear sky. That was when we saw the Milky Way for the first time in all of its glory.

During the years of travel to Vanuatu we have got to know quite a few people there. In 2013 I was asked to apply for the position of honorary consul of Vanuatu in the Netherlands, and I was officially assigned in September 2014.

Now I have started activities to promote Vanuatu in the Netherlands. My main goal is to reach people who are interested in Vanuatu for its pureness and uniqueness. People who want to discover a very special country with very special people. And discover how the world was before modern society took over.

I have so much more stories about Vanuatu and its lovely people. But I think it is much better that you go there yourself and experience your own stories.

Elly Van Vliet

Honorary Consul for Vanuatu in the Netherlands
Amsterdam. The Netherlands

Introduction

Far Flung Places travel books take you off the beaten track, to places that are full of adventure, and deserve to be better known. Vanuatu is no exception.

It has twice won the accolade of being the 'Happiest Place on the Planet' in recent years. At the same time, in a recent UN survey, the country has been identified as the most dangerous place on earth to live, due to its high exposure to natural disasters.

How can these two extremes exist in one place? You can read this book to give you some idea, but you really have to visit to find out.

Vanuatu is a place where stories happen. With active volcanoes, black magic, ancient customs and dances, cargo cults, shipwrecks and white sandy beaches, how could they not!

This book is more than just a guidebook; it also includes a small collection of in-depth stories about places and experiences in Vanuatu.

For the armchair traveller this will hopefully transport you to these beautiful islands, and make you want to learn more.

For the active traveller, we hope it will fire up your imagination to actually go there and discover Vanuatu for yourself. It will be one of the best travel decisions you ever make.

Vanuatu: The Guide

The Rom Dance in Ambrym

Where is Vanuatu?

Vanuatu is located in the South Pacific Ocean, approximately 1750 kilometers from east Australia, 500 kilometers North East from New Caledonia, and only 100 kilometers from the southern edge of the Solomon Islands.

Itineraries

One day allows a cruise ship passenger to get a great taste of Vanuatu, which should bring you back for more. See the section 'Recommendations for the Cruise Ship Passenger' on page 91.

One week will give you the opportunity to explore Port Vila and Efate, with a trip to Pele Island north of Port Vila, and an island hop to either Santo to dive the Coolidge, visit Six Million Dollar Point or swim on Champagne Beach, or Tanna for the short climb to the explosive Mt Yasur volcano.

Two weeks gives you the chance to go further afield, to include both Santo and Tanna, or to visit Pentecost, particularly if the Nagol is occurring, or on to Ambrym to visit more volcanoes and see the wood carving and ancient art of sand drawing.

Three to four weeks allows you to include some of the more remote islands in the Banks and Torres, which require a little more flexibility to reach, with great snorkeling, deserted beaches, more volcanoes and custom ceremonies, or head to the Malekula and the Maskelynes for some custom dancing, or snorkeling over hundreds of giant clams.

You cannot see all of Vanuatu in one visit, unless you are lucky enough to have six months to a year available, which means you will need to return!

Our Top 10 things to do in Vanuatu

❖ Get up close to Mt Yasur, and see lava erupting from close range at this active volcano in Tanna. Page 121.

❖ Snorkel in the Marine Reserve around Nguna and Pele, and then relax on the golden sand beaches of Pele afterwards. Page 107.

❖ Dive the SS Coolidge in Santo, one of the most spectacular, and closest to the surface, wreck dives in the world. Page 174.

❖ Wander around the colourful Port Vila markets and then sit down for a lunch and chat with the locals. Page 76.

❖ Live a Robinson Crusoe experience on the beautiful coral fringed Mystery Island. Page 133.

❖ See the ancient art of Sand Drawing in Ambrym. Page 152.

❖ Watch the Nagol land diving in Pentecost, the forerunner of Bungie jumping. Page 200.

❖ Walk amongst the Second World War debris dumped at Six million dollar point in Santo, from Coke bottles to the remains of US Army vehicles. Page 175.

❖ Get wet while watching the unique Women's water music in Gaua. Page 211.

❖ See the big, or small, Nambas perform the noisy and colourful custom dances in Malekula. Page 158.

A Short History of Vanuatu

Early History

Archaeological remains suggest that humans have lived on Vanuatu for over 3,000 years, with the early Melanesian settlers arriving from the north by canoes from Papua New Guinea and the Solomon Islands.

More settlers came from Polynesia, which today is most noticeable in the southern islands of Aniwa and Futana, where the majority of the populations are Polynesian.

Around 1200 AD Chief Roy Mata rose to become the first leader who united many of Vanuatu's islands, through both battle and negotiation.

When he died, poisoned by his brother, many of his family were buried with him, alive. Forty-six graves have been discovered of those who travelled with him to the afterlife on Retoka Island (also known as Hat Island) now a UNESCO listed site.

European Discovery

The islands reverted back to local clan leadership and independence, until the Europeans set out on their voyages of discovery.

The Portuguese explorer Pedro Fernandez de Quiros, while sailing on a voyage funded by King Philip III of Spain in May 1606, believed he had discovered the great Southern Continent when he found Santo. He named the island *Australia del Espiruti Santo* (Australia to flatter King Philip who came from the House of Austria).

He wanted to start a Spanish colony there, called New Jerusalem, although the local inhabitants were not quite as keen, attacking De Quiros and his crew.

The crew were so homesick that the colony was abandoned. What we now know as Australia was only a further seven days sailing west; if he had continued in this direction De Quiros would have landed at what is now Noosa in Queensland.

The French explorer Louis Antonie de Bougainville further explored and mapped the chain of islands in 1768, before Captain Cook, the legendary British navigator and explorer, named the islands the 'New Hebrides' as some of the scenery, if not the temperatures, reminded him of the original Hebrides, more commonly known as Scotland.

Cook landed on several islands, and was greeted with spears and rocks. The locals were not happy to welcome these foreigners into their life.

Traders and missionaries followed. Peter Dillon from Ireland discovered sandalwood, a highly prized fragrant wood, in Erromango, and started to exploit the nation's resources.

This was a great time of upheaval for inhabitants of many of the islands, as they were either kidnapped by 'Blackbirders' to work the cane fields of Australia and the Pacific islands, or were being encouraged to abandon their centuries old traditional custom beliefs and accept western religions.

British and French citizens set up farms and plantations and there was an increasing rivalry between each group over which country the islands should belong to, and become a governed colony of.

Internationally, with the scramble for colonies in Africa, tensions were high between Britain and France, often threatening to boil over into conflict.

In the last part of the nineteenth century there was a rapprochement between the two countries, resulting in joint projects such as the Suez Canal development, and the two came together to first proclaim the islands as neutral in 1878, and then in 1906 jointly decided to rule the country together, as a Condominium.

The Condominium

An interesting idea from the outset, the reality of two countries jointly ruling another with their own armies, police, judiciary, education systems and currencies often resulted in chaos and ridiculous rivalry. Rather than the Condominium, many referred to it as the 'Pandemonium'.

One example shows the somewhat crazy and wasteful nature of this arrangement. Every morning the flags of Britain and France were raised in

Port Vila, in what is now known as 'Independence Park'. A Swiss national was employed to ensure that neither the Union Jack nor Tricolor was higher.

Not surprisingly the local inhabitants, the New Hebrideans, were not allowed to acquire citizenship in either country, and were basically stateless.

The influx of American servicemen during the Second World War, when the islands became an important base against the Japanese in the Pacific war, was a trigger for change. It helped bring new ideas of equality to the islands, black and white servicemen fought together. It also started Cargo Cults in some of the more remote islands, where the sudden arrival of fantastic and modern goods from silver planes helped establish the 'John Frum' beliefs.

Protests over land rights led by Jimmy Stevens in Santo, and also in Malekula and Efate, in the 1960s, began to increase the pressure on the British and French governments to cede more control back to the New Hebrideans.

Political parties began to form, in particular the New Hebrides National party, which became the Vanaua'aku party, peacefully requesting more rights and independence.

Britain was receptive to this pressure, having gone through a period of granting many colonies independence after the end of the Second World War. The French were less keen, fearing a domino effect with their other colonies, but they reluctantly agreed at the 1977 Paris conference and a date was set for independence in July 1980.

The Coconut War

In early 1980 in Santo Jimmy Stevens and his Nagriamel political group had seen saw their chances of winning any power in the soon to be independent country end when the first national election was won by Walter Lini and his Vanaua'aku party.

Funded and supported by French settlers and elements of the French government, they declared Independence in Santo and renamed the island Vemerama; another rebellion was also staged in Tanna.

The rebels, who were mostly armed with bows and arrows, seized the airport and key bridges in Santo. The New Hebrides government asked for help from the British and French governments. Britain sent Marines to Tanna to act as peacekeepers, and was not involved in any military action.

The French refused to help, despite already having troops stationed on Santo, so the government turned to its neighbour, Papua New Guinea, who sent armed forces and helped to retake the airport.

The war came to an end after Steven's son was killed while trying to speed through a Papua New Guinea roadblock, and Jimmy Stevens and his forces surrendered.

Post Independence

The country gained full independence on 30th July 1980, took as its name Vanuatu, meaning 'Land eternal' and adopted a new flag. The new Prime Minister, Walter Lini, led the new country on a path of non-alignment, which caused upset to its previous rulers when he established relations with Libya, and became a supporter of New Caledonian independence movements.

In more recent years there has almost been a 'revolving door' at Prime Minister level, as leaders are regularly replaced as different political factions group with each other to gain power in parliament.

A big challenge to the political systems occurred in 2015 with the MP Bribery Scandal, which involved 14 Members of Parliament, including Moana Carcasses, an ex-Prime Minister himself. These MPs were given 1,000,000 million Vatu each to change their vote, and help oust the existing government. Democracy prevailed and those involved were jailed, which also brought about yet another change of government.

Cyclone Pam in March 2015 was the worst post-independence disaster to befall the young country. Sixteen people were killed, whole villages were destroyed, and the crop damage required importation of large amounts of food to avoid starvation. Tanna and Erromango were particularly hard hit, when the eye of the cyclone passed over them.

The country, with good support from international aid organisations, is rebuilding itself, and by the time you read this, most villages will have been mostly rebuilt, and most of the tourist accommodation will be operating as normal.

Yet despite natural disasters, and the parliamentary scandals and upheavals it has encountered in its recent history, Vanuatu still remains one of the most peaceful, safe and stable nations in the world.

How to get to Vanuatu

By Air

Air Vanuatu fly from Port Vila to Auckland in New Zealand, Sydney, Brisbane, and Melbourne in Australia, Noumea in New Caledonia, and Nadi in Fiji. One flight a week is operated between Santo and Brisbane.

The airline flies a modern Boeing 737-800 to most of the international destinations, and has a friendly cabin crew with superior service and generous servings of in-flight drinks and tasty food in both Business and Economy cabins.

Air Vanuatu has an excellent safety record. It operates a code share with **Qantas**, so any Qantas flights booked to Vanuatu will actually be operated by Air Vanuatu.

Virgin Blue fly direct from Brisbane to Port Vila several times a week, while **Air New Zealand** does the same from Auckland.

Air Calin and **Fiji Airways** fly to Port Vila from Noumea and Nadi respectively.

Air Niugini has recently started a once a week flight from Port Moresby to Honiara in the Solomon Islands, and then onto Port Vila.

Note that in early 2016 the runway at Port Vila airport started to break up in several places, due to damage sustained during cyclone Pam, resulting in Air New Zealand and Virgin Blue temporarily suspending flights, and Qantas to suspend its code share agreement with Air Vanuatu. Thanks to a World Bank loan, repair works were completed in mid April 2016 with most airlines resuming their services soon after.

Arriving at Bauerfield Airport in Port Vila you are welcomed into the country by a local string band, who immediately get you into a relaxed state of island time, as you wait in the queue at passport control.

By Sea

Cruise ships regularly visit Port Vila, and also Santo and Inyeug (Mystery Island). **Carnival**, **P & O**, **Royal Caribbean** and **Holland America** depart regularly from Sydney and Brisbane, while **Cunard** and **Paul Gauguin Cruises** visit in more comfort once a year.

For the real luxury traveller, both **Silversea** and **Island Escape** use small ships to explore the more remote parts of the islands on annual voyages.

Travelling around Vanuatu

Travelling by air

Air Vanuatu is the main domestic airline carrier, travelling to all destinations in the islands. Using a mixture of an ATR-72 to Santo and Tanna, and smaller De Havilland Twin Otters to the other islands, the airline will get you to some of the most remote parts of Vanuatu, often landing on grass runways.

You are limited to 10kg per person checked in luggage on the small planes to the outer islands, so pack lightly or leave luggage in Port Vila at your hotel.

Carry on is whatever can fit on your lap. There are no overhead lockers, and the carry on can include chickens and well trussed up crabs, as you may see from your fellow passengers.

This does not apply on journeys to Santo or Tanna, where the larger ATR aircraft allows you to take 20kg per person.

Flights may seem expensive, yet they are all subsidised by the Government. You can get a further 20% discount on domestic fares at Air Vanuatu office in Port Vila, if you can show you have an international return ticket on an Air Vanuatu flight. Contact Air Vanuatu on 23 848 or visit their office on the Rue de Paris in Port Vila (**T1** map, page 66).

Belair Airways have started a limited number of flights in competition with Air Vanuatu. The flights are slightly cheaper, but the schedules are not well publicised. Contact Belair on 29 222.

Unity Airlines specialise in tours to Tanna to see Mt Yasur, and to the Nagol in Pentecost. They also arrange charter flights to the outer islands. Contact Unity on 24 475.

When travelling to the outer islands it is good to check your luggage is actually loaded onto the plane. It can, and does get left behind. Air Vanuatu do have a very efficient tracking system, and, from experience, you usually will get your bag within a few days, although this is dependant on flight frequency from your departure point (some destinations only get 1 or 2 flights a week).

Flexibility in your travel plans is important; not only are many of the runways grass strips, which are prone to closure after heavy rain or bad visibility, but Air Vanuatu has a limited number of aircraft, and if one requires urgent maintenance this can cause sudden schedule changes and can delay your flight for a day or more.

This is more likely to be a risk in flights to the more remote islands, and not to Santo or Tanna, which are served by numerous flights each day.

Note that there is a 200 Vatu **departure tax** payable in cash for all domestic departures.

Travelling by boat

Air Vanuatu is often too expensive for the locals to use, and the alternative is to travel by ferry. The most common are cargo ships; these can be overcrowded, and not all of the ships are well maintained.

The best way is to go on the passenger ferry companies, **Vanuatu Ferry** (contact 26 999) and **Big Sista** (568 5225) who run regular routes from Port Vila to Santo, stopping off at Malekula, Epi and sometimes Ambrym on the way. The cost is 7,000 Vatu to go from Port Vila to Santo one way. Business class is available on Big Sista, a quieter area upstairs with better seats for 2,000 Vatu more.

Ferries can be found that travel to Erromango and Tanna from Port Vila, although the journey is not recommended due to the rough seas often-encountered en route.

To travel to Ambae and the Banks and Torres from Luganville enquire down at the harbour where the ferries depart from for the latest schedule.

Where the islands are close together, such as between Maewo and Pentecost, and between many of the Banks and Torres islands, small speedboats can be hired.

As flights are often few and far between on many of these islands, this is worth considering, although the price will be expensive unless your timing is good and you manage to share with locals making the same journey. Lack of fuel may mean the speedboats are not operational, particularly in the remote northerly islands, and life jackets may not be carried.

Vanuatu A to Z

A water musician from Gaua

Accommodation

Vanuatu has a variety of options when it comes to accommodation, from five star resorts to tiny thatched huts made of local materials.

Around Port Vila, Luganville and to a lesser extent the east coast of Tanna, cluster the highly starred, and priced, resorts with all the mod cons including spas, pools, and a huge array of leisure activities.

Of course, there are places to suit every budget, just check out the accommodation listings in each island section to see the options. Once you move off the tourist trail of Port Vila – Santo – Tanna, the choices become more limited, but also will provide you with a greater experience and understanding of life in Vanuatu.

The typical bungalow on the outer islands is made from local materials, mainly pandanus, bamboo, and coconut fronds, which make for surprisingly comfortable places to sleep.

Often with solar panels for a bit of light at night, generally not enough to read, and with either shared western style toilet or a pit toilet (western style toilets are becoming more common as the local owners realise that is what tourists want) and basic shower.

Thanks to Australian and New Zealand aid programs, you will find almost all bungalows have mosquito nets. After a tiring day swimming, walking, and exploring you will find that you go to sleep earlier after it gets dark, and also wake up earlier when the villages come alive.

Art Galleries and Exhibitions

Port Vila has the **Alliance Francaise Exhibition Space** in the centre of town next to the French Consulate. This has regular art exhibitions showcasing local artists.

In October every year there is a major exhibition with a focus on reusing everyday objects to produce new art. Artists re-use Second World War debris such as old coke bottle glass to make jewellery, drink cans for statues, and even old satellite dishes pressed into fish shapes.

At the last event one local artist inventively uses old x-rays from the hospital to produce intricate drawings that would have been carved in wood by his ancestors (see the story on page 289).

Other galleries include the **Diana Tam** gallery at Ellouk near the Erakor ferry, the **Suzanne Bastien** project space, used for contemporary art shows, and the **Michoutouchkine and Pilioko Foundation**, both on Pango road just beyond the Warwick Lagon hotel in Port Vila.

Consulates

Australian High Commission

Contact: 22 777. (**C3** map, page 66) Winston Churchill Avenue, Port Vila.

Belgian Consulate

Contact: 22 306, Rue de Paris, Port Vila.

Chinese Embassy

Contact: 23 598, Rue de Auvergne, Port Vila.

French Embassy

Contact: 22 700, (**C1** map, page 66) Lini Highway, Port Vila.

German Consulate

Contact: 22 331, Rue Rene Pujol, Port Vila.

New Zealand High Commission

Contact: 22 933, (**C2** map, page 66) Rue Pierre Lamy, Port Vila.

Philippines Consulate

Contact: 25 589, Tassiriki Park, Port Vila.

Swedish Consulate

Contact: 22 944, Lini Highway, Port Vila.

Costs and Money

Vanuatu is not a cheap destination, particularly if you just go to the tourist centres and stay in three or four star accommodation, where you will pay prices similar to those of Australian cities.

However there are plenty of options for cheaper accommodation of a good standard, and the further you stray off the well worn Port Vila – Santo – Tanna route, the better the prices and you will see and experience a lot more of what the country has to offer.

Food and drink is reasonably priced, particularly if you avoid resorts and hotels. Eating at market stalls is safe, tasty and very cheap and you get to talk to the locals.

Tipping is not part of the Vanuatu culture, and nor is bargaining (except with taxis).

Changing money

Goodies in Port Vila, with two locations on the Lini Highway (opposite the ANZ bank, and next to the Digicell Phone shop) offers the best rates by one or two percent over the banks for cash and travellers cheques, with no fees.

ANZ (**B3** map, page 66), **Bank South Pacific** (formerly Westpac) (**B2** map, page 66), **Bred Bank** (**B1** map, page 66) and the **National Bank of Vanuatu** (**B4** map, page 66) are also in Port Vila, and you can withdraw money from their ATMs.

Cirrus and Maestro network customers can access their accounts through ANZ and Bank South Pacific ATMs.

In Santo the LCM store in Higginson St is the best place to exchange cash. There are also National Bank of Vanuatu, ANZ and Bank South Pacific branches in the same main street.

Once you get to the more remote islands you need to take cash. Make sure you have small notes as the 5,000 Vatu note will be very hard to change.

Currency

Vatu is the currency of Vanuatu. It is kept relatively strong by the Reserve Bank of Vanuatu linking it to a small basket of currencies including the US$ and Euro.

Notes are printed in denominations of 200, 500, 1000, 2000 and 5000 Vatu.

Coins are in denominations of 5, 10, 20 and 100 Vatu. New lighter designs were introduced in 2015, and you will still find some of the older heavier coins that were used since independence. They are both legal tender.

As of September 2016, the current approximate exchange rates are:

1 US $ = 110 Vatu

1 Euro = 120 Vatu

1 GBP = 145 Vatu

1 AUD = 80 Vatu

1 NZD = 75 Vatu

Australian banknotes are widely accepted in shops and restaurants in Port Vila, due to the number of cruise ships that regularly call in there.

Credit cards are also accepted at most hotels, supermarkets, and up-market shops and restaurants in Port Vila and Luganville.

Custom/Kastom

Custom, spelt Kastom or Kastam in Bislama, is the traditional culture that pre-dates European contact in Vanuatu. You will come across Custom dances, stories, ceremonies, drawings and villages.

Custom villages, particularly in the remoter islands, are where the inhabitants follow traditional practices with a very limited influence of modern western ways. Some villages welcome tourists, while others are off limits to visitors.

Customs Regulations

Visitors over the age of 18 can bring into Vanuatu:

- ➢ 250 Cigarettes, or 25 Cigars, or 250 grams of tobacco
- ➢ 2 Litres of Spirits
- ➢ 2 Litres of Wine
- ➢ 9 Litres of Beer

There is a competitively priced duty free shop on entry to Port Vila, by the luggage collection. It is worth getting your duty free here, rather than at your departure point.

Spirits can be purchased for 10 USD a bottle or less, nice French wine for 6 USD and a case of Tusker beer for 30 USD. Although if you arrive late, they can sell out of items by the end of the day.

Note that the duty free on departure is strangely not competitively priced, and you are much better off purchasing at the duty free stores in Port Vila who deliver to the airport. See 'What to Buy' on page 56.

Meat, fish, dairy products, nuts and fruit cannot be brought into the country. All luggage is x-rayed on arrival, and on-the-spot fines can be incurred if you do not make an honest customs declaration.

Drink

Beer

Frank Zappa once said, that to be a real country you need to have a national airline and to brew your own beer. Well Vanuatu satisfies the first condition with Air Vanuatu, and also the second, with the best beer in the South Pacific.

You may dispute this if you have tried Vailima beer from Western Samoa (it does run a close second thanks to its German heritage), but if you have tasted the bland Fiji Bitter, and the rather metallic tasting South Pacific ales in Papua New Guinea you may agree with us.

The **Tusker** brewery, close to the airport roundabout in Port Vila, uses local spring water, and imported Czech hops to produce the islands' best seller, a lager. All around Port Vila you will see adverts in Bislama promoting the "Bia blong yumi" (the beer that belongs to you and me) and 'Mi Wantem Tusker' (I want a Tusker).

The brewery was set up by the Swedish Pripps Company in 1991, although it has changed hands since. The beer in the bottle is good, but if you can get it on draught it is outstanding. The draught version is unpasteurised, and will only last for five days from the date of brewing so you know it is going to be fresh.

There are not many places in Port Vila that do sell Tusker on draught, and this being Vanuatu, it is often not available. We recommend trying 'The Moorings', down on the Lini highway, where you can sup your beer while dangling your toes in the Pacific Ocean.

The Tusker brewery also does an OP (over proof) variety, which comes in at 7% alcohol content and is perfect for hangovers, and Tusker Lemon, which tastes like a shandy and is very much an acquired taste that we have yet to get.

The **Nambawan** brewery provides competition for Tusker with a changing variety of beers including ale, wheat beer and porter. The ale is the pick of the bunch, and can be tried on tap in a few locations including the Brewery Bar, opposite the Grand Hotel in Port Vila.

Wine and Spirits

No wine is produced in the country, but the local **Pure Spirits** produce an acceptable range of vodka, rum and other varieties. Despite their duty free prices being very reasonable, purchasing spirits in Vanuatu is expensive due to heavy local taxes; so bring a bottle or two in on your way into the country.

French and Australian wines are widely available, although again they are not cheap. The supermarkets have a good range, although the Calvos store, opposite the Grand Hotel, has the best prices for wine, particularly French, undercutting the other shops by a third or more.

Note that alcohol cannot be purchased in shops between midday Saturday and Monday morning, although is still available in bars and hotels for on premise consumption.

Kava

The choice of most Ni-Vanuatu. Cheap, from 50 Vatu a shell, and available at nakamals, the open air Vanuatu version of bars, across all the islands.

Made from the root of the kava, it has a bitter muddy taste, which few would agree is pleasant, but it has the effect of a mild narcotic. A few shells will numb your lips and throat, and relax your body.

Just as with alcohol, over use can lead to medical problems such as kidney or liver failure, but the biggest issue in Vanuatu is drinking and driving under the influence of kava.

If you want to try kava in different forms, such as kava cola and chocolate, or have developed an addiction to it and want to take some home, head to the **Kava Emporium** in Port Vila in the centre of town on the Lini Highway.

For a selection of kava bars to experience in Port Vila, go to page 80.

Mineral Water

The local water in Port Vila and Luganville is fresh and safe to drink, but if you are heading off to the islands, load up with **Vanuatu Water** mineral water from the supermarkets.

Coffee

Tanna coffee beans are flavoursome and organically farmed. If you get the chance, head out to the **Tanna Coffee Roasting Company** on Devils Point Road at Mele for a fresh cup and to watch the roasting of the beans.

Drugs

The importation or use of drugs such as marijuana, cocaine, heroin etc. is illegal and carries severe penalties. **Kava** is generally the drug of choice for most in Vanuatu.

Ecology

The country is itself a distinct eco-region, the Vanuatu rain forest, while being part of the Australian ecozone.

There are nineteen species of reptiles native to the islands, including the endangered flowerpot snake found in Efate. Bats are widespread, including three unique species. European settlers introduced cattle, dogs and pigs.

Note that there are no poisonous snakes or spiders in Vanuatu, although fire ants have recently taken hold on the Banks and Torres islands, whose sting can prove very painful, and poisonous Stonefish and Cone Shells can be found in the sea.

Economy

The Vanuatu economy is based around the three areas of tourism, food and agriculture, and financial services.

In 2013 351,000 tourists visited Vanuatu, cruise ship passengers spending just one day in port account for almost 70% of this figure. Australia provides 60% of all tourists, followed by New Caledonia with 14%, New Zealand with 9%, other Pacific nations with 8%, and Europe with 4%.

Air passengers tend to stay for 11 days or more on average, and spend over 90% of the time in the main centres of Port Vila, Santo and Tanna. The outer islands barely get any foreign visitors.

In food and agriculture, copra (dried coconut shells) and coconut oil provided 70% of income from exports in 2015, followed by cocoa at 9%, beef at 5%, timber at 2%, and kava and coffee tied at 1% each.

The export of beef has increased substantially as markets such as Japan recognise the organic qualities of the beef cattle, mainly from Santo, while coffee is growing rapidly with the increase of plantations in Tanna, where the volcanic soil helps give the coffee a distinctive taste which is becoming popular in boutique stores in Australia and in Europe.

Financial services are an important revenue area for the government. Vanuatu is a tax haven, with no capital gains tax, income tax, or inheritance tax. It does levy VAT of 12.5% on all goods and services, including financial services.

With the growing focus and pressure from western governments on cracking down on tax havens and increasing the transparency of financial transactions, this part of the economy is under threat, and it is currently under review with possibly significant changes likely.

Electricity

Vanuatu runs on 230 Volt, 50 Hz, with a three pin flat plug (similar to Australia, New Zealand and China).

Entertainment

Around Independence Day (30th July) there are many music and dance (modern and custom) events across the islands.

In Port Vila the main seafront stage often has lunchtime events, which can include music and dance. These are mostly not advertised, wander past and see what is happening.

Regular **music festivals** are held in Port Vila, including the Fest Napuan, a Pacific island event where bands come from the Solomon Islands, New Caledonia, Papua New Guinea, New Zealand and Australia (see the story on page 268). The Fest Napuan occurs towards the end of the year around September.

Port Vila has **cinemas** at the Tana Russet Plaza and an outdoor waterfront cinema at the Nambawan Café. Alliance Francaise has regular French cinema evenings at its building on the Rue Mercet next to the French Consulate, contact 22 947.

The **theatre** group Won Smol Bag, located on the roundabout next to the Tusker brewery on the way to the airport, regularly has plays, which are highly recommended. These are often then taken on tours throughout the islands. Check out their website http://visit.wansmolbag.org/ for current plays. Won Smol Bag is also behind the hit Pacific TV series about the police in Port Vila, '*Love Patrol*', which is worth grabbing on DVD from the box office. Local humour and great acting make it an entertaining show.

The Won Smol Bag group is also the home of Vanua Fire, the **fire-dancing** troupe pictured on the front of this book. Trained by Rik Hinton, an English volunteer who is also a circus performer, their spectacular show is perfect to watch on a warm night under the palm trees. They perform most nights of the week; check out visit.wansmolbag.org/vanua-fire for current performance days.

Our favourite sites to watch them are at the Mele Beach Bar on a Friday and the Coconut Palms Hotel on a Saturday. Both are free to enter, but donations for the dancers are encouraged after the show.

Festivals and Holidays

Vanuatu enjoys many public holidays. Shops mostly remain open, except at Easter and Christmas.

Independence Day, and almost the whole week that follows, is a time of great celebration. In Port Vila four or five sports grounds are turned into festival sites, with music, sport, and stalls selling food and kava for 24 hours a day. Well worth attending, although sleep is harder at this time!

Vanuatu observes fourteen public holidays:

- 1 January - New Year

- 21 February – Father Walter Lini Day

- 5 March – Custom Chiefs Day

- 1 May – Labour Day

- 5 May – Ascension Day

- 24 July - Children's Day

- 30 July- Independence Day

- 15 August - Assumption Day

- 5 October - Constitution Day

- 29 November - Unity Day

- 25 December – Christmas Day

- 26 December – Family Day

The Christian holidays of Easter, Good Friday and Easter Monday are also observed. Since these are not fixed, the dates of these celebrations vary and are announced annually.

Food

As tropical islands in the Pacific Ocean, it will come as no surprise that the **seafood** is particularly good in Vanuatu. Tuna, mahi mahi, marlin, as well as the smaller poulet fish are staples of the restaurants in Port Vila and Luganville.

Lobsters are cheap and plentiful on the more remote islands, but not in the main tourist towns, where they can be as expensive as back home.

The indigenous coconut crab is often a menu item, and considered a rare and delicious treat by the locals, although it is now on the endangered list so you should consider whether to contribute to its possible extinction.

The French influence lingers, with **baguettes** being the main type of bread available at restaurants and from bakeries, best when still warm.

The **beef**, which comes mainly from Santo, is one of Vanuatu's biggest growing exports, and with good reason. Free from injected hormones and not fed from genetically altered crops, these cows roam around the grass in Santo. The quality of the meat is now being globally recognised with expensive restaurants in Tokyo shipping in Santo beef as a delicacy

When we first went to Port Vila and went to the main markets for lunch with a local friend, he raved about how good the beef was. Admittedly the choice that day was beef or fish, and he had no understanding of why anyone would ever pay for fish. "If I want fish I go down to the water and I spear them" was his response, but the beef, well, that was worth paying for. And in Vanuatu it is fine dining at a budget price, although there is a tendency to over-cook it.

Root vegetables are staples, many dishes will come with either yam, manioc, taro or sweet potato, as well as rice to ensure you get enough carbohydrates.

Lap Lap is the standard local lunch food, and is one of the best dishes for vegetarians, a mixture of ground root vegetables and coconut milk, baked in an oven and with additional toppings added. Meat can be a topping, so vegetarians should ask first. An acquired taste, it is a filling meal.

Visit the markets wherever you travel and you will pick up seasonal fruit and vegetables at bargain prices. Whatever is in season will be available, and you may be lucky to try the sweet **pineapples**, big bags of **passion fruit** for only 100 Vatu, the huge **pamplemousse** (grapefruit), or tubs of **mangoes**. Of course you are walking or trekking in the islands you may well come across these growing wild in the bush.

For a cheap and tasty snack grab a packet of **roasted peanuts** in their shells, mostly grown on the island of Epi and on sale at the markets for 30 Vatu.

For dessert you cannot go past the locally made **Switi ice cream**. Amazing flavours of ice cream and sorbets (dependant on what fruits are in season), but we recommend the lemon, mango and raspberry sorbets, and the rum and raisin and chocolate ice creams.

The containers they come in are also incredibly useful for storage and you will see them popping up even in the most remote and unlikely locations in the islands.

Geography

Vanuatu is a Pacific archipelago consisting of 82 islands 1,300 km (830 Miles) from north to south, with 65 of the islands inhabited, and two uninhabited islands to the south, Matthew and Hunter, also subject to a claim of ownership by France.

It lies between latitudes 13 and 21 degrees south and longitudes 165 and 170 degrees east.

The size of the country is 12,274 square km (4,739 square miles) although only 4,600 square km (2858 square miles) is actual land.

In the north the country borders the Solomon Islands, in the south, New Caledonia, Fiji in the east, and Australia in the west.

Volcanic in origin, it has many active volcanoes including Yasur in Tanna, Benbow and Marum in Ambrym, Lombenben in Ambae and Gharat in Gaua, and is situated on the western Pacific ring of fire, where the Pacific plate meets the Indo-Australian plate.

Vanuatu has few natural resources, except for sandalwood forests and fishing. It imports 100% of its oil, which makes energy prices high, although wind power and solar power is slowly being implemented in the islands for more renewable, and cheaper, energy.

The use of copra, oil extracted from dried coconut skins, has resulted in a first for Vanuatu: the power generator on the island of Malekula, operated by the company UNELCO, now runs 100% on coconut oil, powering around 700 households with renewable fuel.

It has a tropical maritime climate with a temperature variation of between 28 C (82 F) in summer, and 22 C (78 F) in winter. It has two distinct seasons, the dry season from May to October, and the wet season from November to April, although it does experience rain even in the dry season, often short and powerful in duration.

Due to its location on the edge of two moving plates, Vanuatu is prone to earthquakes, with the associated risk of tsunamis. Cyclones are possible during the wet season, and Vanuatu will generally experience the effects of two to three cyclones a year. Due to it being comprised of many small islands located close together from north to south, there is a high probability of at least some islands being affected by a cyclone each year, although only rarely with the ferocity of 2015's cyclone Pam.

Health

Malaria carrying mosquitoes are present in some of the outer islands (not in Port Vila currently) so take the necessary precautions. Dengue fever outbreaks, including in Port Vila, have occurred in recent years during the wet season.

Ciguatera poisioning does occur in Vanuatu, and with reefs surrounding all the islands, where the toxins can spawn, it is a risk, a small risk but one to be aware of when eating reef fish.

When in the tropics cuts can easily become infected and turn into tropical ulcers. Make sure the wound is cleaned regularly, and obtain some antibiotics.

Pack sunscreen, getting sunburnt is extremely easy in the tropical sun.

As with most destinations, AIDS and sexually transmitted diseases are a health risk. Practice safe sex.

Note that there are no restrictions on pharmacy sales, so drugs that may require a prescription in your home country are available over the counter in Port Vila and Luganville. They are usually more expensive as there are no government subsidies on drugs, although you will find generic drugs are much cheaper than brand names.

Water is safe to drink in Port Vila and Luganville, where it is supplied by the French utility, UNELCO. In the outer islands you will find most water is captured rainwater, except in Pentecost where fresh spring water is often available.

The rainwater is generally safe to drink, depending on how it has been collected and stored, but do note that cases of giardia have occurred on some islands in 2015. If you are concerned, drink bottled water, you will need to bring this with you in the more remote islands like the Banks and Torres, where there are few shops.

The main public hospital for Vanuatu is in Port Vila, staffed by locals and Western volunteers, but is not up to western standards. There are also no ophthalmologists and the locals that can afford it generally seek treatment for most health problems in New Zealand or Australia.

For most medical complaints go to a private practice, they are expensive and a basic consultation will cost at least 7,000 Vatu, another reason to have travel insurance. There is an excellent ambulance service operated by mainly Australian and New Zealand volunteers, **ProMedical**, in Port Vila and Luganville.

Talk to your medical practitioner before you depart to be certain on what inoculations are required, and for any anti malarial treatment needed.

Health Contact Information

Port Vila Private Hospital (Tassiriki) 23 112

Port Vila Pro Medical Ambulance 25 566

Port Vila Emergency and Specialist Medical Centre 22 219

Santo ProMedical Ambulance 37 983

Santo Public Hospital (Luganville) 36 345

Tanna Public Hospital (Lenakel) 88 659

Malekula Public Hospital (Norsup) 48 410

Internet Access

Vanuatu now has three main providers; **TVL**, **Digicel** and **Telsat**, which provide various plans to households, businesses and hotels.

With the construction in 2014 of an undersea cable to Fiji connecting onto the Southern Cross cable linking Australia and the US west coast, Internet speeds and reliability have increased greatly.

Heavy rain can still disrupt Internet speeds when copper cables get flooded, but this is now a rarity compared to previous years.

Internet cafes can be found in Port Vila, Luganville and Lenakel.

Most hotels offer reasonably fast, and often free, Internet in Port Vila, Luganville and Lenakel, but outside these main centres Internet access may only be available over 3G, where available.

To give an idea of cost, currently (2016) Digicell offer 1 GB of data for 1,000 Vatu.

LGBT Travellers

The islands are, like most in the Pacific, conservative in their outlook. Homosexuality is legal, but there is no real gay scene, or bars.

However adult only resorts such as Mangoes, Irriki Island, and Breaka's, are popular amongst LGBT travellers.

Local Transport

Local transport is cheap around the urban areas in Port Vila and Luganville is cheap, with 150 Vatu for adults and 50 Vatu for children, getting you a journey across the city in the converted **mini-buses** which have room for about ten people (these have a B at the start of their number plate).

You ask for your destination before you board, and if the driver agrees, you hop in. You may not get dropped off as quickly as you may expect, as the bus driver will often drop off the passengers in order of who boarded first, even if your requested location is closer. At least it will give you a chance to see parts of the city you would not have otherwise seen!

Taxis (which have a T at the start of their number plate) are available in Port Vila and Luganville. These are generally unmetred and you will have to negotiate a fare, but it should not be more than 500 Vatu within the central parts of the urban area.

Outside of the cities you can catch a **truck**. These are utility vehicles with a cabin holding the driver and a couple of passengers, and a flat bed on which you can sit, or risk standing (beware of low branches). You can hire the whole truck, or if you have the time to wait until it fills up with passengers, share it with locals for a much cheaper fare.

Music

The island is known for its ubiquitous string bands. Guitars, ukuleles and washboards combine to produce songs about love, romance, and of course, custom stories.

You do not have to look too far to find a band performing; they are often at nakamals in Port Vila, or on the stage at lunchtime at the seafront park.

You will be even greeted by a string band on arrival at the international airport, whose tunes sooth you as you wait for your luggage to appear on the carousel.

Each of the islands has its traditional custom music, often only vocals, although it can be accompanied by the percussion of local drums, or the slit gongs and shakers of **Ambrym**, which are mesmerising.

Gaua, has its unique water music (see page 211) whereby the ladies use the water for percussion, and the harmonic vocals also include mimicking the animals of the sea. Worth travelling a long way to see. If you miss them in Vanuatu you may be lucky to see them elsewhere, as they often attend festivals in Europe and North America.

Reggae is incredibly popular. Jamaican bands tour occasionally, but the homegrown music can stand on its own feet. Local legends **Naio** from Tanna have recorded several CD's and toured overseas. Particularly recommended is the album 'New Day' from 2008. Great songs to be played while lying on the sand beneath a palm tree.

Currently **Stan and the Earth force** are incredibly popular, not just for their danceable Pacific reggae songs, but for the showmanship of their lead singer, Stan.

Music festivals are regular events on the Port Vila calendar, ask at your accommodation, or check the newspapers. In particular, the annual **Fest Napuan**, usually in August, brings together the best of local and a couple of invited international bands, including a whole night of string bands and a night of Gospel music at Sarafina park in Port Vila. Eat local foods, drink kava and dance the night away with most of the local populace. And best of all, it is free.

The best, and only, music shop with local CD's of string bands, and local favourites such as Naio, and even the odd cassette from last century, ask behind the counter if not on display, is the **Music Shop** in Port Vila on the Rue Camot, just down from the Rue de Paris.

Packing List

Some of the key things to bring with you to Vanuatu:

- Torch and a solar light if you are going to head outside of the main islands.

- Insect repellant

- Sunscreen (very expensive if bought in Vanuatu) and hat

- Wet weather gear (when it rains, it is torrential)

- Anti malarial tablets if you going to wander far from Port Vila or Luganville (check with your Doctor first). Almost all accommodation will have mosquito nets.

- Powerbank, fully charged, to provide power for your phone and camera when the solar power is not strong enough to charge them.

- Basic first aid kit.

- Sarong, for women to cover their shorts in rural villages

- Reef shoes.

- Sturdy walking boots if you are to climb a volcano.

- Snorkel and mask

- Books

- Refillable water bottle.

- Swiss Army knife.

Do not worry if you forget some of these items, both Port Vila and Luganville have many of them, albeit at much more expensive prices than you would pay back home.

Once you get to the other islands these items will be much harder to find, if at all.

Petanque

Also known as **Boule**. One of the legacies of being, at least partially, a French colony, is that Petanque is played in many places.

In Port Vila watch, or even politely ask to join in, behind the Nambawan Café on the waterfront. Most resorts will provide you with a set of balls and direct you to a spot to play for hours.

Photography

There are many opportunities for great photographs in Vanuatu, whether it is exploding volcanoes, colourful village life, beaches, or Custom dances. Ni-Vanuatu people generally do not have any problems with photographs being taken of them, but it is always polite to ask.

Rarely, often because of shyness, they may say no, respect their wishes and takes some different shots elsewhere.

There are no additional charges for photography at cultural events; this is covered in the entrance fee.

SD Cards and batteries are available in Port Vila and Luganville, but are not so easy to find in the outer islands.

If you wish to make digital prints of your photographs in Vanuatu, there is a Digital Print Shop opposite the library in Port Vila.

Politics

The Republic of Vanuatu is an independent parliamentary democracy. Elections are held every four years to choose the 52 members. The leader of the main party, or coalition of parties, is usually elected Prime Minister.

The parliament and the presidents of the six provinces choose the Head of State, the President, every five years.

Population

Vanuatu has an estimated population of 284,721 in 2016 (from the Vanuatu National Statistics Office). The population is mainly rural, although the capital, Port Vila, with 45,000 people, has a high urban population. The growth rate is approximately an annual 2%.

The local population, known as Ni-Vanuatu, is comprised of 98.5% Melanesian origin, with the small remainder being made up of Polynesian, European and Asian origins.

Life expectancy is 61 for males, and 65 for females.

Presbyterians and Anglicans make up of over 50% of the population's religion, with Catholics at 15% and traditional kastom belief at almost 8%.

There are over 110 local languages, but Bislama, a form of Pidgin English is the national language, alongside English and French. English is spoken widely, particularly in urban areas, and there are still many French speakers in both Efate and Santo.

Post

There are no postal deliveries to homes in Vanuatu. All post is kept at the post office in PO boxes for collection. The service is somewhat slow; all post arrives and departs from Port Vila.

It takes about two to three weeks to send post to Australia and New Zealand, and about four weeks to Europe and North America. If the post begins in the outer islands, you can add extra weeks onto the journey.

If you are staying in Vanuatu for a while, it is worthwhile getting a PO box, it costs 3375 Vatu for a year, at the main post office on the Lini highway, close to the markets.

Vanuatu has some of the more unlikely places for posting a letter, with an underwater post box on Hideaway Island near Port Vila, and a volcano post box on Mt Yasur in Tanna, accompanied with somewhat unique postmarks for postcards and letters sent using them (waterproof postcards are for sale on Hideaway Island).

Provinces

Vanuatu is divided into six provinces:

Malampa: Malekula, Ambrym, Paama

Penama: Pentecost, Ambae, Maewo

Sanma: Santo, Malo

Shefa: Shepherd Islands, Efate

Tafea: Tanna, Aniwa, Futana, Erromango, Aneityum

Torba: Torres Islands, Banks Islands

Responsible Tourism

Many of the remote islands do not have facilities for handling non-biodegradable waste. Try to minimise waste as much as possible, and bring back plastic bottles and other non organic waste with you to Port Vila, where it can be disposed of properly.

Most Ni-Vanuatu people are very tolerant, and forgiving of most inadvertent cultural faux pas. However please be considerate, particular when outside of Port Vila and Santo and their resorts. For women to wander through villages in bikinis or skimpy clothing is inappropriate.

Many sites, including beaches and other attractions charge local custom fees. This money goes to the traditional owners of the land, and is mostly only a token payment. Please do not try to avoid paying it, or even arguing with the owner over payment.

Safety and Security

Vanuatu is a safe country for travel, barring natural disasters. Volcanic activity, earthquakes, tsunamis and cyclones can be considered a risk.

If you do feel a large earthquake move to higher ground in case of a tsunami.

If visiting volcanoes do check out the Vanuatu Geohazards site at http://www.geohazards.gov.vu/ before you travel to a volcano to see if you can safely visit or not.

Common sense is important when travelling anywhere, and Vanuatu is no different. It is safe to walk the streets, but it is inadvisable for women to travel in buses alone after 10 PM by themselves.

The major risk in rural areas is from dogs, which can be over protective of their territory. Keep calm and back away slowly, usually an owner will come out and see what all the barking is about. Rabies itself is not currently a risk, with no cases being reported for over twenty years

There are no breathalysers used by the police and drink driving does happen, both from alcohol and kava, so be wary when on the roads at night.

Sand Drawing

A unique art on Ambrym and the surrounding islands, where old custom stories are represented by complicated drawings on sand or ash. Each drawing is completed on ash or sand without the finger being lifted from the ground.

It is more than a picture, as it was used to educate and communicate history and stories before European languages were introduced to Vanuatu. UNESCO has recognised their cultural importance by listing them in 2003 as a 'Masterpiece of Oral and Intangible History of Humanity'.

See the story on page 272 for more information.

If you do not make it to the outer islands, the Vanuatu Cultural Centre in Port Vila organises regular demonstrations of this art form.

Sport

Cricket

Vanuatu has an excellent cricket team, with the current coach, Shane Deitz from South Australia, helping drive the team to success against other ICC countries and beating Papua New Guinea recently to be the top team in the Pacific Islands.

Cricket is played during the summer, mainly on Efate, although it is starting to grow on Santo also. Matches are played at Independence Park in the centre of Port Vila, and also out at the cricket field next to the Korman Stadium. The games start at 10AM, and are worth watching, particularly the heavy hitting twenty-twenty matches.

The Vanuatu Women's team is also progressing well on the world stage, with matches played at a very high standard. If the men's matches are not on at Independence Park, chances are you will get to see a competitive women's match instead.

The best place to check for fixtures is the Vanuatu Cricket facebook page: www.facebook.com/vanuatucricketassociation.

Football

On each island you will find football (soccer) grounds of varying quality. I would recommend going to watch a match, most are local derbies and you will rarely see the locals so vocal and outward in expressing their partisan support as at a football ground. The games are played in the 'winter', when it is as hot as usual. Check out fixtures in the Vanuatu Daily newspaper or on the Vanuatu Football website www.vanuafoot.vu

Vanuatu does play well on the international stage, with hard fought matches against New Caledonia and New Zealand every year. Port Vila also has a very hotly contested league with matches every Wednesday and Saturday afternoons, often at the Port Vila Stadium.

Big money, particularly for Vanuatu, has got behind the teams and you may be surprised to see imported players from the Italian and French leagues, usually at the end of their careers, both playing and coaching teams.

See the story on page 265.

Rugby

Both rugby codes, Union and League, are followed and are growing in Vanuatu. Mainly popular, as with cricket, in Port Vila.

Ifira Island, in the harbour of Port Vila, has been a strong base for the growth of the game of Rugby Union. In the winter, matches are played at Independence Park and finals at the Port Vila stadium. The Sevens tournaments are particularly entertaining to watch and are played at the Port Vila Stadium for the finals.

For fixtures checkout: www.facebook.com/VanuatuRugbyUnion

Rugby League, only introduced in 2011, is also taking off with funding from the Australian Rugby league body. Matches are also played at Independence Park, usually during the week. Pango, on edge of Port Vila is proving to be a huge growth area for the game. Fixtures and news can be checked at www.vanuaturl.com

AFL

Australian Football League fever has only recently hit Vanuatu. There has been a big push from the AFL in Australia to export the game outside its home country. It is not football, or soccer, as the rest of the world knows it, being closer to Gaelic Football. Fun to watch, and the locals love to play it with more style and athleticism than can often be witnessed in Australia.

It has a huge following in the Port Vila suburb of Mele, and matches can be seen here and at Kazaa field near Erakor Bridge in Vila. Another winter game, fixtures and news can be found at www.aflvanuatu.com

Tennis

Resorts in Port Vila such as the Holiday Inn, Irriki Island Resort, and Le Lagon have courts, but the main and best-kept courts are at the Port Vila Tennis club beside the stadium.

It can get too hot play tennis in Vanuatu, playing in the middle of the day in summer would be almost suicidal, so plan to get out on the court in the early mornings or evenings.

If you are more of a fan of the game than a player, see if you can catch a competition. Check out the Vanuatu Tennis site at www.facebook.com/Vanuatu-Tennis-201305376645317

Golf

There are three golf courses in Port Vila. Resort standard courses at the **Le Warwick Lagon** resort, be careful of the odd wild dog on the later holes, and **Holiday Inn**, and a full 18 hole course at Mele run by the **Port Vila Golf and Country Club**, contact 22 564.

Beach Volleyball

Short mentions since Vanuatu are the world champions in Women's Beach Volleyball, and are hoping for a gold medal at the next Olympics.

The main court is situated as part of the tennis court complex by the Port Vila stadium. Check out www.vanuatuvolleyball.com for fixtures and competition news.

Street Art

Vanuatu is starting to gain some rather nice street art. Locations change, and paintings can get removed, but currently there is some rather beautiful art on the Mele community hall, by the visiting Melbourne artist Rone.

More homegrown art has appeared on the walls outside the university of the South Pacific, with some well-drawn faces and inspirational quotes, which are worth a look.

Surfing

There are great areas for surfing on many of the islands, but the breaks at Pango, on the edge of Port Vila, are considered the best by surfers from

Australia, particularly from April to June. Head out beyond the coral and ride the waves.

Boards can be rented from the local shop there at times. Beware that there are dangerous rips in the area, and you must be a strong swimmer to surf there. Launamoa on Pele, a small island off the north coast of Efate, is also becoming popular amongst surfers.

Ambae Island is surfing's newest Vanuatu frontier, when, weather dependent, great waves can be surfed outside of the reef. We met one surfer from Australia, who described the waves as some of the best he had ever ridden, although he had tremendous problems (and cost) getting his board to the island on the small Twin Otter plane.

If you get the chance, you can also surf down the Yasur volcano in Tanna. An unusual and exhilarating experience (see the story on page 250).

Telephones

The international code to dial Vanuatu is **+678**. In this book the numbers shown are the numbers to dial when within Vanuatu, so to ring Nonda guesthouse in Waterfall on Pentecost Island, you would call 547 3071 within Vanuatu and +678 547 3071 to call from overseas.

To dial out from Vanuatu to your home country, enter 00 first and then your country code.

Within Vanuatu there are two main mobile phone networks. **TVL**, the French incumbent, and **Digicel**, the low cost operator founded by the Irishman Denis O'Brien initially in Jamaica, before expanding in the Pacific Islands.

TVL have lifted their game considerably once Digicel provided competition, and now there is little to choose between the two networks.

In some remote islands you may find you are closer to a TVL or a Digicel transmitter, and often the islanders carry two phones to ensure they can stay in contact as they move around.

There are tourist specials, costing approximately 1,000 Vatu which will give you a sim card pre loaded with calls (including cheap international rates) and data which can easily be topped up at small shops wherever there is mobile coverage.

Time

Vanuatu is eleven hours ahead of Greenwich Mean Time (GMT) and one hour ahead of Australian Standard Time (AST).

There is no daylight saving time.

Travel Insurance

Get some. You are crazy to travel in Vanuatu without comprehensive travel insurance including **air evacuation**. If you needed emergency evacuation, the cost would be in excess of US$60,000.

Hospitals or local clinics will patch you up if you are in need of minor help, although wait times will be long.

Visa Requirements

Vanuatu encourages tourism; therefore entry is not an issue for citizens of most countries.

A recent agreement with the European Union (15th December 2015) allows all Schengen Agreement countries to stay without a visa for 90 days, in any 180-day period.

Visitors from most other countries including Australia, New Zealand, United Kingdom, USA, Canada, Switzerland, Russia, China and India are allowed to stay without a visa for 30 days.

If you are not from any of these countries check to see visa requirements at: http://vanuatutravel.info/index.php/en/travel-services/permits-and-immigration

Note that an onward or return ticket is required for entry to Vanuatu, and a minimum of six months validity before expiry for passports.

Visa Extensions

Extensions can be granted via the Immigration Service office in Port Vila, upstairs in the building opposite the Vanuatu Tourist Office on the Lini Highway.

The costs are:

6,000 Vatu to extend your stay up to 120 days.

12,000 Vatu to extend your stay up to 210 days.

18,000 Vatu to extend your stay up to 365 days.

Proof that the applicant has funds equivalent to 40,000 Vatu per month of the extended stay will be required, alongside a copy of your onward air ticket, and details of where you will be travelling.

Volunteering

A great way to experience Vanuatu, help make a difference, and immerse yourself in its culture.

In Australia contact Australian Volunteers for International Development (AVID) for longer assignments (usually a year or more), and Australian Business Volunteers (ABV) for three to six month assignments.

In New Zealand contact Volunteer Service Abroad (VSA).

In the UK contact VSO.

In Japan contact JICA.

In Canada contact CUSO.

Globally the following organisations require volunteers in different areas:

Red Cross, Care, Oxfam, ProMedical, and Lattitude (for 17-25 year olds).

What's On?

To learn about events, upcoming sports fixtures, concerts and the latest news, buy a copy of the English language **Vanuatu Daily**, on sale from street vendors in Port Villa and Luganville, or the weekly Anglo-French **Vanuatu Independent,** on sale at the weekend.

On social media the **Yumi Toktok Stret** www.facebook.com/groups/ yumitoktok on facebook is a great resource for local events, as well as seeing the latest concerns and occasional conspiracy theory, for social media users in Vanuatu. They have recently added a newspaper also.

The **Vanuatu Tourist Office** and their provincial counterparts are also a great source of information.

What to buy

There are some great souvenirs that you can buy in Vanuatu. Woodcarvings are particularly distinctive (see page 58) whether you want a mask, small figure, or and you may even want to get your very own Tam-Tam for your garden or living room! The larger ones are heavy and difficult to get home, unless you are on a cruise ship.

Check all wooden items for borer holes, else you may have the choice of having them taken from you and destroyed or paying for fumigation at customs on returning to your country, particularly in Australia and New Zealand.

Woven pandanus leaf bags and mats are popular and, as with the carvings, can be purchased from Custom villages you may visit, or in Port Vila at the **Hibernian marketplace** (**S2** map, page 66), opposite Bank South Pacific on the Lini Highway, or at the Vanuatu Handicraft market (**S6** map, page 66) on Wharf road.

It is also worth going to the local art exhibitions at the **French Cultural Centre**, opposite Sound Centre Duty Free on the Lini Highway. The art shown there, including local carvings and more modern offerings, are for sale at the end of the exhibition.

And there is Duty Free. It is worth buying before you fly in town, as the Duty Free store at the airport has a limited selection and is often double the price of the stores in Port Vila. The best places to pre-order are **Vanuatu**

Wine and Spirits, **Fung Kuei** and the **Sound Centre Duty Free**, all on the Lini Highway.

The duty free needs to be ordered at least 24 hours before your flight, and you pick it up after you pass through passport control at Bauerfield Airport.

Cruise passengers are the exception to the rule, as they can pick up and take away duty free at the point of purchase. They are not allowed to open or consume the duty free until back on board the ship. Depending on the cruise operator, alcohol may be taken off you when re-boarding and returned to you before you dock at your homeport.

You can also buy wine and spirits to drink while you are on the islands at the duty free shops, at the **Au Bon Marche supermarket**, and also at the specialist retailer, **Libation**, on Parliament Rd. Duty at least doubles the cost of wine and spirits, but it still considerably cheaper than buying at a hotel restaurant.

What to Wear

Weather conditions are warm to hot all year round, except in winter (June to August) when it can get quite cool at night, so pack summer clothes and a jacket for winter, or for climbing volcanoes.

Outside of the major tourist areas it will cause offence to the locals if women wear skimpy clothing, or bikinis. These are fine on the beach but are considered innappropriate elsewhere.

When to go

Vanuatu has a warm tropical climate, and can be visited all year round.

Best time to visit

The coolest and most pleasant times to visit are from April to October, during the country's warm winter, with low rainfall and low humidity.

The Worst time to visit

The worst time to go is December to March, when the humidity is at its highest, and the rainy season can cause flooding. This is also the cyclone season.

Wood Carving

Most islands in Vanuatu have some specialist wood carving skills, quite distinct from one another. From the spirit figures of Malekula, the human heads of Tanna, and perhaps the most well known, the Slit gong, or Tam Tam figures from Ambrym.

The streets of Port Vila is one of the best places to see some great carvings, Tam Tams are sited at many places. Some of the best are outside the Air Vanuatu offices and the ANZ bank.

Other great places to see wood carvings are at the Vanuatu Cultural Centre and the Alliance Francaise Cultural centre in the centre of Port Vila, which has many art exhibitions throughout the year.

To buy, have a look at the **Hibernian market**, the **Vanuatu Cultural Centre**, and the **Handicrafts market** on Wharf Road in Port Vila. In Malekula the handicrafts centre in Lakatoro has a great selection of local work.

If travelling around the islands you should ask the owners of your bungalow, and you will be directed to the local carvers or artists, who will produce an impromptu exhibition of their current stock.

See the story on page 253.

Vanuatu: The Islands

Flying over the Banks and Torres Islands

Port Vila (Efate)

As the capital and main entry point to Vanuatu, you are going to inevitably visit Port Vila. On the south eastern corner of the island of Efate, the majority of tourists, those coming ashore for day visits from the huge cruise ships that arrive several times a week, never get any further than the main city.

Even though there is a lot more to Vanuatu than Port Vila, it is still an interesting city to visit. Most inhabitants are drawn from the outer islands, looking for work and riches, along with the expats working for aid agencies, running local businesses, or who have just come looking for a quiet Pacific island to retire to.

Port Vila has some of the best food, shopping and entertainment to be found on the islands.

Getting to Port Vila

By Plane

International and domestic flights arrive at Bauerfield airport on the northern edge of Port Vila. Airlines that fly to the airport include the nation's carrier **Air Vanuatu** (which code shares with Qantas) from Sydney, Brisbane, Melbourne, Noumea and Honiara, **Virgin Blue Australia** from Sydney and Brisbane, Air Fiji from Nadi, Solomon **Airlines** from Honiara, **Air Calin** from Noumea, **Air New Zealand** from Auckland, and **Air Niugini** from Port Moresby (due to start in 2016).

The terminal is fairly basic, with a few shops including a small duty free outlet (fairly expensive, for where to buy see the section on Duty Free on page 56). For business class passengers there is a small lounge available to you on departure when you have passed Passport control.

Map of Port Vila and Surrounds

Taxis will transfer you to your hotel for a fixed price, see the board positioned as you leave the terminal, for a fare of between 2000 and 4000 Vatu depending on location.

Alternatively Adventures in Paradise (Phone +678 25200) and Melanesian Tours (Phone +678 26847) arrange pickups and drop offs for most hotels for around 1200 Vatu per person, arranged through your hotel on booking.

If you have not got too much luggage and want to save money, catch a <u>bus outside the Domestic terminal</u> for 200 Vatu into the centre of Port Vila.

By Cruise Ship

Outside of the Caribbean, Port Vila is one of the few places in the world where more tourists arrive by boat than by plane. In 2014 230 cruise ships arrived, bringing in over 250,000 passengers.

The cruise ships dock at the terminal on Wharf Road, which is a 45-minute walk into town, and not the prettiest introduction to Port Vila.

With limited time you are far better off getting a water taxi for approx 1000 Vatu per person right into the heart of the city, or jumping into a crowded bus (an adapted transit van) for 500 Vatu per person.

If you have not booked a tour on board the ship, you can haggle with the bus or taxi drivers for an island tour, this should cost approximately 10,000 Vatu for the vehicle.

By Yacht

Vanuatu is fast becoming a popular stop off for round-the-world adventurers and yacht owners in Australia and New Zealand.

All yachts are required to undergo formal customs clearance, see the following link for the latest government requirements:

http://customsinlandrevenue.gov.vu/index.php/en/travellers/yacht-clearance

For more information on yachting around the islands, download the booklet 'All ports lead to Vanuatu'.

Written by New Zealand authors Anna and Eric Simmons and funded by VSA, New Zealand Aid, it lists anchorages and provides vital navigation, tide timetables, marine services by port, as well as tourist information in an entertaining manner suitable even for non-yachties.

Download it for free at:

https://issuu.com/vanuatucruising.info/docs/all_ports_lead_to_vanuatu

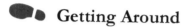 # Getting Around

The city is small; a little over 44,000 people live here according the last census in 2009. This makes it easy to walk around the harbour and the central business district with its shops and restaurants.

Keep an eye out for uneven pavements and the occasional unpaved drainage channel designed to trip you up.

Buses are everywhere, though not resembling a bus as you may expect in first world country, red double deckers they aren't. They are converted transit vans, and you will recognise them as they all have a red 'B' on their number plates.

They are a good way to travel, cheap, 200 Vatu (Children 50 Vatu) for any trip within the city, pushing out to double that if you wish to go as far as Pango or Mele.

You never know whom you will bump into, almost everybody takes the bus, and we have bumped into politicians, Olympic athletes and well-known local musicians while travelling around Vila.

There are a couple of official bus stops in Vila, one outside the Bank South Pacific, the other outside of Air Vanuatu, but in reality you just stick out your hand, or catch the eye of the driver to hail a bus.

You tell the driver your destination and if he is going that way, he will say yes and you jump on. Bear in mind the last passenger to join usually gets the lowest priority in reaching their destination, so it can be a good way to see many parts of Vila that you would not normally come across, in an unhurried fashion.

The buses are in varying states of repair with sliding doors that often do not work. Luckily you cannot go too fast in them thanks to the huge volume of traffic clogging the streets of Vila.

They are safe to travel on, except late at night when it is not recommended for single women to travel alone, and there is also the added risk that the driver might have spent a few hours at his local nakamal drinking kava, which substantially affects driving ability.

Taxis are also easy to find. They can be recognised by the 'T' on their number plates. The cars can also be in poor state of repair.

Except from the airport, where fares into the city are fixed, the cost of a journey is hard to predict, with the driver often quoting a ludicrous fare if he thinks you are a cruise ship passenger, or a bit gullible. You need to negotiate to get the fare you are happy with, but generally most rides around Vila should not be more than 500 Vatu.

The central area is also known as '**Numbawan**', with the next suburb south known as '**Numbatu**', and '**Numbatri**' is next to the first lagoon. The names date back to the Second World War, when the Americans built three radar stations #1, #2, and #3.

Car Hire

Some of the global players are in Port Vila, along with some local companies.

Note, World Car Rentals do good weekend specials, effectively charging you one day's rental from Saturday morning to drop off first thing Monday morning.

Europcar:	26 517
World Car Rental:	26 515
Avis:	22 497

Budget:	23 170
Discount Rentals:	23 242

Thanks to the US Millennium Challenge, money was provided to pave the ring road round the entire island of Efate. Unfortunately not much has been spent on the roads of Port Vila, which are potholed and often flooded after rain due to inadequate drainage.

Vanuatu drives on the right side of the road. During early colonial times the British and French were reluctant to cede to the other's custom and either side was permissible for a while. Luckily there were few cars on the road at this time.

This was eventually resolved with the decision about which side of the road to be used settled by the position of the steering wheel on the next car that arrived on the island. It was French.

By Bike

Mountain bikes are a great way to get around, if you are fit. With a bike you can head to Mele and the Cascades, grabbing a bite to eat at the Mele Beach Bar, before popping into the Secret Garden and heading back before nightfall. It is recommended not to drive at night.

For a longer trip take a tour around the island. Clems Hill, on the west of Port Vila beyond Mele, would be worthy of inclusion in the Tour De France mountain climbs, but if you can get the bike up there, it is long slow drop towards Havannah Harbour and then North. Alternatively head east out of Port Vila and you will encounter mainly flat going around the island, until the climb to Clems Hill and a fast ride back into the city.

Hiring a bike for a few days is a great way to travel around the island, and there is very little traffic outside of Vila.

EcoTours (Contact: 25 299 ecotour@vanuatu.com.vu) come highly recommended. Pascal and his team have new Italian Lombardo bikes, with very comfortable saddles.

They have no shop but will deliver to your accommodation and the bikes include helmets, locks and a map. Cost is 2,500 Vatu per day.

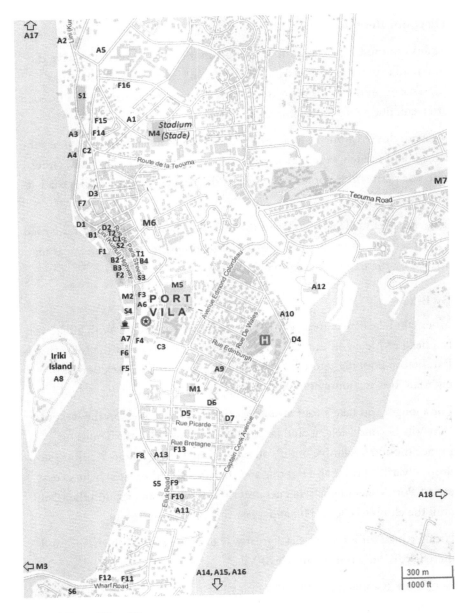

Map of Central Port Vila

Central Port Vila

Accommodation
A1 Travellers Budget
A2 Fatamaru Lodge
A3 Moorings Hotel
A4 Chantilly's
A5 Hibiscus Motel
A6 City Lodge
A7 The Grand Hotel
A8 Iriki Resort
A9 Coconut Palms
A10 Mangoes
A11 Breadfruit
A12 Holiday Inn
A13 Kaiviti Motel
A14 Breakas Resort
A15 Le Lagon
A16 Erakor Resort
A17 Hideaway Resort
A18 Eratap Resort

Food
F1 Nambawan Café
F2 Jill's Café
F3 Au Peche Mignon
F4 Brewery Bar
F5 Waterfront Bar
F6 Le Café Du Village
F7 Flaming Bull
F8 Golden Point
F9 Spice
F10 L'Houstalet
F11 War Horse
F12 Kanpai
F13 Krishna
F14 Harbour View
F15 Kesorn's Thai
F16 Nambanga

Drink
D1 Anchor Inn
D2 Voodoo Bar
D3 Shefa Bayview
D4 Maewo Seaside
D5 Reynold's
D6 Chiefs
D7 Ronnie's

Banks
B1 Bred
B2 Bank South Pacific
B3 ANZ
B4 Vanuatu National

Consulates
C1 France
C2 New Zealand
C3 Australia

Places
M1 Cultural Centre
M2 Markets
M3 Cruise Ship Terminal
M4 Football Stadium
M5 Independence Park
M6 War Memorial
M7 Korman Stadium

Shopping
S1 Tana Russet Plaza
S2 Hibernia Market
S3 Post Office
S4 Au Bon Marche #1
S5 Au Bon Marche #2
S6 Handicraft Centre

Travel
T1 Air Vanuatu Office

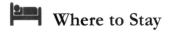 Where to Stay

Travellers Budget Motel. Stade (* FFP Recommended)

Contact: 23 940   www.thetravellersmotel.com

Price: 9,800 Vatu per room

(**A1** map, page 66) A friendly place with a nice pool and at a reasonable price in expensive Port Vila.

Comfortable beds, great breakfasts and outdoor areas to mingle with your fellow travellers. Jack and Janelle will help with tours around town, as well as to the other islands.

The Grand Hotel. CBD (* FFP Recommended)

Contact: 28 882   www.grandvanuatu.com

Price: 22,000 Vatu + per room

(**A7** map, page 66) Formerly the Sebel, the Grand is a 4 star hotel with most rooms overlooking the harbour. Great service, nice food at the restaurant and a small pool to relax in (it could do with a little bit of shade though).

Friday night happy hours on the top floor bar, Hemisphere, are a great place to watch the sunset over the harbour. The hotel also has a casino attached (for the occasional gambler you should grab the lunch special for a 1,000 Vatu, which gives you free casino chips, and then see if you can win back the cost of your lunch at the blackjack table).

Warwick Le Lagon. Numbatri (* FFP Recommended)

Contact: 22 313   warwickhotels.com/le-lagon-resort

Price: 22,000 Vatu + per room

(**A15** map, page 66) A resort facing both the first lagoon and Erakor Island. Three layers of pools, with a swim up bar, make it a great place to relax, but not too far from the rest of Port Vila. It was the hotel used by Princess Anne when she visited Vanuatu in 2014.

Sailing, kayaks, a large golf course and a giant chessboard are provided for guests, and the restaurant, '*Wild Ginger*' does serve very tasty food, although it is expensive.

The landing stage for the ferry out to Erakor Island is beside the hotel.

Eratap Resort. Eratap (* FFP Recommended)

Contact: 35 560   www.eratap.com

Price 50,000 Vatu+ per room

(**A18** map, page 66, and page 61) Thirty minutes from Port Vila is this beach side luxury resort. Twelve very comfortable bungalows make the resort uncrowded. Good and imaginative meals, and all the resort facilities you could expect.

Many activities are included, including fishing and tours to the local village. Free daily shuttle into Port Vila for your fix of urban life, and airport transfers (helicopter transfers from the airport can be arranged at cost).

Children only allowed during specified 'family weeks' (based on Australian school holidays) when there are some great activities, some with Bear Grylls-like adventures in the Vanuatu bush.

Coconut Palms. Numbatu (* FFP Recommended)

Contact: 23 696   www.coconutpalms.vu

Price: 10,000 Vatu + per room

(**A9** map, page 66) Friendly hotel with the cheapest bar in Port Vila.

Cosy rooms with a large pool, and themed evenings where you can get cheap pizza, eat Melanesian feasts, tap your foot to some reggae or watch the Fire Dancing on a Saturday night.

Just up from the Australian High Commission.

Chantilly's on the Bay. CBD

Contact: 27 079   chantillysonthebay.com

Price 18,000 Vatu+ per room

(**A4** map, page 66) A bit of an institution in Port Vila, the hotel was the number one place for businessmen before the Grand Hotel was opened.

Rooms have been recently refurbished, and are comfortable and quiet, albeit expensive. The restaurant has good views but the food does not make it a compelling place to eat.

The latest addition though, the Banyan Beach Bar, is a hit. The beanbags on the beach, and some good happy hour deals, make it a top spot to sip a cocktail and watch the sunset.

City Lodge. CBD

Contact: 26 826   www.citylodge.com.vu

Price: 5,000 Vatu + per room

Cheap small rooms with reasonable wi-fi. Opposite the market, a little noisy, but OK for a quick stopover before heading elsewhere.

Erakor Island Resort. Erakor

Contact: 26 983   erakorislandresort.com

Price: 25,000 Vatu + per room

(A16 map, page 66, and map on page 61) Occupying the entire Erakor Island is this refurbished resort. It had fallen into disrepair, but its new owners are updating and repairing it. Rooms are either facing the garden or over the ocean. Quiet and relaxing, particularly after dark when the gentle lap of the sea sends you to sleep.

No pool, but you have shallow water outside your door, and kayaks, boats, snorkels are all available for guests. Great Sunday barbeques, and activities every night of the week.

Ferry departs from next to Le Lagon resort. Day visitors are welcome with 1,000 Vatu admission, to be spent on food and activities.

Fatamaru Lodge. Fatamaru Bay

Contact: 23 456   www.fatumaru.com

Price 16,000 Vatu + per room

(A2 map, page 66) Quiet spot with access to the harbour and free use of kayaks and other watercraft. Comfortable rooms with kitchens and a fruit filled breakfast. Family friendly.

Moorings Hotel. Fatumaru Bay

Contact: 26 800   www.mooringsvanuatu.com

Price 12,000 Vatu + per room

(A3 map, page 66) Located on the edge of the harbour this is more of a flashpackers' hotel. Small rooms with thin walls, yet with a great view onto the harbour, and only ten minutes walk from the CBD attracting a younger crowd.

One of the best bars in Port Vila, with Tusker Draft on tap, and basic but filling meals. A busy and popular nightclub, run by the Moorings, is next door.

Iriki Island. Iriki

Contact: 22 338   warwickhotels.com/le-lagon-resort

Price: 30,000 Vatu + per room

(**A8** map, page 66) The premier resort island in Port Vila harbour, the home of the British High Commission. Restaurants, music and kava nights, kayaks, boats, several pools located across the island and nice bungalows facing the harbour towards Port Vila.

The ferry out to the island is located next to the Grand Hotel. It has just reopened after damage caused by cyclone Pam, with a multi-million Vatu refurbishments and a new casino. No children are allowed to stay in the accommodation.

Day trips cost 1,500 Vatu per Adult, 500 Vatu per child, payable before you board the ferry. The money can be spent on food or activities on the island, which makes for a good day out. Children are permitted for day trips only as long as families stay at the pool on the western side of Iriki and do not use the main hotel facilities.

Hideaway Island. Mele

Contact: 23 963   hideaway.com.vu

Price: 22,000 Vatu + per room (Dorm beds from 3,750 Vatu)

(**A12** map, page 66, and page 61) The last of the three islands that you can stay at in Vila. The best snorkeling in the area, along with some great dive spots nearby, with a dive shop on the island. And of course, there is the underwater post office to swim out to and post your letter.

Comfortable accommodation and cheap and tasty food make this a fun small island getaway. The ferry departs from next to the Mele Beach Bar.

Day visitors are welcome, with a charge of 1,000 Vatu admission, to be spent on food and activities.

Kaiviti Motel. Numbatu

Contact: 24 684   www.kaivitimotel.com

Price: 12,000 Vatu + per room

(**A13** map, page 66) Popular with volunteers, great position close to the Au Bon Marche supermarket, and a short walk into the CBD.

Older rooms in need of refurbishment, but the price reflects that, and there is a nice pool.

Breadfruit Apartments. Numbatu

Contact: 754 7147   www.apartmentsportvila.com

Price 8,000 Vatu + per room

(**A11** map, page 66) Tucked away in a quiet side street from Au Bon Marche supermarket, these five quiet self-contained units are ideal for longer stays and are reasonably priced. Facilities include a small pool , car parking, and barbeque area

Mangoes. Nambatu

Contact: 24 923   www.mangoesresort.com

Price 19,000 Vatu + per room

(**A10** map, page 66) Boutique resort set amidst tropical gardens. Some rooms have their own private pool, as well as three larger pools to share with the other guests. Perfect for couples, as no children are allowed. Nice, but pricey restaurant. Big breakfasts and yoga sessions are included in your room price.

Breakas Beach Resort. Pango

Contact: 25 884   www.breakas.com

Price 12,000 Vatu+ per room

(**A14** map, page 66) Wake to the waves crashing in on Port Vila's best surfing beach. Adults only and a little way from the rest of town.

The only drawback is the somewhat inflated prices at the restaurant.

Hibiscus Motel. Stade

Contact: 24 289   vilahibiscus.com

Price: 3,000 Vatu + per room

(**A5** map, page 66) One of the cheapest hotels in Vila. Basic rooms, with road noise. We stayed a few nights but the lack of sleep meant it could not be a long-term option.

Holiday Inn Resort. Tassiriki.

Contact: 22 040   vanuatu.holidayinnresorts.com

Price: 24,000 Vatu + per room

(**A12** map, page 66) The refurbished Marriott has a good position next to the Second Lagoon set over 60 acres. Tropical gardens surround the pool and the dining areas. You have the option of staying in over water bungalows.

Great kids club, and all the features that you could expect from a resort, plus a casino

Malampa Travel Lodge. CBD

Contact: 23 137   Price: 3,000 Vatu per room

Olympic Hotel. CBD

Contact: 22 464   Price: 8.500 Vatu + per room

Shefa Guesthouse. CBD

Contact: 25 110   Price: 2,000 Vatu per person

Tafea Guesthouse. CBD

Contact: 25 412   Price: 2,000 Vatu per room

Aquana Beach Resort. Eratap

Contact: 551 8060   Price: 30,000 Vatu + per room

Coral Motel and Apartments. Fatumaru Bay

Contact: 24 755   Price: 7,000 Vatu + per room

Island Breeze Apartments. Fatumaru Bay

Contact: 7763 774   Price: 6,000 Vatu + per room

Benjor Beach Club. Mele Bay

Contact: 26 078   Price: 8,500 Vatu + per room

Island Magic Resort. Mele Bay

Contact: 29 015   Price: 14,000 Vatu + per room

Melanesian. Numbatu

Contact: 22 150   Price: 9,000 Vatu + per room

Paray Lodge. Nambatu

Contact: 552 6289   Price: 4,000 Vatu per room

Pasi Lodge. Nambatu

Contact: 24 840   Price: 3,000 Vatu per room

Poppy's on the Lagoon. Numbatu

Contact: 23 425   Price: 15,500 Vatu + per room

Terraces Boutique Apartments. Numbatu

Contact: 24 923   Price: 18,000 Vatu + per room

Tradewinds Resort. Numbatu

Contact: 772 7018   Price: 8,000 Vatu + per room

Vanuatu Holiday Hotel. Numbatu

Contact: 29 930   Price: 8,000 Vatu per room

Whispering Coral Bed and Breakfast. Numbatu

Contact: 26 505   Price: 5,000 Vatu + per room

Pacific Lagoon Apartments. Numbatri

Contact: 23 860   Price: 13,000 Vatu + per room

Blue Pango Motel. Pango

Contact: 775 0085   Price: 3,000 Vatu per room

Conquistadors Resort. Pango

Contact: 775 5394   Price: 12,000 Vatu + per room

Treetops Lodge. Pango

Contact: 22 944   Price: 4,000 Vatu + per room

Vale Vale Beachfront Villas. Pango

Contact: 23 528   Price: 40,000 Vatu + per room

Angelfish Cove Villas. Paradise Cove

Contact: 557 7034   Price: 15,500 Vatu + per room

Coco Beach Resort. Paradise Cove

Contact: 772 2200   Price: 14,000 Vatu + per room

Koyu Apartments. Paradise Cove

Contact: 774 6173   Price: 19,000 Vatu + per room

Paradise Cove Resort. Paradise Cove

Contact: 25 701   Price: 22,000 Vatu + per room

Le Maison Du Banian. Second Lagoon

Contact: 535 7495   Price: 15,000 Vatu per room

Starfish Cove. Second Lagoon

Contact: 28 160   Price: 18,000 Vatu + per room

Sunset Bungalows. Second Lagoon

Contact: 29 968   Price: 12,000 Vatu + per room

Tropicana Lagoon. Second Lagoon

Contact: 772 2202   Price: 20,000 Vatu + per room

Vila Chaumieres. Second Lagoon

Contact: 22 866   Price: 11,000 Vatu + per room

Pacific Paradise Motel. Tassiriki

Contact: 28 989   Price: 3,500 Vatu per room

¶¶ Where to Eat

You are spoilt for choice in the nation's capital. Most hotels and resorts have their own restaurants, some are great quality and value — Coconut Palms deserves a mention here — some less so, but do get out try some of the great food options around Port Vila.

L'Houstalet (22 303) – (**F10** map, page 66) A French institution in Nambatu, opposite Au Bon Marche supermarket, being here for over forty years. Has a reputation for obscure dishes such as stuffed flying fox, but we kept going back for the pizza, beautifully made at a reasonable price.

Nambawan Café (771 4826) – (**F1** map, page 66) on the seafront. Standard café fare with an unbelievable vista. See the boats come in and out and enjoy the Port Vila sunset. Free Internet with a purchase.

A highlight is its regular weekly movies. Check to see what is showing here, www.nambawan.com/#moonlight . There is nothing to beat watching a good movie with the southern stars above, a glass of wine, and the harbour behind the screen.

Waterfront Bar and Grill (23 490) – (**F5** map, page 66) At the start of the hill up to Numbatu, a favourite of the yachties. Its seafood platters are recommended. Go at lunchtime and get to visit the salad bar as often as you want, with your meal.

Harbour View Chinese Restaurant (23 668) – (**F14** map, page 66) Overlooking Fatumaru Bay is the very popular Chinese. Its spicy crab is worth a mention, as are all its fish dishes. Book ahead for a table with a view.

Kesorn's Exotic Thai Restaurant (773 1751) – (**F15** map, page 66) Above the Moorings Hotel, near Fatumaru Bay, Kesorn's adds spiciness to local food, its Ginger Beef is a very popular dish, and the Tom Yum soup will clear your sinuses. The Thursday all you can eat buffet for 2,200 Vatu per person is highly recommended.

Le Café Du Village (27 789) – (**F6** map, page 66) Next to the Grand Hotel, views over the water and reasonably priced French inspired menu. Good vegetarian options, and the breakfasts are recommended.

Jill's Café (25 125) – (**F2** map, page 66) In the main street before ANZ Bank is this value for money café. Great for a big breakfast or burger for lunch. Also has a book swapping facility.

Chill – (22 578) - (**S4** map, page 66) Family restaurant next to the Au Bon Marche supermarket. Pizza, burgers and ice cream at a reasonable price in air-conditioned comfort.

The Markets – (**M2** map, page 66) Unbeatable value, at the very back of Port Vila market. Virtually every stall offers beef, chicken or fish, with rice, root vegetables and salad for 500 Vatu. Santo beef is an expensive luxury exported to Japan, here it is a bargain. Ask for it to be cooked the way you like it, or it may come out rather well done.

Sit at the shared wooden tables and chat with the locals, it may prove to be the most interesting meal you have in Port Vila. Get there early, as even by 1PM many stalls have run out of popular dishes.

Au Peche Mignon (27 271) – (**F3** map, page 66) Opposite the Markets, it has some of the best French patisserie in Vanuatu, go early in the morning for the best choice. Enjoy a coffee, and nibble on a chocolate croissant, and watch the world go by.

Stonegrill (546 5406) – (**S6** map, page 66) Now at a new location at the Handicraft market in Wharf Road. Great local steaks and seafood cooked the way you like it, by yourself on the stone grill in front of you. Generous portions and you have only yourself to blame if the food is over cooked.

Le Jardin Des Saveurs (25 405) – (**A15** map, page 66) One of the top restaurants in Port Vila. Located just before the Warwick Le Lagon. Beautiful French cuisine with a price to match, the degustation menu is perfect for special occasions. Good selection of French wines.

Flaming Bull Steakhouse (27 716) – (**F7** map, page 66) Located just beyond the Fung Kuei duty free store on the Lini Highway. Maybe not the best beef in town, as it proudly proclaims, but not bad at all, and reasonably priced with friendly service. The lunch specials are good value.

Golden Port (22375) – (**F8** map, page 66) A Chinese restaurant opposite the Melanesian Hotel in Numbatu. It used be the memorable Le Rendez Vous, and before that a luxury bolt hole for a well-known Australian criminal. Now you really go for one of the best sunset views in town. The food is average Chinese at a reasonable price, with MSG or too much salt making you very thirsty.

Joe's Vietnamese Restaurant (26 907) – In the centre of Port Vila on the Lini Highway, go for the Pho or the many vegetarian dishes. Tasty food at a good price, and goes down perfectly on a hot day with a glass of cold beer.

The Brewery Bar (28 328) – (**F4** map, page 66) Opposite the Grand Hotel. Serves draft Nambawan beer, and has all the usual suspects on the bar menu, as well as some nicely done Mexican dishes, although a little bit light on chilies. Every night there is a special, from cheap pizzas, Mexican dishes or free beers with your meal, which can make for an economical, as well as tasty, night out.

Spice (24 406) – (**F9** map, page 66) Indian eatery located opposite Au Bon Marche supermarket in Numbatu. Food is average, although light on the spice you might expect in an Indian, but it is somewhat expensive, unless you go for the lunch specials.

War Horse Saloon (26 670) – (**F11** map, page 66) On Wharf Road. Tex-Mex style food. Draft beer, darts and rowdy Friday nights when the DJ gets going. Average quality food, a little bit expensive, even for Port Vila, but the expat crowd loves it, and it can make for a good night out.

Kanpai (26 687) – (**F12** map, page 66) On Wharf Road. Port Vila's only Japanese restaurant has the requisite great views, and reasonable Japanese food. Nice but pricey sashimi, and all the standard teriyaki dishes, which are good but not memorable. However the lunchboxes are good value.

Krishna – (**F13** map, page 66) In a rather unusual setting, the car park of the Colorite Printers in Numbatu, this small hut serves up the tastiest and cheapest Fijian – Indian curries in Port Vila. Using a traditional thali tray, you can load up with vegetarian dhal, or beef and chicken, with rotis for around 700 Vat, and eat in the thatched hut next to it. One of the best vegetarian options in town. Only open for lunch.

Nambanga Training Restaurant (26 830) – (**F16** map, page 66) A little unusual, this is the part of the Vanuatu Tourism School, which provides training for chefs, kitchen and wait staff for Ni-Vanuatu. This small restaurant is open on Thursday evenings for tasty French influenced meals. There is a set three-course menu for 1,800 Vatu, with beer and wine available. The funds provide a source of income for the school.

Jenny's Rasta Van – Behind the BSP and ANZ banks on the seafront car park sits Vanuatu's version of a food truck. Jenny's tasty 'Kick Ass Spicy Chicken and Rice' and 'Spicy Rasta Burgers' are great to take and sit and eat looking out to the harbour. Ask for them extra hot if you can stand the heat of the locally grown chilies! The Van appears around lunchtime and in early evenings.

Where to Drink

Western Style

Port Vila has some of the best bars in the country. Grab a beer or cocktail, nibble on the bar menu and relax beneath the waving coconut palms.

Nambawan Café, **The Brewery Bar**, **War Horse Saloon**, and **The Waterfront Bar and Grill**, mentioned in the 'Where to Eat' section, are all worth checking out for a drink, but there also are some other great bars to try.

Mele Beach Bar (560 1132) – One of the best-designed and well-run bars in Port Vila. A Converted shipping container placed on a beach, and it works! Palm trees, the sand beneath your toes, and the view out to Hideaway Island and the Pacific Ocean, make this a rather special place. If you are staying on Hideaway Island, you will end up catching the free ferry to spend many an evening here, if you are in Port Vila it is only a 300 Vatu bus fare or 1,000 Vatu taxi fare.

Tasty wood fired pizza goes well with the draft beers, wines and spirits available, and this is one of the best places to see the Fire Dancing (see page 37) on the beach on a Friday night. Other regular events include a circus on the beach and live music nights.

The Anchor Inn (555 1319) – (**D1** map, page 66) On the north end of the seafront is the Anchor Inn. Another haunt of expats on a Friday night, it was badly damaged by cyclone Pam. It is now back up and running and is a great place to grab a beer and watch an Australian or New Zealand sports match on the big screens.

The Moorings (26 800) – (**A3** map, page 66) Sit on the landing stage overlooking the harbour in Fatumaru Bay and be cooled by the breeze. Great location and cheap beer, particularly if you a buy a ten beer discount card. Get the draft Tusker.

Banyan Beach Bar (27 079) – (**A4** map, page 66) Owned by Chantilly's hotel, a cool spot with bean bags on the beach. Go there for sunset, luckily timed with its happy hour.

Hemisphere (28 882) – (**A7** map, page 66) On the top floor of the Grand Hotel, it has great sunset views towards Iriki Island and the harbour. Go on a Friday night from 5PM to 7PM for Happy Hour. The drinks are cheap, the place is buzzing, and there are free bar snacks brought around to munch on.

Voodoo Bar (26 670) – (**D2** map, page 66) Opposite Bred Bank on the Lini Highway, open from 11PM. More of a nightclub, with some of the best Ni-Van DJs, the bar is famous its flaming shots. The melted areas on top of the bar are testimony to their popularity. Also serves reasonably priced beers and spirits.

Vanuatu Style

You cannot visit Vanuatu and not go to a kava bar, known locally as nakamals, catering to the locals, but they welcome visitors and some offer beer and soft drinks also.

Many of the kava bars are situated in such great locations; they are worth visiting for the view alone. But, of course, there is also the kava to try.

Kava is a narcotic made from the roots of the *piper methysticum* plant. Traditionally the roots were broken down by chewing, now it is more likely to be pounded by hand, and mixed with water.

It is an earthy, muddy taste, which is not that pleasant, but it has an immediate numbing sensation, often of the throat first, and then acts as a muscle relaxant. Over use produces similar effects to alcohol, with loss of balance and inability to converse properly.

In Port Vila there are over 100 nakamals, and unlike the more conservative and traditional remoter islands, women can drink kava at them. A half shell of kava, often the shell of a coconut, is 50 Vatu, a full shell 100 Vatu.

Nakamals open late afternoon, and close when the day's kava runs out, which being Vanuatu, can occur quite early on if they have not made enough.

Some of our favourite nakamals include:

Shefa Bayview – (**D3** map, page 66) Walk through the Shefa government buildings off the Rue De Paris, and there is a small path down at the end. The nakamal has great sunset views, and ice-cold Tusker beer.

El Manoro – In Bellevue, involves an expedition, but is well worth it. Located on top of a hill, with several small huts in tropical rainforest. The nakamal serves consistently good kava, and also has snacks and beer.

Popular with expats and locals from Freshwota. They have a facebook page at www.facebook.com/el.manaro.kava

Maewo Seaside – (**D4** map, page 66) Behind the hospital and close to Mangoes in Nambatu. It has a great position above the Holiday Inn and Second Lagoon, but is down a dark path, so bring a torch.

The kava is made from fresh rainwater. Bus drivers may know it by its old name, 'Korna'.

Sophie's – In Nambatri. Lots of seating, very popular at weekends. Not the most beautiful of settings, but a great place to meet up with friends.

Hannington's – Just past the Erakor Bridge on Second Lagoon, near the Korman stadium, with a small deck over the water so that you can sit on the edge of the lagoon.

The affable Mr. Hannington comes from Ambae, and imports his Royal Ambae kava to his lagoon side bar. Local aficionados recommend the kava here. Bus drivers may know it by its old name 'Felix'.

Reynolds – (**D5** map, page 66) Across the road from the stage at Sarafina Park. Lots of tables in the courtyard. Popular with expats, beers and soft drinks also available.

Ronnie's – (**D7** map, page 66) In Nambatu close to the Melanesian Hotel. Old school nakamal run by local character, Ronnie Watson. Badly damaged by cyclone Pam it is back up and running, serving its Malekula sourced kava. They have a facebook page at www.facebook.com/pages/Ronnies-Nakamal/137805169624140

Annie's – In Pango, across the road from Breakas Resort. Long benches to sit on, beer and soft drinks also available.

Chiefs – (**D6** map, page 66) Just behind the Vanuatu Museum at Sarafina Park is the large iconic ceremonial building, destroyed by cyclone Pam, but now rebuilt, with a few tables and chairs hidden in the gloom. Always full of a mixture of politicians, expats, tourists and even the odd chief.

Last Flight – Situated just beyond the end of the runway at Bauerfield airport, the last place to get kava before you leave! Popular with the French community, it serves some of the strongest kava in Port Vila.

It has a facebook page at www.facebook.com/pages/Last-Flight-Nakamal-Port-Vila/285150891505178

Things to See and Do

Vanuatu Cultural Centre   vanuatuculturalcentre.vu

(**M1** map, page 66) On Rue d'Artois, next to Sarafina Park, and a five-minute drive or 15 minute walk from the centre. Some great exhibits from across the islands of Vanuatu, and the history of the Condominium. The admission includes a sand drawing demonstration (see story on page 272 for more information on sand drawing).

Admission is 700 Vatu for Adults, 350 Vatu for Children. (Open Monday to Friday 09:00 to 16:00, and Saturday 09:00 to 12:00).

Port Vila Markets

(**M2** map, page 66) A riot of colour in the centre of Port Vila. Tropical flowers mingle with tables laden with seasonal fruit and vegetables. Tread carefully as even the floor has produce, including piles of coconut crabs brought in from the outer islands.

If close to lunchtime, go to the back and pick up a tasty meal from the stalls there.

The market is open 24 hours a day, the stallholders sleep underneath their tables at night, from 06:00 AM Monday to 12:00 AM Saturday.

Mele Cascades Waterfalls

5km from the centre of Port Vila are the Cascades. Perfect on a hot day. You walk through tropical rainforest before you climb to the top of the waterfalls, with fresh water pools to swim in. It can be slippery as you climb, so take care.

2,000 Vatu for Adults, 1,000 Vatu for Children. A bus from Port Vila would be 300 Vatu for Adults, 100 Vatu for Children each way, or transfers from Evergreen Vanuatu (25 518).

Secret Garden   www.vanuatusecretgarden.com

An introduction to local culture, food and drink, accompanied by a humorous local guide. A bit touristy, but good for families. Dancing and a filling Melanesian feast on Thursday nights.

1,000 Vatu for adults, 500 Vatu for children. A bus from Port Vila would be 300 Vatu for adults, 100 Vatu for children each way.

Ekasup Cultural Village

(See map on page 61) If you are not heading off to the outer islands, this is a great introduction to rural island life. You get a tour of the village near Erakor and learn about traditional medicine, hunting (including how to catch pigs and chickens, not as easy as it sounds, or looks, as you can have a go), cooking and family life. The tour finishes with a custom dance.

Tours are in the morning and afternoon, and on Thursday night there is a big Melanesian feast.

4,500 for Adults, 2,250 for Children including transport. Make a booking at your hotel, or call 24 217.

Hideaway Island and Marine Sanctuary   hideaway.com.vu

(See map on page 61) Located off Mele Bay, this is a great day excursion. Some of the best snorkeling in Port Vila on the reef that is close to shore. Beyond are decent drop-offs for divers (the island has its own dive shop).

Hideaway is also where the world's only underwater post office is, you can swim to it and post the waterproof cards back home, when it is operational (ask at the resort).

Alternatively just relax in the loungers and grab a beer and a tasty fish burger for lunch.

The ferry departs from next to the Mele Beach bar, and you can combine with the Friday night fire dancing there. The cost for a day trip is 1,000 Vatu. A bus there would be 300 Vatu for Adults, 100 Vatu for Children each way.

Vanuatu Zipline   www.vanuatujunglezipline.com

A stomach-churning adventure set high in the hills above Mele. You are attached to a zip line and launched over canyons and trees and even a waterfall, before coming to a gradual stop.

The safety standards seemed high when we checked it out, which is important for this sort of activity. If you keep your lunch down, you will want to do it again.

Situated at the Summit Gardens, transport is included in the price from beside Nambawan café on the waterfront. The cost is 9,500 Vatu for Adults, 5,000 for teens (13-19), and 4,000 for Children.

Summit Gardens   www.thesummitvanuatutours.com

Beautiful rainforest gardens above Mele, with great views across to Port Vila and beyond. Also the location of the Vanuatu Zipline. A nice little add on to a Zipline adventure, or a trip to Mele Cascades, which are below the gardens.

A café and essential oil distillery are also on site.

Currently admission is free due to the damage received during cyclone Pam.

Wet 'n' Wild Adventure Park   wetnwildvanuatu.com

If you have ever wanted to strap yourself into a big plastic bubble ball and roll down a hill, then this is for you. This was the first Zorbing we had ever tried and it was quite unnerving to have no control as you move through 360 degrees again and again, and see the world at unusual angles out of the clear sides. Exhilarating and dizzy stuff.

On Devils Point Road, beyond Mele. There are also Segways, Go-karts and water slides to try out. The cost is 7,000 Vatu per adult, and 5,500 Vatu per child. Transfers are available from near the Numbawan Cafe at 1,000 Vatu per person.

Vanuatu Ecotours   vanuatu-ecotour.com.vu

Environmentally friendly tours into different locations in the bush around Port Vila. Working with local landowners and communities, small groups are taken to undisturbed natural locations for a half-day of adventure. Kayak down rivers, take a mountain bike off-road past small local villages, or trek to the Lololima waterfall for a swim.

The Kayak trip is highly recommended. You get to travel slowly through the rainforest, and slip past local villages on quite shallow rivers, before returning to your hotel tired but happy.

The owner and chief guide, Pascal, a French ex-professional footballer, is both knowledgeable and entertaining. Book early as the small group sizes means tours can fill up quickly.

5,900 Vatu per person, including hotel pickup. Contact 25 299.

Tanna Coffee Factory   http://www.tannacoffee.com/

Good place to stop off if you are in Mele for any of the other attractions. Watch the fresh beans from Tanna being roasted, learn about the coffee making process, and grab a coffee and cake for 500 Vatu and sit in their gardens. A bag of Tanna coffee is a nice souvenir, as are the hand painted coffee sacks.

On Devils Point Road. Free Admission.

Congoola day Cruise   southpacdivecruise.com.vu

Set off from Havannah on the Congoola, a 23 metre ketch, around the large natural Havannah harbour, which was a major US navy base in the Second World War. Stop off on Moso Island to see the Turtle conservation rookery before heading on to a private beach for a barbeque and snorkel.

A little expensive, but a good day out on the water in good weather. Transfers from Port Vila are included, 12,000 Vatu per adult and 6,000 Vatu for children

Erakor Island

(**A16** map, page 66, and page 61) Head over to Erakor for either a day of water sports, or to relax on its white sand beach. Great snorkeling in the clear waters, where different coloured starfish like to live in the shallows. Explore the island and see the graves of the early missionaries who lived there.

Good lunchtime specials at the bar, or wait until evening for their nightly specials, from pasta specials to Melanesian feasts.

The ferry leaves from besides the Warwick Lagon Hotel, and day visitors pay 1,000 Vatu for adults, and 500 for children, which can be redeemed against food and drink, the spa, or water sport hire.

A bus from Port Vila would be 150 Vatu for adults, 50 Vatu for children each way.

Iriki Island

(**A8** map, page 66) Opposite the main centre of Port Vila is Iriki Island. The former home to the British High Commission, it is now an up market resort. You can still visit for a day trip, and make use of their facilities for a small fee.

When you arrive at the landing stage you have to turn left to access the pools and watercraft. Only those who are staying are allowed to go right to their accommodation, restaurant and infinity pool.

The facilities available for day visitors are good, with a number of inter-connected pools, a reasonably priced café and bar, and some great beanbags under a wooden shelter where you can watch the harbour traffic from close quarters.

Be there for cruise ship departure time, between 5PM and 6PM on cruise ship days, it is worth seeing the huge ships glide by close to the shore as they leave the harbour.

The ferry leaves from besides the Grand Hotel, and day visitors pay 1,500 Vatu for adults, and 500 for children, at the small hut by the dock, which can be redeemed against food and drink, or water sport hire.

Diving

With its clear blue water, Port Vila is well suited for diving. There are several operators in town who offer both dive trips and courses. Nautilus (Contact 22 398 www.nautilus.com.vu) and Big Blue (Contact 27 518 www.bigbluevanuatu.com) are recommended.

There are some good reef dives and drop offs near Pango and Mele, as well as some interesting wrecks to explore. Two shipwrecks, *The Star of Russia*, a square-rigger built in 1874 and lost at sea in 1953, and the *Konanda*, a small cargo ship sunk in 1987 specifically to create a dive site.

Perhaps the most interesting wreck is a *Qantas Sandringham* flying boat, which had an accident with a dugout canoe in 1951 in the harbour. It is in well-preserved condition, but quite deep down at 40 metres, which makes it a great site to explore only for experienced divers.

Shopping

Some of the best shopping for souvenirs can be done at the **Hibernia Market** (S2 map, page 66), opposite Sound Centre duty free on the Lini Highways in the centre of Port Vila, and at the **Handicraft Centre** on Wharf Road.

The main high street, the Lini Highway, has many shops where you can buy mainly cheap Chinese clothes, DVDs and tat. But there are also some gems in this street.

The **Kava Emporium** just before the French Embassy, has a range of kava and associated products, including kava flavoured chocolate bars (they do taste as bad as they sound!)

Head to **Philippe Metois Photography**, opposite the Library, not only for some great photographs of Vanuatu and coffee table books, but for a selection of products from the **ACTIV** organisation, who support local communities' produce and market their products, including tasty chocolate, spices, oils, vanilla, pepper, as well as handicrafts and art.

I recommend trying the chocolate nibs, small shavings of cocoa beans which taste rather nice when added to ice cream, or on their own. Better still head out to their main building by the Second Lagoon, where they have a chocolate factory, exhibitions, and much more produce and handicrafts for sale. For more information check their website www.activassociation.org.

The **Vanuatu Post Office** (**S3** map, page 66) just after the Market Centre has some nice photographic greeting cards and postcards, and fine sets of the islands' colourful stamps for a philatelist.

If you want to hear some local music wander into Rue Camot to the **Music Shop** which stacks CDs and tapes by local artists, mainly of the reggae persuasion, but also string bands.

The main supermarket chain in Port Vila is **Au Bon Marche**, and it has stores next to the Market (**S4** map, page 66), and larger ones at Numbatu (**S5** map, page 66), and Manples on the way to the airport. Lots of expensive imported Australian and French products, great for French cheese, wine and paté in particular.

With **Tana Russet Plaza** (**S1** map, page 66), Port Vila has now got its own modern shopping mall. If you need your fix of boutique shops, fast food restaurants and a small cinema, head over to the northern edge of the CBD in Fatumaru Bay.

For **Duty Free** shopping see page 56.

A Walk around Port Vila

Port Vila is a fairly compact town, and a three to four hour walk will give you a good introduction to most of the key sites, as well as building up an appetite for that Melanesian feast later.

Using the map on page 56 as a guide, start at the **Markets (M2)** and see and smell the fresh produce the ladies are selling. Buy some peanuts blong Epi as a snack for your walk for 30 Vatu.

Next head south towards the **Grand Hotel (A7)** before crossing the road and walking up the large flight of steps towards the Australian High Commission (**C3**). In the mornings the clear view out towards Iriki Island and the Pacific Ocean is more than photo worthy. There is a seat at the top for you to recover your breath before heading along Rue Winston Churchill and turning right into Rue d'Artois. Walk past the new **Port Vila Conference Centre** and then the **Vanuatu Parliament building**.

Cross the road into Sarafina Park and visit the **Vanuatu Cultural Centre** (**M1**, opening times and more information on page 82) and see a demonstration of the impressive sand drawing from Ambrym, and then wander around the exhibits. If later in the afternoon you can try a shell of kava in the **Chiefs Nakamal (D6)**, else retrace your steps to the Rue d'Artois and walk up the road, past the roundabout, before cutting across **Independence Park (M5)** where the flags of Britain and France were raised, with a Swiss observer ensuring they were of equal height, during the Condominium. Nowadays you may well see a rugby or cricket match (the national team plays and practises here during the cricket season).

Turn right into the Rue General De Gaulle and then right up the steps besides the Rue Mercet to the **War Memorial (M6)**. There is a beautiful outlook here right across the harbour to Mele and beyond. Walk back down the Rue Mercet, cross the Lini Highway, and on to the harbour **seafront**. This is slowly being rebuilt and beautified in a NZ Aid project, yet it remains a hive of activity. On warm days watch the school kids throw themselves into the water to cool down, usually on the slide on the edge of the harbour wall, which dumps them into the deep ocean.

Walking north you will reach the boule court on the right, (also known as petanque) and watch the locals play hard fought games. Turn right onto the Lini Highway and you will walk past the **library**, which also sells books and pamphlets about Vanuatu (and will gratefully accept any books that you may have finished on your travels). Outside is an anchor from the *Astrolabe*, one of the boats from the expedition of the French explorer La Perouse, who explored this part of the Pacific in 1788.

Walk back to the seafront and head towards the **Nambawan café (F1)** and sit down and relax after the walk. If you get here at the end of the day you might be able to have the unforgettable experience of watching a movie on the big screen at the edge of the harbour.

A Day in Port Vila

Recommendations for the Cruise Ship Passenger

There is a lot to see in Vanuatu, and your day here will hopefully give you a taste to come back for longer. There are many tours on board the ship, often focussing on water sports or island tours, which sell out quickly.

To enjoy your seven to eight hour stop, get off the ship early, and brave the chaotic bus and taxi free-for-all, which is not really the best introduction to the island and its people.

You can get a boat across to the Port Vila waterfront (cost approx 1,000 Vatu per person) from the cruise ship terminal, which takes you to the waterfront by the Nambawan Café, grab a cup of tea or fresh juice and check out the tour providers next door, who have a range of tours such as the Zipline (see page 84).

Alternatively take a **DIY** tour, following our suggestions, which can be combined and would include:

> Hire a taxi, or bus and driver to take you **around the island**. To avoid finding and haggling with a driver on cruise ship day, pre- book a trip (see page 94 for contact details) and you can enjoy a relaxed tour stopping off at the Tanna coffee factory, Havannah Harbour, Ernest's World War II museum, and beautiful secluded Eton beach (check out the Efate section on pages 98 to 100 for other things to you may want to see). Do not worry that you will miss returning to the boat as with the new road the island can be easily circumnavigated in two to three hours.

> Head to **Hideaway Island**, with some of the best snorkeling close to Port Vila, and home to the unique underwater post office. Snorkel equipment and kayaks can be hired, and diving can also be arranged on the small island. Alternatively grab a Tusker beer and a fish burger and just relax on a sun lounger. The island charges 1,000 Vatu admission fee, and the bus journey will cost 300 Vatu for Adults, 100 Vatu for Children each way from the centre of town, and takes about twenty minutes.

> Take in some culture and visit the **Vanuatu Cultural Centre**. See some interesting artifacts and a sand drawing demonstration. (see page 82). Combine with a visit to the Chiefs Nakamal behind the museum, where you can taste a cup of the local drug of choice, kava.

> Scoot across the harbour to **Irriki Island** resort. An up market resort, formerly the British Ambassador's residence, where you can head to Mitcheners restaurant for some fresh island food, or just swim in the pools. If you are feeling more energetic hire a kayak, boat, or even take a ride in the seaplane. The ferry departs from next to the Grand Hotel in the centre of town (it is easy to spot as it is the only high rise in town) and the cost is 1,500 Vatu per person (Children 500 Vatu) with the added benefit that the money is a credit to be used for food, drinks or boat hire.

> Swim in the **Cascades Waterfalls**. A beautiful tropical walk through lush rainforests and an easy, albeit sometimes slippery, walk up to the various levels of waterfalls, with pools to swim and cool down in. They are in Mele, and are easily combined with a trip to Hideaway Island, as they are only five minutes apart. Cost is 1,500 Vatu for Adults, 750 Vatu for Children. A bus there would be 300 Vatu for Adults, 100 Vatu for Children each way.

> Go south to **Erakor Island**. Another island, but this one is less busy than the previous two, it has some beautiful gardens to walk through and one of the best over water restaurant views in Port Vila. All water sport equipment can be hired, and there is a small beach to relax on. The experience of getting to the island is one of the highlights, as the low-slung craft speeds you across the water, over multi coloured starfish. The ferry departs from next to the Le Lagon Hotel approximately ten minutes from town. Admittance is 1,000 Vatu per Adult, 500 Vatu per Child., this can be used as credit for food and equipment. A bus from the centre of town would be 150 Vatu for Adults, 50 Vatu for Children each way.

> Take a stroll around the **Fresh Food Market**. A riot of colour and fresh food. Great photographic opportunities (ask first if you want to take a photo of a local) and a chance to taste some very tasty local produce. If in season, try the tasty pineapples, pamplemousse (grapefruit), mango

and other fruits all for between 100 and 500 Vatu a big bag. Get a small packet of the always available roasted peanuts form the island of Epi, the signs proclaim 'Peanuts blong Epi' for a tasty 30 Vatu snack. If you are feeling more adventurous, and hungry, grab a sit down meal at the back of the market, where you will have a chance to chat to friendly locals and eat fresh steak from the island of Santo, or local fish, for a bargain 500 Vatu a plate with vegetables and salad. Admittance is free, and the market can be found just after the Grand Hotel when coming from the cruise ship.

➢ Get your souvenirs at the **Handicraft Market** on Wharf Road, the road to the ship terminal before you head back to your cabin. T-shirts, jewellery, beautifully carved statues, and much more can be purchased here.

Efate

Although Port Vila dominates the island of Efate by both its size and being the gateway to the country, there is still a lot to be seen on the rest of the island.

Now that the old potholed and rutted road has been given a brand new smooth surface there is no reason not to venture out of the capital, and explore the beaches, World War II sites, seafood restaurants, and even a chocolate factory.

Efate has the largest island population in Vanuatu, with over 66,000 inhabitants, although two thirds of that total live in Port Vila.

Once you leave the capital you will be in the tropical countryside, and you will pass very few other vehicles.

Getting Around

The island can be circumnavigated in just over eight hours by running, as happens in the annual relay race held every July. You can of course drive around it in a much faster time, but it is better to take it at a leisurely pace and stop off at the many places of interest on the way .

You can hire a car in Port Vila, see page 64, or negotiate for your own bus to take you around the island (this will cost upwards of 12,000 Vatu for the day) but will not include a guide, or you can or go on an organised island tour.

For organised tours, we recommend both **John's Authentic Island Tours** (Contact: 540 7386, 775 5193 authenticislandtours.weebly.com) who do tours for 8,000 Vatu for Adults, and 4,000 Vatu for Children, **Manples Tours** (Contact 561 4190, 779 4826 manples-tours.weebly.com) with tours for 7,500 Vatu for Adults, and 3,750 Vatu for Children with bi-lingual (English and French) guiding.

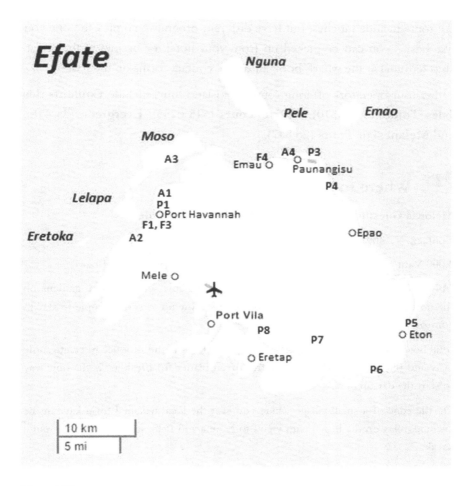

Map of Efate

Accommodation

A1 The Havannah

A2 Havannah Eco Lodge

A3 Tranquility Resort

A4 Malowia Guesthouse

Food & Drink

F1 Francesca's

A2 Gideon's Bar

F3 Wahoo Bar

F4 Orovy Beach

Places

P1 Ernest's WW II Museum

A2 Survivor Beach

P3 Quoin Hill Airfield

P4 Nasinu Hot Springs

P5 Eton Beach

P7 Eden on the River

P8 Chocolate Factory

All tours include lunches, but have different programs, so pick the one you like best. You can be picked up from your hotel, or be met at the cruise ship terminal at the wharf, book ahead via contact forms on their web sites.

Other tour operators offering round the island tours include **Couleurs des Isles Tours**, (591 5510), **Native Tours** (545 0253), **Evergreen** (25 418), and **Melanesian Tours** (26 847).

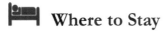 Where to Stay

Malowia Guesthouse. Paunangisu (* FFP Recommended)

Contact: 777 4091, 598 9809   www.malowiaguesthouse.com

3,000 Vatu per person (incl Breakfast), 4,000 Vatu per person (Full Board)

(A4 map, page 95) Modern and comfortable bungalow set in tropical gardens on the northern tip of Efate. Two separate rooms allow up to seven people to stay in comfort.

Full board is highly recommended as Janet use fresh island produce to create some tasty and filling meals. The massive fresh fruit platter for breakfast is the only way to start the day up here.

On the edge of a small village where you visit the local nakamal for a kava in the evening, relax on the beach with views to Nguna and Pele, swim, snorkel, or rent a kayak.

The Havannah. Port Havannah (* FFP Recommended)

Contact: 35 600   http://www.thehavannah.com/

Price: 50,000 Vatu + per room

(A1 map, page 95) One of the most luxurious hotels on the island, if not Vanuatu. Private beach, villas with their own plunge pools, with all activities included such as kayaking and tennis, and a daily sunset cruise.

The meals at the impressively designed restaurant are a great mix of local, French and Australian influences.

A place to go if you want to get away from it all on a Pacific island, and are without children, which are not allowed. There is a free daily shuttle into Port Vila to remind you that you are still in Vanuatu.

Havannah Eco Lodge. Port Havannah

Contact: 591 9949   www.havannahecolodge.com

Price: 6,000 Vatu per room

(**A2** map, page 95) Located right on the water, with a protected reef to snorkel or kayak around outside your door.

The new bungalows, further away from the bar, are the best, with decks to relax on and soak up the views. You can eat meals, and grab a beer at Gideon's restaurant and bar on site.

Tranquility Island Resort. Moso

Contact: 25 020, 27 211   tranquillitydive.com

Price: 8,500 Vatu + per room

(**A3** map, page 95) A spot for divers, to do courses or go out on the many dive trips offered. Stays can include packages for dives as well as meals. Very much an eco-resort with solar power and a limited environmental footprint.

The beachfront bungalows are highly recommended. Great for a weekend getaway from Port Vila

Trees and Fishes Resort. Port Havannah

Contact: 556 2111   www.treesandfishes.com

Price: 65,000 Vatu + per room

Vatapua Beach Bungalow. Emua

Contact: 546 2052   Price: 3,000 Vatu per person (Includes Breakfast)

Raymond's Bay View Bungalow. Emua

Contact: 710 0969   orovybeachrestaurant.weebly.com/accommodation

Price: 3,500 Vatu per person (Includes all meals)

Nicky's Homestay. Emua

Contact: 710 0969   orovybeachrestaurant.weebly.com/accommodation

Price: 3,000 Vatu per person (Includes Breakfast)

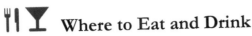

Where to Eat and Drink

Orovy Beach Restaurant. Emua (540 0026) – (**F4** map, page 95) Don't miss the small turn off to the beach in Emua village. Locally owned and run, great meals at a reasonable price and you get to relax on the beach afterwards.

Perfect for a stop on the around the island route, and also a top spot for a cold beer at sunset also. Lunch served 7 days a week, breakfast or dinner by appointment. Chief Kai also runs great local cooking classes.

Francesca's. Port Havannah (24 733) – (**F1** map, page 95) Modern Italian in an open plan building on the water. Menus change regularly but the grilled seafood, and fresh pizza are excellent. Degustation menus held on Saturdays, and Francesca also runs cooking classes.

Gideon's Bar. Port Havannah (591 9949) – (**A2** map, page 95) Standard pub grub in a waterfront location. A bit pricey, but good place to stop for a beer and a burger.

Wahoo Bar. Port Havannah (773 6232) - (**F3** map, page 95) Built down at the water's edge, with free rental of masks and snorkels for guests, which is a nice touch. Only open during the day, go for the fish of the day special for lunch, you might be lucky and get a plate of its spicy namesake.

Good for families also, with well priced kids meals.

Things to See and Do

Ernest's World War II Museum

(**P1** map, page 95) In Havannah harbour is the roadside shack full of the world war two artifacts collected by the delightful Ernest. He started off collecting coke bottles left by the Americans who used the harbour as a major naval base during the war, but has since found a huge amount of discarded and rusting relics, from guns to grenades.

Worth a stop to look at the collection, talk to Ernest and look out at the view to the harbour. Entry by donation.

Survivor Beach

(**A2** map, page 95) Next to Gideon's Bar and Restaurant in Havannah Harbour is where much of the US Survivor TV series was shot. If you are a fan you can see the beach where much of the action took place. With a decent bar so close, maybe appearing in the series was not as hard as they made it look.

Nasinu Hot Springs

(**P4** map, page 95) For those who want to roll about in hot mud pools, fed from volcanic sources, before cleaning off in a cooler pool next to it. A little basic with no changing facilities.

Entrance fee is 1,500 Vatu per person.

Second World War Sites

On the far north of Efate is the remains of **Quoin Hill** runway (**P3** map, page 95), which along with Bauerfield and the runway at Havannah, was the home to the aircraft attacking the Japanese forces in the Pacific, particularly at the battle of Guadalcanal in the Solomon Islands. The runway is still there, although covered by large patches of grass. At the end of the runway, near the road, you can still make out the earthworks that spell USA.

North of Quoin Hill next to Paunangisu village, in four metres of water, is a fairly intact **Corsair** from the war. Erick (777 7205) will take you to it, so that you can swim down and sit in the cockpit. Cost is 2,500 Vatu.

The Best Public Toilet in the South Pacific

Not a huge amount to see here unless you need to stop! In Paunangisu, near **A4** on the map, and opened in 2016. Clean, functional and strategically placed half way around Efate. One of its claims to fame is that it is possibly the only public toilet in the world with its own website http://bestpublictoilet.org/. 200 Vatu to spend a penny.

Eton Beach

Our favourite beach on Efate (**P5** map, page 95). A small lagoon protected by coral outcrops, the azure water is the temperature of a warm bath and you want to stay all day. Picnic tables are provided, bring your own food and drink from Port Vila. Do not swim out beyond the coral as there are dangerous rips.

Entrance fee is 300 Vatu per person.

Blue Lagoon

500 metres on from Eton Beach is this swimming hole. Similar to Santo's blue holes, although not so deep, it is a great place to cool off, or to try swinging on a rope before you fall into the water. Can get very busy at weekends.

Entrance fee is 500 Vatu per person.

Coconut Beach

(**P6** map, page 95) On the East coast, this is the only beach that is free and open to the public. Not so good for swimming as the waves can be quite large, but is popular with locals for picnics and has some remains from shipwrecks on the southern part.

Eden on the River   edenvanuatu.com

(**P7** map, page 95) A farm, which has embraced eco-tourism. Walking tours that will take you over the river on small suspension bridges, and come back on a small zip line., introduce you to local flora and fruits, or see the farm animals. Good for families, although if you take each tour the costs do mount up.

ACTIV Chocolate Factory www.activassociation.org/aelan-chocolate-makerstrade

(**P8** map, page 95) On the way back into Port Vila at the edge of the second lagoon is the Chocolate Factory. Not as large as Willy Wonka's, nevertheless it is worth seeing and tasting the first chocolate to be produced on the island and also supporting the local farmers getting fair prices for their produce.

Entrance is free, but it is worth loading up on chocolate, or some of the local handicrafts displayed here.

Nguna and Pele Islands

Off the north coast of Efate are the islands of Nguna and Pele. As with much of the Shepherd Islands, they were hit hard by cyclone Pam in 2015. They are recovering fairly quickly, with the tarpaulins on the roofs gradually being replaced, and they remain as well worth visiting now as they were before the cyclone hit.

The larger of the two islands, Nguna, has a population close to 1,500, while Pele has only approximately 300 people living on the island.

The reason for visiting them is easily apparent on arrival, the ability to experience rural island life so close to Port Vila, with beautiful sandy beaches and great snorkeling in clear waters.

The islanders have been very progressive, establishing a marine conservation area of over 3,000 hectares covering much of the sea surrounding the islands in 2002. The payback has been swift, with populations of hawksbill and green sea turtles, reef sharks and rays growing rapidly, and now inhabiting the easily accessible waters and coral reefs off the shore.

Getting to Nguna and Pele

The islands are only 18km from the capital, Port Vila. The lack of airstrips on the islands is therefore not a major issue, you can travel up from Port Vila by road in just over forty minutes, before catching a ferry out to them from Emua wharf.

You can use public transport. The car park of the Au Bon Marche supermarket, by the petrol station, is where the trucks and buses leave for the north of the island. Not all go there, so you will have to ask first. The best time to catch one is in the morning, you may find no transport departs in the afternoon, and also on Sundays there will be few if any departures. The cost in shared transport to Emua wharf will be 500 Vatu per person.

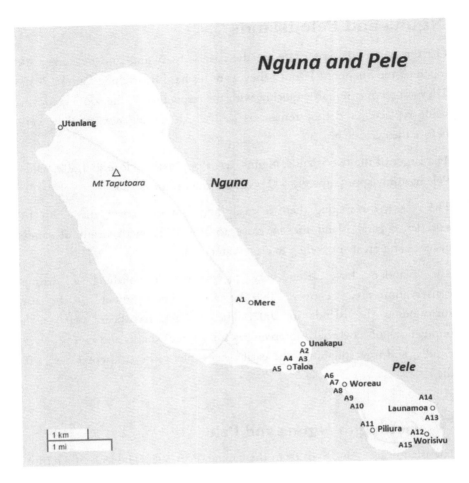

Map of Nguna and Pele

Accommodation

A1 Mere Sauwia Homestay

A2 Paunvina Guesthouse

A3 Island Breeze

A4 Nakia Guesthouse

A5 Mangamus Bungalow

A5 Uduna Cove

A6 JJ's Bungalows

A7 Jowi's Bungalows

A8 Sunset Frangipanu

A9 Simoa Bungalow

A10 Sene Pap-pa

A11 Serety Bungalow

A12 Nabanga Bungalow

A13 Wora Namoa

A14 Sunrise Bungalow

A15 Bella Bungalow

Alternatively you can hire a car in Port Vila (see page 64) and park safely at the wharf for 500 Vatu per day, or negotiate a fare with a bus driver in Port Vila, remembering to get the driver's phone number to arrange a pickup again from Emua.

At Emua Wharf you can share a speedboat across to either island for 500 Vatu. They do not run to any timetable and only depart when they are full, which can take a while. If you are not that patient, then you can hire the whole boat for a quick trip across for 3,000 Vatu.

If you can only spend a day, then both **John's Authentic Pele Tours** (775 3273 authenticislandtours.weebly.com) and **Evergreen Tours** (25 418) offer day tours including all transport from Port Vila and lunch on the beach.

🏝 Getting Around

Do as the locals do and walk. You can travel easily between villages on the grass paths. Between the islands you can catch a boat across for 500 Vatu, or swim, but bear in mind the current is very strong in the middle of the channel.

🛏 Where to Stay

Uduna Cove Beach Bungalows. Taloa, Nguna (* FFP Recommended)

Contact: 776 6263   Price: 3,500 Vatu per person (Includes Breakfast & Dinner)

(**A5** Map, page 102) These five brightly painted bungalows are on a long stretch of white sandy beach ten minutes' walk from Taloa.

The marine reserve is on your doorstep, making it a good place to snorkel from. Great for groups, as up to twenty people can be housed in the accommodation.

Lunch is 500 Vatu extra.

Mere Sauwia Homestay. Mere, Nguna

Contact: 779 0734   Price: 2,500 Vatu per person (Includes Full Board)

(**A1** Map, page 102) Set in a conservation area on the way up to the volcano. Ten single room bungalows, made from local materials, are located across the village, and you are looked after by one local family per bungalow. A real village experience. A porter (500 Vatu) may be required to carry your luggage up the forty-five minute hike from the wharf.

Paunvina Guesthouse. Unakapu, Nguna

Contact: 541 9486, 534 8523   Price: 3,000 Vatu per person (Includes Full Board)

(A2 Map, page 102) Originally a bush retreat, the cyclone has now given the guesthouse sea views. Sleeps up to seven people in three rooms, with a great communal verandah and extensive library.

John's kava bar is nearby, perfect for a sunset shell.

Island Breeze Guesthouse. Taloa, Nguna.

Contact: 772 6488, 777 1606   Price: 4,500 Vatu per person (Includes Full Board)

(A3 Map, page 102) Facing Pele on Undine Bay, is this two-bedroom guesthouse. You can even access wi-fi (1,000 Vatu per device) while relaxing in the hammock watching the sunset.

A small kitchen means self-catering is possible (enquire when you book).

Nakie Women's Guesthouse. Taloa, Nguna.

Contact: 711 3375, 564 00439, 779 4506   Price: 3,000 Vatu per person (Includes Full Board)

(A4 Map, page 102) A sold concrete bungalow, which survived the cyclone with only a few scars. Community owned and run by the village women, Nakie has two bedrooms and a large communal area, which can have ten mattresses on the floor, ideal for large groups.

Set in the middle of the village, it is a good way to immerse yourself in village life. Self-catering is a possibility, but with the tasty fresh food on offer, at a very reasonable price, why would you?

Mangamus Bungalow. Taloa, Nguna.

Contact: 711 3443   Price: 3,500 Vatu per person (Includes Full Board)

(A5 Map, page 102) Close to Udana Cove Bungalows is this single bungalow directly facing the beach and marine conservation area. It has a double bed, but a single mattress can also be provided.

JJ's Bungalow. Worearu, Pele

Contact: 772 6476   Price: 3,500 Vatu per person (Includes Full Board)

(**A6** Map, page 102) Sleeps up to five people in two rooms, one with a double bed, one with bunk beds and a single bed. Close to a white sand beach with a verandah overlooking the sea.

Jowi's Bungalow. Worearu, Pele

Contact: 562 2221   Price: 3,500 Vatu per person (Includes Full Board)

(**A7** Map, page 102) Sleeps up to three people in two rooms, one with a single bed, one with two single beds..

Sunset Frangipanu. Worearu, Pele

Contact: 534 8534   Price: 3,500 Vatu per person (Includes Full Board)

(**A8** Map, page 102) Sleeps up to five people in two rooms. One with a double bed, one with a single bed and bunks.

Simoa Bungalow. Worearu, Pele

Contact: 568 6685, 773 2670   Price: 3,500 Vatu per person (Includes Full Board)

(**A9** Map, page 102) Actually on the beach with good snorkelling just footsteps from the bungalow. Sleeps up to five people in two rooms, one with a double bed, one with a double and single beds.

Sena Pa-pa. Worearu, Pele

Contact: 542 4728, 772 2206   Price: 3,500 Vatu per person (Includes Full Board)

(**A10** Map, page 102) Another bungalow right on the beach. Sleeps up to four people in two rooms, divided by a calico sheet. One with a double bed, one with a single bed and extra mattress on the floor. Beach camping can also be arranged at a lower cost (bring your own tent).

Serety Bungalow. Piliura, Pele

Contact: 563 0979, 7717113   Price: 3,500 Vatu per person (Includes Full Board)

(**A11** Map, page 102) The most remote bungalow, a bit of a Robinson Crusoe experience, located at the edge of the bush overlooking a long deserted white sandy beach. A brightly painted bungalow that sleeps up to three people in a double and a single bed. Beach camping can also be arranged at a lower cost (bring your own tent).

Nabanga Bungalow. Worisivu, Pele

Contact: 563 0315, 778 7850   Price: 3,500 Vatu per person (Includes Full Board)

(**A12** Map, page 102) Sleeps up to five people in two rooms, divided by calico. One with a double bed, the other with two single beds. The host, Kenneth, can cook some great meals with freshly caught fish a highlight.

Wora-Namoa Bungalow. Launamoa, Pele

Contact: 5913 890   Price: 3,500 Vatu per person (Includes Full Board)

(**A13** Map, page 102) Sleeps up to two people in a double bed.

Sunrise Bungalow. Launamoa, Pele

Contact: 5649 102   Price: 3,500 Vatu per person (Includes Full Board)

(**A14** Map, page 102) On the windy side of the island, perfect for surfing. If the water is too disturbed for snorkeling, you can walk thirty minutes across the island to the sheltered side. Sleeps up to ten people in five rooms Beach camping can also be arranged at a lower cost (bring your own tent).

Bella Bungalow. Worisivu, Pele

Contact: 562 6956   Price: 3,500 Vatu per person (Includes Full Board)

(**A15** Map, page 102) Facing the Efate coast, and sleeping up to four people in two rooms. One with a double bed, and the other with two singles. The coral gardens are located almost opposite the bungalow.

Note: Mobile reception on Nguna and Pele is patchy, if you cannot get through, contact the Shefa Tourist office on 5526028, and they will help you book accommodation.

⑪ Where to Eat

At your accommodation. All include full board, and meals are mostly chicken and seafood based, with root vegetables such as taro and yams, and fresh seasonal fruit for dessert.

If you have any specific dietary requirements bring your own food from Port Vila.

🏛 Things to See and Do

Snorkeling

As both islands are part of a marine protected area, there is an abundance of corals and sea life to view, including many turtles. All sheltered areas are good for snorkeling, although the main channel between the islands does have a strong current, and is popular with sharks.

Bring your own gear, and ask permission from the village chief before snorkeling (check with your accommodation on how to do this). Joel Kalfua (711 3443) on Nguna will take you on a snorkeling tour over some of the best corals and hidden fish playgrounds. Cost is 500 Vatu per person, 200 Vatu per child.

Mt Taputoara Volcano

Dominating the island of Nguna at 593 metres (1,946 ft) is this extinct volcano. To climb it you will need a guide, and pay a small custom fee, your accommodation will help arrange this. It is a good half-day climb up to the top and back, with great views of the surrounding islands, from Efate to Epi. Tane Kalo (711 0422) will guide you for 1,000 Vatu per person.

Garden and Cooking Tours

The fertile volcanic soil means that the islands vegetable and fruit gardens surround the volcanic cone. Jack (594 7341) organises a half-day tour where you visit the gardens, select the food, and prepare a fully locally self-sourced meal.

Beaches

Pele's Sunset Strip at Worearu has one the beast beaches in the Shefa province. Golden sands with snorkeling at your door.

The five bungalows here are located close together along the beach, most only sleep two or three people, so if you are going as a group it makes sense to book a few of them together.

Surfing

Pele's wild east coast makes for great surfing amongst the breakers, as well as hosting the occasional kite surfer from Port Vila. The best area for this is down from Launamoa village.

Coral Gardening

Help preserve the marine conservation area in the village of Worasivu on Pele by working with locals in removing foreign invasive species. There is some great snorkeling for pleasure here also, and newly developed giant clam sanctuary. Contact Willie on 568 4429 for more details.

Shepherd Islands

In between Efate and Epi lie a number of populated volcanic cones, the Shepherd Islands. Only twenty minutes by plane from Port Vila, most tourists only get to see them as they fly north to the more popular northern islands.

The islands have a population of over 3,600, although with Port Vila so close, many choose to move there to find work, they even have their own football team, Shepherds United, in the Port Vila Football League.

The main islands are Emae and Tongoa, both were hit badly by cyclone Pam but are recovering rapidly. Those who make the short trip will experience scenery as good as any of the outer islands, as well as trekking, white sandy beaches, and some great diving and snorkeling sites.

Getting to the Shepherds

Emae and Tongoa are the only islands with landing strips. Air Vanuatu fly to Siwo Airport on Emae on Monday and Friday and to Tongoa Airport on Wednesday and Friday, both from Port Vila.

The cost is approx 7,400 Vatu each way. Check out the travel section (page 23) to learn about ticket discounts using your international ticket.

Note that Emae's airport is a very short runway at Siwo. Flights can be cancelled if there is low cloud cover, or high winds, so be flexible in your travel plans, and do not plan to travel out the day before an international flight home.

The Tongoa airport, near Puele, is easier to land on, but note it can also be closed during high winds and low cloud conditions.

There are regular boats from Port Vila. Both the *Brooklyn* and *Island Claws* depart several times a month, for approximately 3,000 Vatu one way. Check out the actual departure times at the harbour in Port Vila.

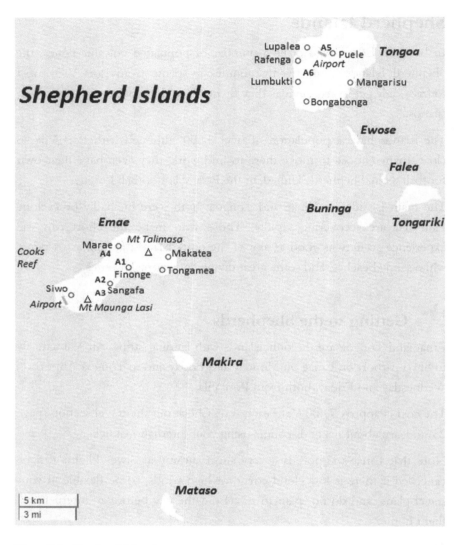

Shepherd Islands

Lupalea ○ A5 ○ Puele *Tongoa*
Rafenga ○ *Airport*
A6
Lumbukti ○ ○ Mangarisu
○ Bongabonga

Ewose

Falea

Buninga

Emae *Tongariki*

Cooks
Reef
Marae ○ Mt Talimasa
A4 △ ○ Makatea
A1
○
A2 ○ Finonge ○ Tongamea
Siwo ○ A3 Sangafa
Airport △
Mt Maunga Lasi

Makira

Mataso

5 km
3 mi

Map of the Shepherd Islands

Accommodation

A1 Nampauwia Bungalow   **A4** Sunset Bungalows

A2 Jaytee Guesthouse   **A5** Kammy's Guesthouse

A3 L & Pako Homestay   **A6** Papatua Guesthouse

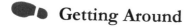 # Getting Around

Both Emae and Tongoa have island roads of varying quality. You can travel from village to village, or from the airport to your accommodation, for 1,500 Vatu per trip, but always check with the driver first.

Depending on where you are staying, walking may be the best option.

Inter-island transport by boat is possible, with a bit of patience, as the *Brooklyn* and *Island Claws* call between the different islands and Port Vila on a somewhat irregular schedule.

To fly between the islands on Air Vanuatu requires an expensive dog leg via Port Vila, as their planes do not fly between the islands. Alternatively Belair have started a service between Emae and Tongoa. They fly on most days, weather permitting. Contact them on 29 893 to check their timetable. The more expensive option is to charter a flight through Air Taxi, contact 554 4206 to enquire about the costs of hiring either a 5, 6 or 9 seater plane.

Where to Stay

Nampauwia Bungalow. Finonge, Emae (* FFP Recommended)

Contact: 779 7324, 535 3655   Price: 2,000 Vatu per person (Full Board)

(A1 Map, page 110) Newly built after the cyclone, and made from traditional materials with a natangora roof, coral floor and palm tree wood walls. It has three rooms, and sleeps up to three guests in single beds.

Set in the garden behind the owners' house, who also have a small store selling basic supplies. James and Marie will help you plan walks and snorkeling (bring your own gear). The beach is five minutes away, and the surf breaking on the reef will lull you to sleep at night.

Jaytee Guesthouse. Sangafa, Emae

Contact: 778 7200, 544 0384   Price: 1,500 Vatu per person (Full Board)

(A2 Map, page 110) Two rooms in another traditional island home. A private dining room and a bedroom with two single beds. The best feature is the shaded area outside that is shared with the owner, his family, and the locals who call round.

L & Pako Homestay. Sangafa, Emae

Contact: 776 1006   Price: 1,500 Vatu per person (Full Board)

(A3 Map, page 110) The largest village on Emae with 250 people has this traditional yet comfortable single roomed house for rent, sleeping two with a mattress on the floor.

Five minutes walk to the nearby beach.

Sunset Bungalows. Marae, Emae

Contact: 569 1407   Price: 2,000 Vatu per person (Full Board)

(A4 Map, page 110) One of the first bungalows built in the Shepherds for tourists in 2010, Sunset Bungalows was badly damaged by cyclone Pam. It is still being rebuilt, but should be fully completed by the time you read this.

Two basic bungalows that each sleep three people on single beds, with a great position facing the coral beach. Eat your meals in the dining room overlooking the sea.

The owner, Jimmy, can also organise day trips out to the Cooks Reef.

Kammy's Guesthouse. Peule, Tongoa

Contact: 539 0212, 537 4321   Price: 1,500 Vatu per person (Self-Catering)

(A5 Map, page 110) Close to the end of the runway. Two bedrooms, and a well equipped kitchen. There is a shop next to the airport to purchase food and fresh bread, or there are supplies of seasonal fruit and vegetables from the nearby market.

Alternatively there is a small kava bar nearby where meals can be purchased for 20 Vatu a dish.

Papatau Guesthouse. Peule, Tongoa

Contact: 543 9046   Price: 1,500 Vatu per person (Self-Catering)

(A6 Map, page 110) On the road between Peule and Lumbukti. Modern building with western toilet and shower and a good kitchen. There is a small market two hundred metres down the road to load up on fresh produce to cook.

Two bedrooms and a verandah overlooking the tropical garden, with a great solar system which charges phones in record time!

⑪ Where to Eat

At your accommodation. Most include full board at a very reasonable price. Meals are mostly seafood based, with root vegetables such as taro and yams, and fresh seasonal fruit for dessert.

The other option is self-catering, with fresh produce available at the local markets. If you have any specific dietary requirements bring your own food from Port Vila.

🛉 Things to See and Do

Emae

Ringed by reef, with white sand and coral beaches, Emae is a typical idyllic Pacific island. Trek around the island on traditional paths or along the grass roads and climb the old volcanoes of Mt Lasi (644 m) and Mt Talimasa (434 m) that rise on the opposite sides of the island.

Both Finonge and Sangafa access the same long beach, and it is an easy thirty-minute walk between the two villages. The best time to snorkel is at high tide, when the reef, which is close to shore, is fully covered with water. At low tide the water is only ankle deep and that is when the villagers wade in, collecting shellfish, octopus, and reef fish for dinner.

The island is also ecologically focused, with the chiefs declaring that Emae had become an organic island in July 2016, with all 290 farmers producing food in an organic way.

Emae women are known for their fine handicraft skills, you can purchase their work in the villages, or if you are interested you can arrange a lesson in traditional weaving.

Cooks Reef

Five km off the west coast of Emae is Cooks Reef. This large atoll is thought to have been first mapped by Captain Cook on his Pacific voyages.

It has brought more than a few ships to grief as the coral only pops above the surface in a few places. A mariner's nightmare is now a recognised snorkeling and diving site, with deep drop offs and very clear water. The corals are colourful, and recent surveys have found that the highest fish diversity and abundance in Vanuatu can be found at the Cooks Reef.

Jimmy Kalo (contact 568 1407) arranges trips out here from Marae in Emae. He also runs the Sunset Bungalows in Marae. Bring your own gear.

Tongoa

The largest and most populated island in the Shepherds, although you are still unlikely to bump into anyone as you walk across the 8km by 7km island.

Tongoa has a steamy, verdant jungle interior of fifteen extinct volcanic cones with deep valleys in between, and a rugged coastline of steep cliffs and black sand beaches, ideal for trekking.

On the west coast is the Tongoa wall, a favourite spot for diving tours from Port Vila who explore this large drop off

The almost deserted village of Rafenga has a stony beach overlooking the water to nearby Epi Island. The underwater volcano, Kuwae (see page 166) may be active, leaving mustard coloured slicks on the water. This can also often be seen when coming into land, or taking off from Tongoa.

Mataso and Makira Islands

The towering volcanic cones on these islands are visible from Emae and Tongoa. If you wish to visit these islands, a boat trip from Emae will cost approximately 5,000 Vatu, or 500 Vatu on a shared boat if your timing is right. Choose a day that is calm, else you may get extremely seasick as the channel crossing can be extremely rough.

You are actually travelling across the caldera of the Makura volcano, Mataso is the remains of the southern rim of the massive crater. Makura is now a submarine volcano, although no eruptions have been recorded in recent history.

The population of Mataso only numbers about 70 now, but they have a reputation for seafaring and cannibalism, and their adventures have entered oral history.

Not only do they own much land in North Efate, but also on Tanna around the Mt Yasur volcano, where a sailor from Mataso once challenged a the local chief to a wrestling match. He won, and as a result some of the land around the volcano there belongs to the Mataso people.

Tanna

Tanna has the second largest population in Vanuatu with 30,000 people living here. Its huge draw card is the mighty Yasur volcano, the easiest active volcano to climb in the world, but there is much more to the island than this.

More of its people follow traditional Kastom lifestyles than on many of the other islands, and its many villages host a number of unique belief systems, from the John Frum cargo cult, to those that revere the British consort, Prince Philip, as their unlikely god. The coral reefs also provide some great diving and snorkeling.

✈ Getting to Tanna

Air Vanuatu operates two daily flights to White Grass airport in Tanna. The cost is approx 13,500 Vatu each way. Check out the travel section (page 23) to learn about ticket discounts using your international ticket.

There are also regular ships from Port Vila, stopping off at Erromango. If you have the time to enjoy a slow journey, contact Vanuatu Ferry to see if they are running south (26 999) or ask around at the Port Vila wharf to see if other cargo ships are travelling there.

Very basic accommodation on cargo ships (no bunks and hard seats if you are lucky) and they can take up to 24 hours to arrive. Note that the channel between Efate and Tanna can get quite rough. The cost is approx 4000 Vatu.

Getting Around

Local buses (converted mini-vans) ply the route from White Grass airport to Lenakel, the main township, approx 5km away, for 300 Vatu a trip. To get around the island you have to be patient and wait for a truck (utility vehicle) where you sit or stand on the tray behind the cab, unless you are lucky and get to ride in the passenger seat.

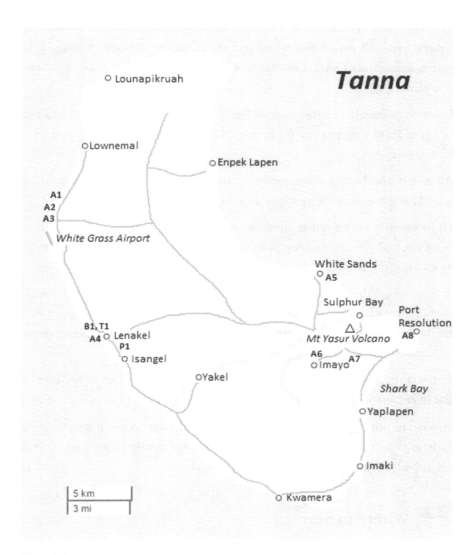

Map of Tanna

Accommodation

A1 Rocky Ridge Bungalows
A2 White Grass Resort
A3 Evergreen Resort
A4 Talupua Guesthouse
A5 Friendly Beach Villas

A6 Volcano Island Paradise
A7 Banyan Castle
A8 Port Resolution Y C

Banks

B1 National Bank

Places

P1 Lenakel Market

Travel

T1 Air Vanuatu Office

The cross-island road is in varying states of repair. AusAid is funding repairs, you will realise this when you travel on the concrete paving. It is worth asking near Lenakel market to see if any trucks are heading to where you want to go.

Fares are somewhat elastic, with different local and foreigner prices and can be up to 5000 Vatu per person to ride to the villages around Yasur and Port Resolution.

All hotels and bungalows either offer transportation, or will arrange it for you. This is the easiest way to get around.

Unfortunately only a rather small amount has been upgraded, which makes for a fun and bouncy journey from the airport and west coast resorts to the volcano.

A four-wheel drive vehicle is required (which also helps explain the high costs to travel across the island). The bumpy journey can take up to two hours and is very scenic, passing through small villages and with great views of Yasur and the east coast.

Importantly, the journey to the volcano is not possible after heavy rain as the river crossing in the ash plane, just before reaching Yasur, is impassable.

If you are not staying close to the volcano and want to see it erupting, go early in your trip, which also gives you the opportunity to go again if you love it, which you will!

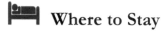 Where to Stay

Volcano Island Paradise. Imayo (* FFP Recommended)

Contact: 771 7460   Price: 2,000 Vatu per person (includes full board)

Email: via web site - www.volcanoparadise.com

(**A6** map, page 117) Morris and Sue will welcome you to these beautifully well-kept bungalows. Deservedly a runner up in the Vanuatu tourism awards for excellence, the view is outstanding. Yasur can be seen as it erupts.

At night time relax in the large dining bungalow and watch the ever-present plume turn red from the lava lake below. A shared western style toilet and three clean bungalows in a tropical garden make for a great stay with locals.

Imayo village nearby provides an opportunity to try kava, see local dancing, and photographic opportunities in the shadow of the volcano. Morris can arrange all tours to Yasur, John Frum villages and Port Resolution.

White Grass Ocean Resort. Near Lenakel (* FFP Recommended)

Contact: 30 010   Price: 29,500 Vatu + per room (includes breakfast)

Email: info@whitegrasstanna.com

(**A2** map, page 117) Luxury four-star resort with all mod cons for tourists including pool, kayaks, golf and tennis on the West coast. A great place to kick back and enjoy the views from the cliff top or garden bungalows.

Tours to the volcano (two hours by car from this side of the island) and village tours organised.

Banyan Castle. South West Valley (near Yasur)

Contact: 535 2449, 779 5622   Price: 2,500 Vatu per person (includes breakfast)

(**A7** map, page 117) An opportunity to stay in a tree house at the foot of the Yasur volcano. An interesting experience and not as unique as expected, as more tree houses are being built at John's neighbours next door.

The only downsides of being perched in the branches of a tree is if you need a nocturnal toilet visit, even with a torch the climb down is scary, and the occasional mouse in search of food (lock your bags up and do not bring anything edible into the room).

If you have not got a head for heights stay in the bungalows below. All tours organised.

Port Resolution Yacht Club. Port Resolution

Contact: 541 6989, 887 791   Price: 2,000 Vatu per person (includes half board)

(**A8** map, page 117) A great spot overlooking the deepwater bay. Six bungalows and shared facilities with a nice bar/restaurant and close to beaches and hot springs.

Busy with yachties from May to October, which brings the bar, in particular, to life. Weary can arrange volcano and other local tours.

Friendly Beach Villas. Near White Sands

Contact: 26 856   Price: 20,000 Vatu + (includes half board)

Email: res@friendlybeach.vanuatu.com

(**A5** map, page 117) Located on the East coast with wonderful sea views. The villas were badly damaged by cyclone Pam, and had actually been looking in need of renovation, but the rebuilding effort has created good modern accommodation using local materials.

It has a bar overlooking the sea and large meals using local seafood. All tours can be booked here, although the volcano tour from here, thirty minutes from Yasur, is as expensive as those booked on the West coast resorts, which is a little odd.

Evergreen Resort. Near Lenakel

Contact: 88 774   Price: 15,000 Vatu + per room (includes breakfast)

Email: tevergreen@vanuatu.com.vu

(**A3** map, page 117) Good snorkeling and great food make this a great place to stay on the west side of the island. Garden and ocean view bungalows, all with en suite facilities. Tours throughout the island can be booked.

Rocky Ridge Bungalows. Near Lenakel

Contact: 541 7220   Price: 4,000 Vatu per person (includes breakfast)

Email: tannarockyridge@gmail.com

(**A1** map, page 117) Opposite the blue hole, the best snorkeling spot on Tanna, these three homely bungalows have the bonus of being located close to the White Grass Ocean resort, enabling you to pop in there for a meal or to book tours.

Talupua Guesthouse. Lenakel

Contact: 88 612   Price: 5,000 Vatu per person (includes breakfast)

(**A4** map, page 117) If you want to be in Lenakel, this is the place to stay. Walking distance to the market, local beaches and shops. Six rooms and shared facilities. Tours can be organised to the volcano and local villages.

Sunrise Bungalows. Port Resolution

Contact: 88 050   Price: 3,500 Vatu per person + (includes breakfast)

Lenakel Cove Resort. Lenakel

Contact: 88 060   Price: 6,000 Vatu per person + (includes breakfast)

Sunset Bungalows. Lenakel

Contact: 88 683   Price: 3,500 Vatu per person (includes breakfast)

Sunshine Coast Bungalows. Loukas

Contact: 543 6795   Price: 3,000 Vatu per person (includes breakfast)

White Beach Bungalows. West Lenakel

Contact: 88 866   Price: 3,500 Vatu per person (includes breakfast)

Volcano Whispering Lodge. South West Valley (Near Yasur)

Contact: 88 000   Price: 2,500 Vatu per person (includes breakfast)

¶¶ Where to Eat

There are a couple of restaurants in the main town Lenakel and in Port Resolution, but you will find that your accommodation will provide most meals, whether you are staying at a resort or in local bungalows. All produce will be local, whatever is available in season, and fish will commonly be the main course.

If you have particular dietary requirements buy your food in the supermarkets in Lenakel or in Port Vila and bring it with you. Kava is always available at a local nakamal, and you should try it if you get the chance.

It is worth stopping at the market in Lenakel (**P1** map, page 117) open every day except after 12PM on Saturdays and all day Sunday, where you can purchase fixed price food at cheap prices. Depending on season, oranges, pineapples, grapefruit (pamplemousse), raspberries, passion fruit, custard apples, root vegetables, tobacco and more can be obtained.

↟ Things to See and Do

Mt Yasur

The most accessible active volcano in the world, Yasur is rightly the highlight of any trip to Tanna. All accommodation will provide a guide and transport to the volcano. If you are staying close by it is not too a strenuous climb, you walk over the ash plain and through jungle to the admission kiosk and then walk up the track for 45 minutes to the car park.

As from April 1st 2016, Admission is 7,500 Vatu per person (reduced by half if you keep your original ticket on subsequent visits). Note that at times of high volcanic activity, you will not be able to get close to the rim, or it may be closed. Check out the Vanuatu volcano monitoring website at www.geohazards.gov.vu to see the current status.

The walk up to the volcano from the car park is via a set of concrete steps, which takes only ten minutes before you arrive at the crater. A short walk to the left or right along pebble marked paths brings you to the sights and sounds of a live volcano.

Explosions are approximately every fifteen minutes, with a huge one every hour. You will see lava thrown into the air before it cools, darkens and falls back down into the crater. The noise of the explosion will likely cause you to step back and blur your camera shot; a tripod is a useful thing to have if you are serious about your photography.

The volcano has three vents, each of which can be active, and is 400 metres across and 360 metres above sea level. The crater is tiered; do not get too close to the edge as it overhangs over the tier below, which is swamped with lava in each explosion.

Even though it is the top attraction in Tanna you will probably find yourself sharing the rim with only thirty or so other tourists. Listen and follow your guide.

There are no railings and there is no insurance that will pay out if you are killed or injured, remember this is a live volcano. Your guide will position you in the best spot, based on wind direction so that the lava is carried away from you, and keep an eye on any material heading your way.

Essential items to bring are a jacket, it can get very windy on the crater rim, and a torch. The volcano is at its best in darkness, and when you have to return to the car park there are no lights to guide you back.

For more details see the story on page 243.

Custom Villages

Tanna is a very traditional island where Christianity has made some of the least impact on the population. The remoteness of many of the villages undoubtedly helped this, as did the locals' desire to eat rather than listen to the early missionaries. Many of these villages do not welcome tourists and are happy continuing in their kastom ways. Those that are open to visitors provide an interesting window into their way of life.

Yakel is one of the best-known villages to visit, the subject of numerous documentaries and the award winning 2015 film 'Tanna' it has embraced tourism with regular tours and dances. All accommodation on the island should be able book you on a tour to the village. For more details see the story on page 293. Carvings and jewellery are available for purchase at the end of the tour.

Perhaps the most unusual and interesting custom village in Sulphur Bay, near the base of the Yasur volcano. This is the heart of the **'John Frum'** movement; a cargo cult, which believes the US Army will return one day bringing gifts and wealth. The use of Tanna as a forward base during the Pacific campaign of the II World War introduced these isolated villages to wealth and western goods brought in on landing strips by cargo planes.

And then they disappeared. If you are there on February 15th the annual celebration encompasses bare chested soldiers with bamboo rifles marching under the US flag. Unmissable.

All is not lost if you are not there on this day, as every Friday Sulphur Bay hosts a John Frum evening with local music and dancing which gives an insight into the culture, albeit with none of the military marching.

Tours may be available from your accommodation, or contact 543 8773 for information on the next dance. A contribution is expected. For more on the John Frum Annual Celebration Day, read the story on page 234.

Depending on where you are staying, other villages close by will often offer tours and dancing. Some of the others include:

Epai – includes hunting demonstration, food preparation and dances. Contact Angela on 542 5077.

Imayo – includes tour of village, dances and kava tasting underneath the imposing Yasur volcano. Contact Poita on 771 7460.

Laul – includes farming methods, kava preparation and tasting and dances. Contact Tony on 566 1665.

Lowinio – including food preparation and dances. Contact George on 771 7336 or 560 0801.

Volcanic Ash Surfing

Yasur and Cerro Negro in Nicaragua are the only two places that you can currently surf down the sides of a volcano. Great fun, although falling off at speed can hurt.

Bring goggles if you know you want to do this, ash gets everywhere and I recommend a dip in the ocean at Port Resolution afterwards as the only way to remove those bits of annoying black cinder.

Surfboards are provided and an hour's entertainment is 1000 Vatu. Your accommodation should be able to book it, if not contact Volcano Island Paradise to arrange a booking. For more details read the story on page 250).

Port Resolution

The deep bay where Captain Cook landed in 1774 has enough to keep you entertained for a day. Close enough to Yasur to hear the regular explosions you can visit the white beaches nearby, or swim in the bay.

Nearby are hot springs, fed by the volcano (good for baking a banana, not for swimming) and cliffs from where you can see sharks and dolphins on a good day.

Best of all is relaxing in the Yacht club with a beer, surrounded by all the paraphernalia the visiting yachties have left behind, listening to Yasur making its presence known.

Diving

Relatively new to Tanna, with **Volcano Island Divers** (Contact 30 010) only opening in 2015. Located at the White Grass Ocean Resort the enthusiastic team will take you to new dive spots, which are being added to every year.

Currently the dives include the *MV Jean Percy* which hit a reef and sank in a storm in 2010, with its cargo still in its holds, 14 metres beneath the surface.

There are also the Blue holes, a series of inter-connected sink holes, which boast tunnels and swim-throughs, with coral formations and abundant fish life, which are at depths of between 6 and 9 metres.

Lenakel

With a population of only 13,000 the main town in Tanna is rather small, which makes it easy to walk through. Hosting a post office, National Bank (with ATM) (**B1** map, page 117), Air Vanuatu office (**T1** map, page 117), a number of shops and restaurants, a hospital and a market.

The market, opposite the main rocky beach, is the real attraction. Wander past the ladies selling all sorts of produce, from bananas to live pigs. Grab a bag of passion fruit for VT100, or the locally grown peanuts as a snack.

For those who enjoy a smoke, the fresh tobacco sold in woven strings, for VT200 a string, is worth buying, bring your own rolling paper. Next to the market is a store, which sells cartons of Tusker beer, useful for those staying in local bungalows without a bar.

Futana

The most easterly island in Vanuatu, the remains of an extinct uplifted submarine volcano, is home to 550 people. Served by Air Vanuatu from White Sands Airport on Tuesday and Thursday for 7,400 Vatu each way.

The Chiefs believe tourism will diminish their cultural values, and no efforts have been made to encourage it. There are no facilities or any accommodation available for tourists. Respect their wishes; you should only go if you have been invited by a Futana local, in whose house you will stay.

Aniwa

A coral island, with its highest point only 42 metres above sea level, Aniwa is considered one of Vanuatu's best-kept secrets for snorkeling, with a marine sanctuary ensuring that a vast array of sea life can be seen in the shallow bay.

It is an adventure; less than 50 tourists a year make it to Aniwa, but the accommodation is excellent, and the fresh seafood is the envy of five star resorts in Port Vila, at a fraction of the price.

Located 24km north west of Tanna it is unusual for its population of just over 350 people being Polynesian in origin, having come originally from the areas around Samoa, and Wallis and Futana, unlike the Melanesian origins of the rest of Vanuatu. The local language is Futanan, although Bislama and English are widely spoken.

Getting to Aniwa

Air Vanuatu fly to Aniwa airport on Tuesday and Thursday from White Grass Airport in Tanna, via the island of Futana.

The cost is approx 5,000 Vatu each way. Check out the travel section (page 23) to learn about ticket discounts using your international ticket.

There are boats from Tanna, but with no set timetable it is rather hit or miss if you can catch one. Ask at Lenakel Wharf.

Getting Around

There is a road from the airport that runs across the island, and a few trucks are available for hire.

The trucks will be at the airport when you arrive and will take you to your accommodation for 2,000 Vatu per person, and are available to run you to and from the lagoon at negotiated prices.

The island is flat and easy to walk around.

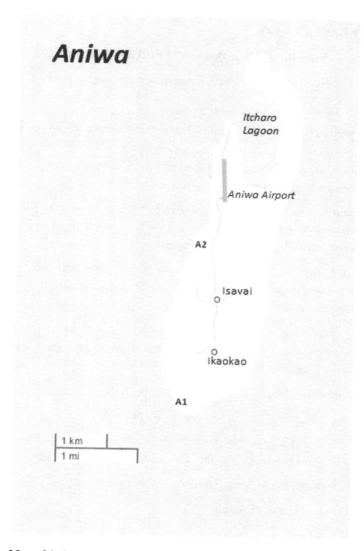

Map of Aniwa

Accommodation

A1 Aniwa Ocean View Bungalows
A2 Fatutu Bungalows

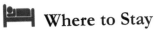 **Where to Stay**

Aniwa Ocean View Bungalows. Ikaokao (* FFP Recommended)

Contact: 561 6506   Price: 2,500 Vatu per person (including breakfast)

Email: aniwaoceanviewbungalows@gmail.com

(**A1** map, page 127) Joshua and Jethro and their families make this a very hospitable place to stay. Three bungalows set in lush gardens opposite the beach and its reef to snorkel on. Small and basic but comfortable with mosquito nets, solar power, solar showers and shared western style toilets.

Fifteen minutes' walk south from the village; you will only be woken by the sounds of the waves crashing on the coral beach. Your host will help take you on local tours, lend you snorkels, and the food is superb.

Lunch and dinner are 750 Vatu each. Fresh seafood and vegetables from the garden are used in most of the meals, and for 750 Vatu extra Jethro will catch a fresh lobster for dinner.

In whale season (July to October) you can see humpbacks in front of the bungalows, and all year round dolphins will play. At night the distant orange glow of Mt Yasur in Tanna can be seen.

Fatutu Bungalows. Isavai

Contact: 535 2951, 535 7795   Price: 2,000 Vatu per person

(**A2** map, page 127) Community owned bungalows in the North West close to Itcharo lagoon, and a short walk to the airport. Meals are 500 Vatu extra.

Local tours include Game Fishing, snorkeling and canoe hire.

Manu-tai Guest House. Ikaukau

Contact: Alfred James in Ikakau village.   Price: 2,500 Vatu per person

Fateika Guest House. Isavai

Contact: Alfred James in Ikakau village.   Price: 2,500 Vatu per person

¶¶ Where to Eat

At your accommodation. Or catch your own fish by line.

Jethro at Aniwa Ocean View Bungalows will teach you how to catch lobster if you ask him nicely, and are good at holding your breath.

¶¶ Things to See and Do

Itcharo Lagoon

In 2007 the islanders decided to create a marine sanctuary here by making taboo the netting and spearing of fish. This has made its lagoon a great place to snorkel, even for those who do not feel comfortable in ocean snorkeling. Even at high tide you can stand up in most of the lagoon. Bring your own snorkel.

Turtles in particular have become numerous since it became a sanctuary, and from November to April you can see Green and Hawk Nosed turtles laying their eggs in the white sand beach of the lagoon on organised tours. Note beach access is closed during this time except for tours.

Snorkeling

Away from the lagoon the reef is very close to the island with big drop offs allowing you to see many fish, and even free dive with the reef sharks if you are more adventurous.

Deep Sea Fishing

Boats can be organised by your accommodation to take you a few km off shore, where you can catch your own meals. Fish that can be caught include Tuna, Barracuda, Marlin and Mahi-Mahi amongst others.

John Frum Village

Every Friday night there is a John Frum cargo cult celebration and dance in Ikaokao, which you are welcome to watch and join in with.

Aneityum

Aneityum, also known as Anatom, is the most southerly inhabited island in the Vanuatu archipelago with a population of just 1300. Mountainous in the interior, this rarely visited island is good for trekking, or visiting the offshore tropical island of Inyeug, or Mystery Island, a spot once favoured by Queen Elizabeth II for a picnic on her trip aboard the royal yacht *Balmoral* in 1974 and now on the itinerary of most cruise ships who visit Vanuatu.

Aneityum was a favoured destination of the 'Blackbirders', slave traders who kidnapped the inhabitants to force them to work in the cane fields of Australia and Fiji in the nineteenth century.

This caused the extinction of local languages, and almost totally depopulated the island. Traders followed, cutting down the island's sandalwood trees, and then the whalers set up station there.

Nowadays it is only the occasional cruise ship that disturbs the tranquility of the island.

✈ Getting to Aneityum

Unless you are travelling on a cruise, the only way to get to and from the island is on the regular Air Vanuatu flights from Tanna on Tuesday and Thursdays.

The cost is approx 7,400 Vatu each way. Check out the travel section (page 23) to learn about ticket discounts using your international ticket.

Getting Around

You walk. There are no cars (except for forestry officials). Catch a local boat to and from the airport on Inyeug.

Aneityum

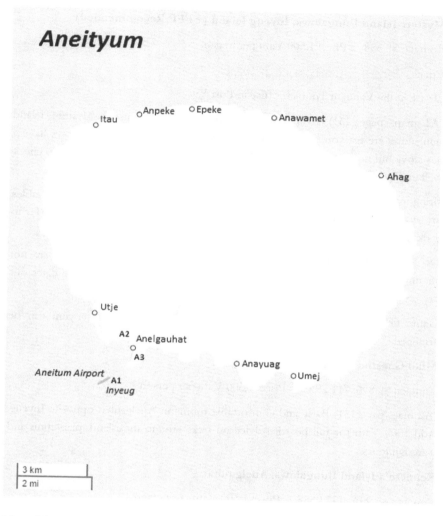

Map of Aneityum

Accommodation

A1 Mystery Island Bungalows

A2 Miko Guesthouse

A3 Kenneth's Island Bungalows

 # Where to Stay

Mystery Island Bungalows. Inyeug Island (* FFP Recommended)

Contact: 88 888   Price: 1,500 Vatu per person

Email: aneityumtourism@vanuatu.com.vu

Or ask at the Vanuatu Tourism office in Port Vila.

(**A1** map, page 131) Ever wanted to be Robinson Crusoe? Mystery Island bungalows are for you. A community based operation; the two bungalows have a gas stove but no electricity. The can be closed at certain times of the year, so check well in advance.

Bring insect repellant and all the food and drink you need. Seafood and vegetables are available on the main island As the airport is on the island you have not far to walk to carry everything you need.

Do look up the cruise timetable before you book, to ensure that you are not sharing the island with thousands of Australian day-trippers. Check the dates out via www.cruisetimetables.com

Game fishing and boat trips around the island and around Aneityum can be arranged.

Miko Guesthouse. Anelgauhat

Contact: 88 896, 711 2957   Price: 1,500 Vatu per person

(**A2** map, page 131) Basic and comfortable rooms in Anelgauhat opposite Inyeug. Add 1000 Vatu for full board. Advice on treks around the island, plantation and waterfall tours.

Kenneth's Island Bungalows. Anelgauhat

Contact: 88 907, 777 0588   Price: 1,500 Vatu per person

(**A3** map, page 131) Also known as 'Breeze Bungalows'. Small bungalows right on the beach with water views, on the edge of Anelgauhat..

Add 1000 Vatu for full board. Kenneth is a guide and will take you on treks, or organise others to take you. Your friendly host is more than willing to take you on a trip to the local kava bar also.

♈ Where to Eat

At your accommodation, unless you are on Mystery Island, whereby you should bring your own food and drink. There are a number of small shops in Anelegauhat, and your host will be able to get you fresh fruit, root vegetables and fish, maybe even a lobster if you are lucky.

Note that Anelegauhat is a dry town and no beer or wine is available.

Things to See and Do

Trekking

Day or multi day trips around and across the island can be arranged upon arrival (bring your own camping gear).

The abandoned Catholic mission (from 1840), ancient rock carvings, old kauri forests, waterfalls and an extinct volcanic crater can be visited, as well as the remains of the old whaling station.

The hardest walk is the cross-island trek to Anawamet, taking you past beautiful waterfalls, but always climbing or dropping, with very few easy sections. Allow two days to complete the trek, and then you have to get back, either by expensive speedboat or on an around the island trek, going east or west.

Analegauhat

The main town and starting point for all the treks. Relax a day or two and snorkel in the bay, there is a wreck of an old whaling boat at the base of the reef, or head over to Mystery Island (500 Vatu per person each way) for its reefs and beaches.

Mystery Island (Inyeug)

Surrounded by sandy beaches, palm trees and a marine sanctuary with a coral reef perfect for snorkeling, it matches the stereotypical image of a south Pacific island.

There are no roads, shops, electricity, Internet access, or other distractions. A perfect place to get away from it all. On cruise ship days the locals from Analegauhat come across and set up stalls selling food, clothes and tourist paraphernalia to the large numbers of passengers who come here by tender from their ship.

To see Mystery Island on a non-cruise ship day is highly recommended. Tradition has it that the island is haunted at night so you will be likely left alone here until your arranged boat comes to pick you up to take you back to the mainland.

The nickname Mystery Island was created due to its hidden runway. This was built in World War II during the war in the Pacific and is very well camouflaged, being invisible from the sea.

Visiting the island today it is hard to believe what an important base it was for the American bombers being sent north to the Solomon Islands to attack the Japanese occupiers. Nothing remains except the bungalows to stay at, and of course the impressively long runway itself.

The runway itself was the cause of a cargo cult on nearby Aneityum, the island that can be seen in the background above. The islanders had rarely seen a white man before, and now they were confronted by hundreds of them, accompanied by large numbers of aircraft. Similar to the John Frum cult in nearby Tanna, the islanders were captivated by the sight of the silver planes flying in, unloading huge amounts of cargo, and then flying off again. Cargo cults are peculiar to this region, the sudden and dramatic meeting of cultures caused them. The short lived nature of the contact (being only the last few years of World War II), contributed to the local myth making and belief that this time of wealth and change will come again.

There are still members of the cult today on Aneityum patiently waiting for the day when the planes return and provide goods for all, accompanied by their messiah.

Erromango

Heavily forested and with little in the way of tourist infrastructure, Erromango does not feature on many tourist itineraries. Don't let that put you off, it has some of the best trekking in Vanuatu and some great historical and natural sights to see.

As with the other southerly islands in Vanuatu, Erromango suffered heavily from 'Blackbirding' with islanders being captured by slave traders and shipped to work on plantations in Australia and other Pacific Islands.

Captain Cook paid a short visit in 1774 but was attacked and after a brief battle in which several locals were killed, he hurriedly departed. In 1852 an Irish trader, Peter Dillon, came looking for the French explorer La Perouse, who had disappeared in this area forty years previously and set up an early trading venture, with the main bay on the west coast now named after him.

Today the island has a population of just under 2,000, and is heavily dependant on Sandalwood trees for income. These are still logged manually and exported overseas.

Getting to Erromango

Regular flights from Air Vanuatu to Dillon's Bay in the north and Ipota in the south can be taken from Port Vila, on Tuesday and Thursday mornings.

You can even use this flight to cross the island, or as part of a trip to Tanna as the itinerary is Port Vila -> Dillon's Bay -> Ipota -> White Sands, Tanna. The return journey later in the day is exactly the same in reverse.

Note that both airports have grass strips which means they are closed after heavy rain. Dillon's Bay airport can be closed when there is low cloud, as with no ground radar, flights are based on visual approaches and if the pilots cannot see the airport they will continue on.

The cost from Port Vila is approx 9,000 Vatu each way. Check out the travel section (pages 23) to learn about ticket discounts using your international ticket.

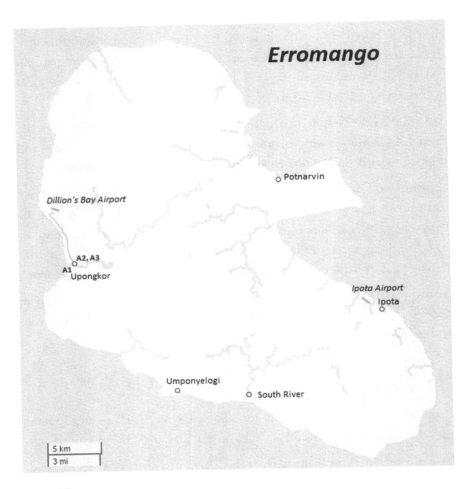

Map of Erromango

Accommodation

A1 Waneo View Yacht Club

A2 Metsons Guesthouse

A3 PWMU Vetunam Guesthouse

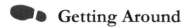 # Getting Around

There is one road from the airport at Dillon's Bay to the main village, which is known both as Upongkor and Dillon's Bay. It is little more than an 8 km grass track.

You should be able to share transport to the village for approx 1,000 Vatu per person. The transport can be out of fuel, or broken down, then you have to walk for approximately two hours.

To get around the island you either walk or catch speedboats. It is easier to catch speedboats on Air Vanuatu flight arrival days, and then you can share. Else you will be paying approximately 12,000 Vatu to South River and then have to walk across the island to Ipota.

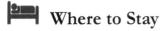 # Where to Stay

Waneo View Yacht Club. Upongkor (* FFP Recommended)

Contact: Book on arrival   Price: 2,000 Vatu per person

(**A1** map, page 136) Newly finished two story buildings set in tropical gardens by the beach, with modern showers and toilets and good local food cooked by David and his family.

Metsons Guesthouse. Upongkor

Contact: 68 993   Price: 2,500 Vatu per person

(**A2** map, page 136) Modern building with two rooms. Add 1,000 Vatu for full board. William can arrange guides for treks, and local tours.

PWMU Vetunam Guesthouse. Upongkor

Contact: Book on arrival   Price: 1,500 Vatu per person

(**A3** map, page 136) A tin shed with space for up to ten people. Mattresses placed on pandanus leaves on the floor. Add 1,000 Vatu for full board. All tours and treks can be arranged.

Sompu-L Guesthouse. Upongkor

Contact: 545 3813   Price: 1,500 Vatu per person

Camping

Price: Custom fee may be payable depending on location.

Bring your gear and camp elsewhere on the island.

Homestays

Homestays may be available in Ipota and Potnarvin, ask upon arrival.

¶¶ Where to Eat

In Upongkor, Potnarvin, and Ipota, the main villages, you can easily obtain fresh fruit, vegetables, eggs and seafood from your accommodation hosts if you wish to prepare your own meals.

However all bungalows will offer you full board for around 1,000 Vatu and you will get to eat family meals which are fresh and tasty. If you are hiking bring in the supplies you need.

¶ Things to See and Do

Upongkor

Situated on the Williams River, the village is a quiet place to relax, swim in the blue water, and prepare for a hike. A thirty-minute walk from the village takes you to the rock where John Williams's body was marked out after he was murdered in 1839.

An unfortunate missionary from England, Williams was the last white man to be eaten on the island. The marks can be seen clearly on the rock, next to a small plaque. Further up the hill are the marks for another missionary, John Gordon, and his wife, who were killed 22 years later (although not eaten).

A short canoe ride away is Suva beach, behind which lie the ceremonial Cave of Skulls where the ancient leaders were buried. Bones and the possessions of the dead can still be seen, as well as rock carvings (A Custom fee must be paid, and a guide is required for entry). The beach itself has a lovely reef, and offers great snorkeling.

Nearby there are other attractions including waterfalls and ancient Kauri forests. Traditional outrigger canoes can be hired for local tours.

Trekking

There are two main treks, timed to fit in with the Air Vanuatu flights arriving on a Tuesday and departing on a Thursday, although you may find this too rushed and may want to linger in Upongkor or on other parts of the island.

The main trek starts (or finishes if you are doing it in reverse) at Upongkor. Leaving the Williams River you climb through the ancient Kauri forests before dropping down to a coastal walk to Umponyelogi village, where you can stay or travel another hour to the South River where you can set up your tent on the flat ground nearby. Mosquito repellant is recommended for nighttime. The river offers a great place to relax and bathe and catch freshwater prawns for dinner.

The next day is a very pleasant walk mostly through forests on an old logging trail. Sleep at Ipota before catching the flight to Tanna or Port Vila the next day.

You will need to provide your own water (you can obtain it in Upongkor, but it makes more sense to bring it with you from Port Vila) and food, and will need to hire a guide (approx 3,000 Vatu per day), as the paths are not clearly marked.

There are steep climbs involved as you travel to South River, but those with at least a moderate level of fitness will not have any problems. The South River needs to be crossed, there may be a canoe available, otherwise you have to swim so bring your costume and protective covers for your bags in case you drop them.

Rain and mist makes the paths slippery in places so wear good shoes, and get your guide to cut you a walking stick.

Ambrym

Ambrym is the island of volcanoes, black magic, carving and dance. Although lush and green around the fringes, it is dominated by the large caldera in the middle upon which the active volcanoes of Benbow and Marum sit. If you climb up to the volcanoes, you see the dramatic contrast from the black beaches and palm trees into a moon-like scene of desolation on the ash plain where nothing lives.

Named by Captain Cook on his voyages through the Pacific in 1774 after asking a native what he called the island, he answered "Ham Rim", although it is debatable whether the question was understood. Ham Rim means 'Hear are Yams' in the Ranon language (spoken only in the south east of the island).

The culture, as with most islands in Vanuatu, is unique to the island, with its own languages in each geographic corner. Black magic is an important part of the belief system, with sorcery and magic being practiced widely. This causes other islands to often be fearful of the people of Ambrym. Maybe not surprisingly, Ambrym had been one of the least successful islands for missionaries to convert the locals to Christianity (see the story on page 272).

The locals are renowned for their specialised carving of Tam-Tams, large wooden statues with a slit in the middle, used to communicate between villages, and for their drawings in the sand to communicate community (or kastum) stories.

Getting to Ambrym

Regular flights from Air Vanuatu to Craig Cove (pronounced 'Kracoff') which can be taken from Port Vila, twice a week on a Sunday and Tuesday, and Santo, once a week on a Tuesday, will get you to the west coast village.

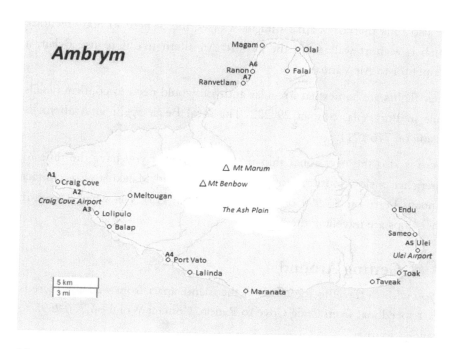

Map of Ambrym

Accommodation

A1 Sylinne Guesthouse

A2 Sam's Guesthouse

A3 Ter Ter Hot Springs Bungalows

A4 Vanuatu Island Experience Bungalows

A5 Sea Beach Bungalows

A6 Solomon Douglas Bungalows

A7 Ranon Beach Bungalows

The local Air Vanuatu booking agent/airport manager is Sam on 776 7129. He also runs the cosy Sam's Bungalows (see the 'Where to Stay' section), which is a short walk from the airport. An alternative is to use Belair, a competitor to Air Vanuatu.

Their flights are somewhat irregular and you would need to confirm details while in Port Vila, contact 29 222. The local Belair agent in Ambrym is Lissing on 776 1711.

There is also the occasional ship from Port Vila. If you have the time to experience a slow journey stopping off in Epi and Malekula also, contact Vanuatu Ferry on 26 999 or ask around at the Port Vila wharf to see if other ships are travelling there.

Getting Around

If you wish to travel to the north of the island, apart from walking, there is a fast speedboat from Craig Cove to Ranon. Contact Wolul on 776 2595 to arrange a journey.

The cost is 12,000 Vatu (highly dependant on fuel prices, and as with most things in Vanuatu, not negotiable) for the boat, so the more people with you the better. If you are lucky a boat may meet the plane and you may pay share the cost with others.

The view of the cliffs as you travel north on the two-hour journey makes it enjoyable; if the seas are rough it is more of an ordeal. Wolul's boat provides life jackets. If you find an alternative make sure that life jackets are available.

There is no round island road, and transport is limited to basic mud roads between local settlements. There are a number of trucks (also known as utility vehicles) where you tend to end up standing on the tray behind the driver. Exhilarating, but keep an eye out for low branches. Their availability is both dependant on fuel and spare parts.

Ambrym Trucks Contact Details

WEST

In Craig Cove contact Tomsen on 771 3602 or Walter on 710 5379. (Both are Seventh Day Adventists, and do not work on Saturdays)

In Port Vato contact Edwin on 771 4426.

In Meltougan contact Sandy on 777 3718 or John on 773 4398.

NORTH

In Ranon contact Sandy on 593 3801, who is also a French speaker.

In Magam contact Towsy on 541 3393.

EAST

In Endu contact Nakon on 593 2520.

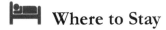 Where to Stay

Ter Ter Hot Springs Bungalows. Lolipulo (* FFP Recommended)

Contact: 772 6534   Price: 2,550 Vatu per person (includes breakfast)

Email: via Malampa Travel Centre - http://www.ambrym.travel/

(**A3** map, page 141) Lovely bungalows with the huge plus of having their own beach and geothermal pools to relax in. Particularly wonderful if you have just done the trek to the volcanoes and back.

Great breakfast full of seasonal fruits. Approximately 20 minutes walk from Craig Cove airport or 700 Vatu by truck.

Sam's Guesthouse. Craig Cove

Contact: 776 7129 Price: 2,250 – 3,000 Vatu per person (includes breakfast)

Email: via Malampa Travel Centre - http://www.ambrym.travel/

(**A2** map, page 141) A short walk from Craig Cove airport, where Sam works, are the bungalows. You can take the truck for 500 Vatu. One has an en suite with shared facilities for the other two. Solar power in the evening. Full board is available for 500 Vatu a meal.

Sylline Guesthouse. Craig Cove

Contact: 540 5280   Price: 2,000 Vatu per person (includes breakfast)

Email: via Malampa Travel Centre - http://www.ambrym.travel/

(**A1** map, page 141) Small and with basic facilities. Great position near the coral beach and fifteen minutes from Craig Cove airport.

Vanuatu Island Experience Bungalows. Port Vato

Contact: 774 2661   Price: 2,000 Vatu per person (includes full board)

(**A4** map, page 141) Located in Port Vato, requires a truck from Craig Cove (enquire when booking, approx 5,000 Vatu). Close to a black sand beach, run by volcano guide John Taso.

Solomon Douglas Bungalows. Ranon

Contact: 541 2615   Price: 3,500 Vatu per person (includes all meals)

(**A6** map, page 141) In north Ambrym, several bungalows close to the bush with basic facilities. Near Ranon village, requires a boat (approx 15,000 Vatu) to return to Craig Cove airport, or walk through the ash plain. Close to a black sand beach

Ranon Beach Bungalows. Ranon

Contact: 593 3801   Price: 2,550 Vatu per person (includes breakfast)

Email: via Malampa Travel Centre - http://www.ambrym.travel/

(**A7** map, page 141) Great position, overlooking the beach with a verandah to gaze out at the sea.

Sea Beach Bungalows. Ulei

Contact: 48 888   Price: 2,550 Vatu per person (includes breakfast)

Email: via Malampa Travel Centre - http://www.ambrym.travel/

(**A5** map, page 141) Unusual double storied bungalows, located near Ulei airport on east Ambrym.

Sanoli Guest House. Endu

Contact: 545 1486   Price: 2,000 Vatu per person (includes breakfast)

Savuli Bungalows. Toak

Contact: 23 167, 534 5250   Price: 2,000 Vatu per person (includes breakfast)

Rambelao Guest House. Toak

¶¶ Where to Eat

There are no restaurants in Ambrym, but your accommodation will provide breakfast and an opportunity to purchase other meals at reasonable prices (approximately 800-1,000 Vatu per meal) made of local ingredients and what is available in season.

If you have particular dietary requirements buy your food in the supermarkets in Port Vila and bring it with you. Kava is always available at a local nakamal, and you should try it if you get the chance.

The local shops will have a small variety of food, mainly tinned, and infrequent supplies of Tusker beer, depending on when the last cargo ship from the capital arrived.

↑ Things to See and Do

The Volcanoes

The mighty Benbow and Marum volcanoes, as well as the spectacular unworldly landscape of the caldera, are what brings most tourists to Ambrym. Not as accessible as the 'park and ride' Yasur in Tanna, you have to work, at least a little, to visit these mighty volcanoes, and it is worth every step and every bit of sweat to do it.

The volcanoes dominate the islands life, and beliefs. A huge Plinian explosion two thousand years ago produced the massive caldera, and their constant activity is an ever-present part of daily life. The soil is rich and crops can grow quickly some years, but in others the eruptions create acid rain and all are destroyed.

The last major eruption in 1913 caused the evacuation of the whole island to Efate in the south. The village of Mele, 5 kms from Port Vila, still remains a transplanted Ambrym village, populated by those who decided not to return to the dangers of living beneath the volcanoes.

They are still very little visited, and the last time we climbed them, only our guide and us were present on the vast plateau. We started from Craig Cove, and the walk was made even longer by the breakdown of the only truck available, but it was two very memorable days that were highlight of our Ambrym stay.

If the volcanoes are the only reason for you to visit Ambrym, check the Vanuatu Geohazards site (www.geohazards.gov.vu) for the latest safety information, and whether the volcanoes are too dangerous to visit.. In late 2014 the volcanoes started to get very active, with a major eruption in August, followed by minor eruptions.

The result was a Level 2 warning, with parts of the caldera and both craters part of an exclusion zone. Take these warnings seriously and do not push your guides to break them, this happened once on Tanna with sadly the guide and tourists all being killed by an eruption.

The Ambrym Volcano Guides

The current list of government approved volcano guides are:

Name	Location	Contact	Language Spoken
Bae Wilpen	West Ambrym	771 3610	English
John Taso	West Ambrym	774 2661 or 544 6190	English & French
Joses Wilfred	West Ambrym	548 7405	English & French
Philimon Paul	East Ambrym	535 4948	English
Gideon Enok	East Ambrym	595 0670	English
Jeffery Bong	East Ambrym	592 3994	English
John Willie	North Ambrym	779 3369	English & French
Edwin Da	North Ambrym	598 7405	English

Alternatively your accommodation can organise a guide, usually on arrival, and a tent for a journey up to the caldera and the volcanoes. If you wish to organise this before you arrive, either contact Malampa Travel www.malampa.travel or contact the guides listed above.

Malampa Travel is an Australian and New Zealand aid funded call centre, created to encourage tourism to the Malampa province (Malekula, Ambrym and Paama islands).

They do charge more than booking direct, although this commission is used to cover running costs, and all profits are pushed back into improving the development and marketing of tourism in the province.

It is also the only way to pay by credit card for tours and accommodation, in advance, on the island.

The tents provided are of varying quality, and are often left behind by previous tourists (you may wish to do the same). It is definitely worth bringing a small US$50 tent with some waterproof capabilities, new tents have these, older tents less so, as you may discover when out on the caldera at night.

The volcanoes have their own weather system, and these are predominantly composed of sudden and torrential showers. You can almost guarantee, whatever the weather on the coast, that it will rain, and rain hard while you are there. Being flooded in a tent is certainly an experience, but one you may wish to avoid having!

Also bring a torch and batteries, or better still a solar torch, these are both extremely useful and highly prized by the guides, and it is a nice way to thank them for safely guiding you up and back.

In recent years the treks have become more organised and include an experienced guide, one porter per person, food, and entrance fees. There are three small campsites available around the two volcanoes.

Note that the fees include the trek only. To get to the trek starting point you will need to pay for boat or truck transfers if required.

Volcano tours and their Costs

- **Volcano Day tour** (only available from the North): 7,000 Vatu per person (single supplement 2,000 Vatu)
- **Volcano return tour**. 2 days/1 night camping: 11,900 Vatu per person (single supplement 4,000 Vatu)

- **Volcano coast to coast** (either north to south or vice versa). 2 days/1 night camping: 16,200 Vatu per person (single supplement 5,500 Vatu)

- **Volcano coast to coast extended** (either north to south or vice versa). 3 days/2 nights camping: 21,150 Vatu per person (single supplement 2,000 Vatu)

The official tariffs may change, check on the board at the arrival shed at the airport for any updated prices. All include one guide (a maximum of four people per guide), one porter per person, all meals during the trek and all entrance and custom fees.

The Routes to the Caldera

The climb to both volcanoes can be done in a very long day, but we strongly recommend sleeping at the west or east camp, and enjoying a two day trek. It makes for a more leisurely adventure, and gives you time to stop and investigate the caldera and its surrounds.

There is also something quite unique about sleeping beneath an active volcano, with the question often coming to mind as you try to sleep of "Is that thunder or an eruption?".

Bring wet weather gear and a change of clothes. There are very few living things on the caldera, and consequently no shade, so wear a hat and apply sunscreen.

There are three major routes to the caldera, from the north, west and east. The walk from the north is the easiest (note that a certain level of fitness and fortitude is still required), from the west it is the longest but avoids the need to get an expensive boat to Ranon and it is quite strenuous in places, while the trek from the east is by far the hardest single climb.

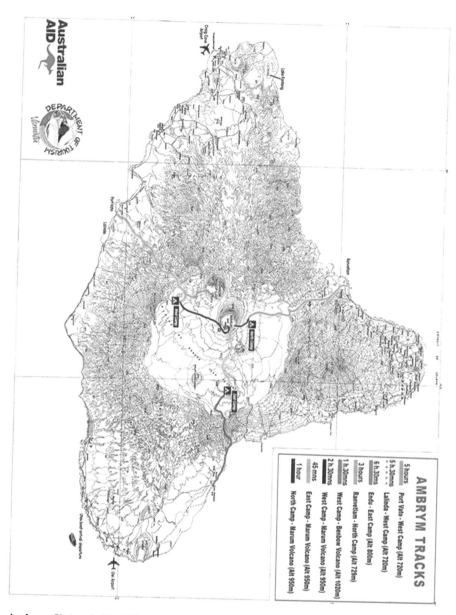

AMBRYM TRACKS

5 hours	Port Vato - West Camp (Alt 720m)
5 h.30mns	Lalinda - West Camp (Alt 720m)
6 h.30mns	Endu - East Camp (Alt 800m)
3 hours	Ranvetlam - North Camp (Alt 729m)
1 h.30mns	West Camp - Benbow Volcano (Alt 1020m)
2 h.30mns	West Camp - Marum Volcano (Alt 950m)
45 mns	East Camp - Marum Volcano (Alt 950m)
1 hour	North Camp - Marum Volcano (Alt 950m)

Ambrym Volcanic Trek Map

149

Climbing from the north

Starting from Ranon it is 15 minutes by truck to Ranvetlam village (3,500 Vatu) or an hour or so easy walk through gardens and trees. Close to Ranvetlam is the official north camp, and the furthest one from the volcanoes. Then it is a 5 hour walk to Marum, and a further 2 hours to Benbow. The walk to the caldera is approximately 7 km. It is an enjoyable walk through rainforests, along river beds (which may have water flowing depending on weather conditions), and with great views of Marum and Benbow in the distance. As you get closer you will walk through fields of wild cane, and then climb over previous scoria lava flows.

Climbing from the west

Starting from Craig Cove it is 30 minutes by truck to Lalinda where the ash river begins (5,500 Vatu) or two to three hours walk down a bush track. It is a 9.5 km journey to the caldera taking 6 hours.

You will walk through a wide ash river, before you reach the canyons made from mudflows and rivers, and encounter some hard climbing. Parts of the route are quite steep and need to be taken slowly.

The West camp is below Benbow, with a 90 minute climb to the top, and upon your return to the caldera a 2 ½ climb to the top of Marum.

Climbing from the east.

The hardest route, it takes approximately 7 to 9 hours to get to the caldera and the east camp from Ulei. The route takes you through rainforest, dunes, and many steep gulleys and small cliffs.

Much of the journey is over difficult terrain, and when you do arrive at the east camp, close to Marum, you will need a rest before attempting to climb to the top of the crater.

Climbing from the caldera to the craters

The climb to the top of Marum (950 Metres) is relatively straightforward, albeit a steep climb, and you will have a fine view of the lava lake below unless obscured by rain and of steam. Take care on the lip as you peer over to the bubbling orange mass below, the unusual slurping lava noise sounds similar to the sea washing onto a beach.

Some hikers like to rest up here and watch the lava at night. This is quite spectacular, but go slow on the return journey to the camp, it is very hard to get medical help for a fall out here.

The climb to the top of Benbow (1,020 metres) is much harder, walking up the knife edge walls of gullies at times, crawling to maintain your grip, and then facing slow progress in the ash near the top as you go two paces up and slip back one.

Not recommended at all if you suffer from vertigo, as you will often be walking slowly with steep drops on either side of you. When you reach the top you look down the steep crater walls to the distant lava lake, and may be able to see explosions, depending on Benbow's activity.

Note that the actual lave lake is mostly hidden from view unless you descend into the crater. Do not do this unless you have the requisite climbing equipment (ropes, carabiners, helmet), oxygen masks and heat resistant equipment. You will also need to be accompanied by a vulcanologist for your safety.

The Rom Dance

One of the most colourful and spectacular dances in Vanuatu is the Rom Dance. Rom means masked, and the dance is a secret male only affair, portraying the old story of good versus evil and the use of black magic, with the elaborately masked dancers representing the evil spirits.

The masks and costumes are beautifully designed, and are destroyed at the end of the dance season so that the evil spirits will not take root within the dancers portraying them.

The Tam Tam statue is used alongside shakers and the dancers' voices to make a mesmerising musical accompaniment to the whirling and fast body movements of the dancers. The shakers are smashed into the ground in front of the Tam-Tam at the end of the dance.

The dance is performed during the harvest period from July to September each year, and for special festivals, and can usually only be attended by males. It is not easy to get to see, if you are in Ambrym from June to September ask at your accommodation to see if any Rom dances are occurring, or call the following people.

- Fanla (North Ambrym). Contact Jamis on 543 2960 or Freddy on 772 2853.

- Awor Sansam (West Ambrym). Contact Chief Jonas on 593 3703 or Chief Louis on 777 9548.

Sand Drawings

Sand drawings are a unique art form in Ambrym. They are used to tell stories and pass on wisdom from one generation to the next. The artists are highly skilled, using one finger to trace quickly through sand or ash to produce intricate artwork, in an amazingly quick time, without lifting the finger from the ground. These are often given as gifts to people.

See the story on page 272 for more on sand drawings.

Malekula

Malekula is the second largest island in Vanuatu with a population of over 20,000. The north of the island, where a major earthquake lifted the land by 40 cm in 1965, is the most accessible, although access, apart from the coast road, is still by walking.

The island is home to the tribes of the big and small Nambas, whose aggressive cannibal tendencies meant much of Malekula was unexplored until last century. It has some the best trekking in Vanuatu, and some of the most remote beautiful beaches hidden away in the rarely visited Maskelynes.

Getting to Malekula

Regular flights from Air Vanuatu to Norsup can be taken from Port Vila, every day except Sunday, and Santo, four times a week (Tuesday to Friday) and will get you to the north east coast town.

To get to Lamap in the south or South West Bay (located descriptively), Air Vanuatu fly on Monday from Port Vila, returning Thursday, and from Santo on Mondays only both ways. The cost is approx 15,000 Vatu from Port Vila to Norsup, and 10,000 Vatu to the southern airports each way. From Santo to Norsup costs approx 5,800 each way. Check out the travel section (page 23) to learn about ticket discounts using your international ticket

There is also the occasional ship from Port Vila. If you have the time to experience a slow journey stopping off in Epi first, contact Vanuatu Ferry (26 999), or Big Sista (568 5225) who run a catamaran to Malekula, stopping at the Maskelynes, Lamap, Atchin Island and Litzlitz, en route to Santo on a Monday, returning on a Thursday. Economy is 6,000 Vatu each way, 2,000 Vatu extra for business class (top level of the boat with better seats, air con and non stop movies) or ask around at the Port Vila wharf to see if other ships are travelling there.

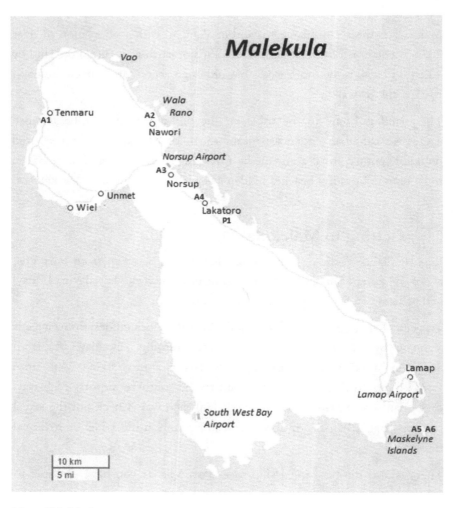

Map of Malekula

Accommodation

A1 Nig Nambas Bungalow

A2 Nawori Sea View

A3 Nabachel Bungalows

A4 Sunrise Bungalows

A5 Senelich Bungalows

A6 Batis Seaside Bungalows

Places

P1 Malampa Handicraft Centre

Speedboats can be hired from both Craig Cove in Ambrym (approx 15,000 Vatu to Lakatoro) and Luganville in Santo (approx 30,000 Vatu).

Getting Around

There is a coastal road, which connects Lamap in the south to Lakatoro, the main town, and Norsup, and then up and around the 'Dogs Head' as the top part of the island is known. Look at the map of Malekula and you will see it is shaped like a dog sitting down.

The road can be closed after heavy rain as the many creeks it crosses flood, this will also make even bigger ruts for vehicles to get stuck in afterwards.

Buses run from the airport in Norsup into Lakatoro, and cost 400 Vatu per person. Taxis are also available for arriving flights. Trucks run up and down the east coast road, and shared rides can be fairly easy to find, although you may have to wait for a few hours, except on Sundays when there is very little traffic.

Shared rides cost from 500 to 3,000 Vatu depending on distance. If you need to hire an entire vehicle, the costs will be much higher, as much as 12,000 Vatu to go from Norsup to Lamap.

An alternative is to hire a speedboat, the only viable alternative after heavy rain. Costs vary, according to distance, but are similar to hiring a truck.

Where to Stay

Nawori Sea View Bungalows. Nawori (* FFP Recommended)

Contact: 541 5570   Price: 2,750 Vatu per person (includes Breakfast)

Email: via Malampa Travel Centre - www.malekula.travel

(A2 map, page 154) Perched on top of a small cliff with a great view out to Wala Island. Approximately 20 minutes by truck from Norsup airport (arrange transport in advance) in the heart of Small Namba territory.

There is a generator for a short time in the evening, and western style flushing toilets. The local village is a source of great food and entertainment (kava in particular), and Etienne can arrange local tours, including to Wala.

Senelich Bungalows. Maskelynes. (* FFP Recommended)

Contact: 711 7096   Price: 8,500 – 10,000 Vatu per room (includes Breakfast)

Email: senelich@gmail.com

(A5 map, page 154) A bit of luxury with two over water bungalows and solar power. Great food from the local chef who used to work at Le Lagon in Port Vila. Try the local lobster.

Nabachel Bungalows. Norsup

Contact: 774 0482, 48 899   Price: 2,500 Vatu per person (includes Breakfast)

Email: via Malampa Travel Centre - www.malekula.travel

(A3 map, page 154) A very short walk from Norsup airport. The owners are great cooks, and ever so helpful in arranging tours, or snorkeling gear for the beach close by. The garden is a great place just to kick back in.

Sunrise Bungalow. Lakatoro

Contact: 48 888   Price: 2,800 Vatu per person (includes breakfast)

Email: via Malampa Travel Centre - www.malekula.travel

(A4 map, page 154) Modern and comfortable bungalow only a short walk from the centre of Lakatoro, but in a quiet location.

Batis Seaside Bungalows. Maskelynes

Contact: 775 1463   Price: 2,500 Vatu per person (includes Breakfast)

Email: batisseasideguesthouse.vanuatu@gmail.com

(A6 map, page 154) Next to Senlich Bungalows, with a choice of sea or garden views. Owner Sethric can arrange many local tours, including snorkeling and village experiences, as well as pickup from Lamap airport.

Big Nambas Bungalow. Tenmaru

Contact: 48 888   Price: 2,500 Vatu per person (includes Breakfast)

Email: via Malampa Travel Centre - www.malekula.travel

(A1 map, page 154) One of the more unique options in Malekula, the bungalow has been built on a large coral outcrop, and you reach it via a rickety bamboo walkway. Great views out to sea from the wonderful verandah.

Close to all Big Namba tours, and end point for the Big Nambas trek.

Yake Guest House. Norsup

Contact: 48 663, 535 8158   Price: 2,000 Vatu per person

Amelenear Guest House. Norsup

Contact: 48 489   Price: 2,500 Vatu per person (includes Breakfast)

Ameltoro Resort. Norsup

Contact: 48 431, 536 8944   Price: 4,000 Vatu per person (includes Breakfast)

MDC Guest House. Lakatoro

Contact: 48 642   Price: 2,500 Vatu

Lakatoro Trading Centre Guest House. Lakatoro

Contact: 48 554, 48 656   Price: 6,500/8,500 Vatu per room (includes Breakfast)

Malampa Provincial Guest House. Lakatoro

Contact: 48 491, 49 571   Price: 2,500 Vatu per person

Amodoteper Bungalows. Rano Mainland

Contact: 541 5159   Price: 6,500/8,500 Vatu (per room includes Breakfast)

Rose Bay Bungalows. Wala Island

Contact: 541 6891   Price: 2,500 Vatu per person (includes Breakfast)

Karuma Guest House. Lamap

Contact: 48 594   Price: 1,500 Vatu per person (includes breakfast)

Tamlam Bungalows. Vao Island

Contact: 536 8648   Price: 2,500 Vatu per person (includes Breakfast)

Limereh Guest House. Maskelynes

Contact: 48 908   Price: 750 Vatu per person (includes Breakfast)

Pelong PWMU Guest House. Maskelynes

Contact: 544 9997   Price: 500 Vatu per person (includes Breakfast)

Malog Bungalows. Maskelynes

Contact: 547 9041, 48 514   Price: 4,000 Vatu per room (includes Breakfast)

¶¶ Where to Eat

There are a few choices in Lakatoro, at the markets and in the occasional cafe in the main street, but as with most of Vanuatu's islands the best options are at your accommodation where you can ask for full board for a reasonable price (usually 1,000 to 2,000 Vatu).

If you do make it as far south as the Maskelynes, do see if you can eat at the Senlich Bungalows, which has a restaurant with full bar overlooking the sea.

¶¶ Things to See and Do

Big Nambas

Ceremonial dances with insights into the Big Namba culture, including kastom stories and kava and food preparation. With painted bodies, feathers in their hair and wearing just a large pandanus penis sheath, the Big Nambas stomp, sing and dance in a colourful and memorable performance.

These can be seen in Mae and at Unmet, near Lakatoro, and cost approximately 5,000 Vatu per person.

Small Nambas

If you see the Big Nambas you cannot miss the Small Nambas. The two tribes, distinguished by their size of their penis sheath, were mortal enemies for hundreds of years on Malekula.

There was rarely a ceasefire lasting more than a few months before attacks would resume and the victors cooking and eating those who lost, which would definitely add more than a little motivation to the fighting.

The Small Nambas ceremonies are similar but involve the use of the Tam Tam, tribal drum, as seen regularly in Ambrym. Magic and fire ceremonies are also regularly performed by the Small Nambas.

See the ceremonies at Vao and Rano, and occasionally on Wala. Cost is 5,000 Vatu per person. For more information see the story on page 298.

Cannibal Tour

There are a few sites where tours are run to the places where the victims of cannibalism were cooked and their bones placed but the best is on the island of Rano.

The practice only ended in the middle of last century, and it is not something that the locals wish to promote.

The site is an eerie and strangely quiet place in the bush, a short walk from the beach. The bones of victims can still be seen, but the skulls have now been buried.

The pits in the earth where the bodies were cooked are still visible, Cost, including boat transfers, 3,000 Vatu per person.

Lakatoro

The main town on Malekula has a National Bank, Post Office, shops and a busy fruit and vegetable market, but one of the best reasons to visit would be to see the Malampa Handicraft Centre (**P1** map, page 154).

If you wish to purchase beautiful tribal masks, clothes and woven mats and bags, this is the place to go. The nearby Cultural Centre has a limited but interesting display of art and carvings from the island.

Trekking

The lack of roads into the interior of Malekula means the island has many traditional paths connecting villages. These are now also used as the basis of several treks across the island.

Although not mountainous, these do involve steep climbs at points and a general level of fitness is required. One of the most popular is the 'Dogs Head' trek, two days from east to west (return by speedboat unless you want to repeat it in reverse).

Somewhat challenging in places, an alternative shorter, although still energetic, one-day hike across to Tenmaru known as the 'Big Nambas' trek, can also be completed.

The cost is 20,000 Vatu per person for the two day trek, and 14,000 Vatu for the one day, including guides, and a porter for the longer walk. Transport costs for the return journey are extra. To book a trek contact the Malampa travel centre www.malekula.travel

Maskelyne Islands

Reached by boat from Lamap, or on the Big Sista boat from Port Vila, the Maskelynes are a number of low lying islands off the south coast.

Very rarely visited, less than 100 visitors made in there in 2014, they have beautiful white sandy beaches and some of the best snorkeling in Vanuatu.

Uliveo Island, has a unique **clam sanctuary**, where you can snorkel out and see hundreds of giant clams in this locally driven project to halt the decline of this increasingly rare mollusc. Try and avoid any nightmares about getting a limb stuck in a closing clam (stories of humans getting caught in them are more apocryphal than a real threat, as the jaws close very slowly).

As well as spending time in the water there are some good walking tours that can be taken as well as an impressive stone-carving lesson from Sam, a skilled artist.

Ecotours, www.vanuatu-ecotour.com.vu (+678 252 99) arrange highly rated 3-4 day trips out to the islands if you would like it all organised for you.

Epi

In the Port Vila markets are tables stacked high with 'peanuts blong Epi' (Peanuts from Epi). For 30 Vatu you get a taste of this small island north of Efate, which should tempt you to go there in person.

An island of around 5,200 people, its fertile volcanic soil means that agriculture and fishing are the main industries here, while tourism is growing slowly.

There are beautiful spots to snorkel, a chance to get up close with a turtle or dugong, and great treks across the island. And then there are those huge bags of fresh peanuts available almost everywhere!

Getting to Epi

Air Vanuatu operates return flights to Lamen Bay in the northwest on Wednesdays and Fridays, and to Valesdir in the southwest on Mondays and Friday. Note that both are grass strip runways, and Valesdir in particular will be closed to aircraft if there has been heavy rain.

Travel time is forty minutes and the cost is approx 8,000 Vatu each way Check out the travel section (page 23) to learn about ticket discounts using your international ticket.

Big Sista (568 5225) runs a catamaran to Lamen bay, en route to Santo on a Monday, returning on a Thursday. Economy is 6,000 Vatu each way, with 2,000 Vatu extra for business class (top level of the boat with better seats, air-con and non stop movies).

The schedule is subject to change due to weather conditions. The *Brooklyn* and *Tina 2* vessels also sail regularly to the island. There may be other boats travelling from Port Vila, ask around at the wharf to see who is travelling there.

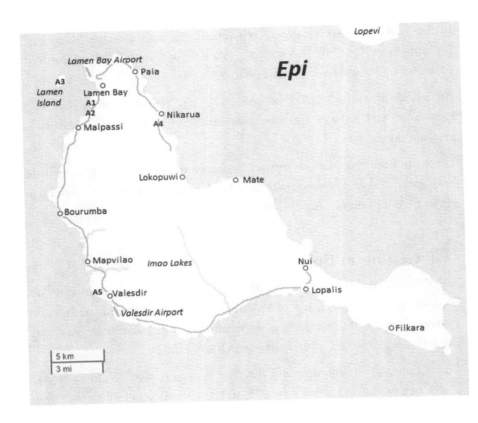

Map of Epi

Accommodation

A1 Paradise Island Sunset Bungalows

A2 Coral Guesthouse

A3 Pulkum Guesthouse

A4 Nikaura Sunrise Bungalows

A5 Epi Island Guesthouse

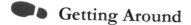 Getting Around

There is one road, connecting Lamen Bay with Valesdir. A bit rough in places, you will be holding on tightly to the back of the small truck (Ute) as you bounce over the ruts in the road.

It is a long two-hour journey, with frequent stops to pick up/drop off passengers, and there are some stunning views towards Ambrym and Malekula on the coastal journey. If shared the trip costs 2,000 Vatu per person, this involves waiting for the next time a small truck decides to do the journey, or you can hire the whole vehicle for approximately 10,000 Vatu.

 Where to Stay

Epi Island Guesthouse. Valesdir (* FFP Recommended)

Contact: 552 8225, 28 225   Price: 10,000 Vatu (includes Breakfast)

Email: epiguesthouse@gmail.com

(**A5** map, page 162) A unique gem in Vanuatu. Alix and Rob Crapper have built their beautiful house from local materials and powered it using hydro energy from the waterfall behind.

The house faces the sea, and it is a short walk down to the beach, and snorkeling in the water. Shared meals make for a very social stay, and Alix's cooking of local produce will more than satisfy you. They also have an extensive library if you get tired of looking at the view of the turquoise waters.

Camping is also available in the large garden for 1,000 Vatu per person.

Paradise Island Sunset Bungalows. Lamen Bay

(* FFP Recommended)

Contact: 28 230, 564 9107   Price: 3,000 Vatu per person (Breakfast and Dinner).

(**A1** map, page 162) Great spot opposite the black ash beach. A large guesthouse and bungalows with shared western toilets. The local chickens and pigs will get you up nice and early in the morning. Tasso will help you with snorkel gear and free rentals of kayaks, or with a tour across to Lamen Island.

Full board is worthwhile as the meals are very tasty, particularly the fresh fish dinners. Tusker beer is available for purchase, unless it has all been consumed by a visiting yacht (the bay is very popular with yachties). 500 Vatu extra for lunch.

Coral Guesthouse. Lamen Bay

Contact: 564 9107   Price: 2,000 Vatu

(A2 map, page 162) Quiet guesthouse in a bush clearing set back a short distance from the sandy beach. Sleeps four, with one double and two single beds. Tasso at Paradise Island can help book overnight stays. Self-catering, although you can arrange to eat at the nearby Paradise Island Sunset Bungalows.

Pulkum Guesthouse. Lamen Island

Contact: 572 0953, 733 2282   Price: 1,500 Vatu per person.

(A3 map, page 162) Built using traditional materials on the edge of the village on Lamen Island, across from the beach. Sleeps up to five people in two rooms. No meals, self-catering using the small kitchen. You will need to bring supplies with you.

Nikaura Sunrise Bungalows. Niakaura

Contact: 535 6289, 534 2659   Price: 2,500 Vatu per person (Full board)

(A4 map, page 162) On the eastern side facing the Lopevi volcano. Community built and operated. Tasso at Paradise Island can help both to get you there and to book overnight stays. Great for snorkeling with a small coral reef in front of the bungalow.

¶¶ Where to Eat

There are very few shops, and the only restaurants are part of the accommodation. Paradise Island Sunset Bungalows in Lamen Bay is very popular with yachts for dinners, and you will often share a meal with visiting yachties.

If you have special dietary requirements, bring your own food.

🏠 Things to See and Do

Lamen Bay

The beach at Lamen Bay is sheltered and great for swimming and snorkeling. And one of the major draw cards here is the chance to see Dugongs.

It has an unusual beach in that it has black volcanic sand to the south and white coral sand to the north. The shallow coral reef in the bay allows good snorkeling with excellent visibility.

There used to be one very friendly and inquisitive Dugong who would let you swim with her. Unfortunately she has died, but families of these strange looking creatures still regularly visit the calm waters of the bay, although they can be somewhat scared of humans and may swim the other way when you approach.

There are also many turtles and schools of tropical fish to be seen in this protected area.

Power of the Plants.

Join Artis in Lamen Bay on a tour of his spectacular garden and nearby forest as he explains the healing power of various local plants, which are used in traditional medicine.

He will also explain how other plants will protect you from evil spirits and can organise a great BBQ after the tour. Contact Artis on 590 0537.

Lamen Island

A small traditional community living less than 1km from Lamen Bay. The 450 inhabitants are rarely visited and enjoy showing visitors around. It its remarkably clean and tidy, with its paths fenced with small coral walls.

The islanders will take you on a tour of their market gardens, and explain and show you food preparation. There are beautiful white sandy beaches to snorkel from. A strong swimmer could easily make it across from Lamen Bay; everyone else can catch a ferry for 500 Vatu each way.

Kuwae Volcano

A submarine volcano off southern Epi, which produces huge amounts of pumice, found around the shores of Vanuatu, and further afield to the east coast of Australia. You can hire a boat to see bubbling waters when it is active, along with large yellow streaks of sulphur on the surface. Not as visually impressive as the nearby land based volcanoes, but with an unusual historical pedigree.

A massive eruption in 1452-1453 has been linked with the Little Ice Age, when crops failed across Europe, China and America, while the fiery sunsets that were produced led the Christians under siege in Constantinople to believe the Turks had broken through the walls and were burning the Hagia Sophia.

Lopevi Island

A volcano above ground and very visible from the north east coast. The last major eruption was in 2007, but in 2015 a new cone appeared on the flank of the volcano, and Vanuatu Geohazards, a government body, advised there was a growing risk of a major eruption.

You can visit on a boat from Lamen Bay, depending on the current risk rating, check at www.geohazards.gov.vu but climbing the volcano is unsafe at this time.

The island is slowly growing with each eruption, and the black lava flows from its last eruption are very clear. Lopevi only had minor eruptions spaced many years apart in previous centuries, and it was inhabited with a growing population taking advantage of the fertile soil until 1960.

That was when the volcano lurched into hyper-activity destroying crops and villages with massive lava flows, a pattern that is still continuing with nine eruptions in the last 15 years. The islanders departed for Port Vila and Paama, none have returned. You can see the remains of the abandoned village on the west coast.

The best way to actually see the volcano if you have not got time for a visit, is on the flight to and from Ulei in Ambrym. Sit on the right side going there, and the left on the return to Port Vila. The stratovolcano is quite spectacular, although its crater is often shrouded in mist.

Trekking

There are some great routes into the lush tropical interior of Epi from both Valesdir and Lamen Bay. Longer walks can be arranged with guides, ask at your accommodation.

An easy four-hour walk from Lamen Bay will take you up to the hills overlooking the village and give you views north to Lopevi, and west to Ambrym and Malekula.

With waterfalls to swim and relax in, and a cool breeze when you are high up, it is a great way to spend an afternoon. When we did it we soon collected a local group of schoolchildren who showed off their foraging skills, giving us all fruit from the bush, and climbing the palm trees to get us fresh coconuts.

Bring a torch, and return from the hills after dark, and you should see the eerie orange glows given off by the lava in the craters of the volcanoes Benbow and Marum in Ambrym.

Espiritu Santo

Espiritu Santo, or Santo for short, is the largest island in Vanuatu. With a population of 32,000 it vies with Tanna to be the second most visited island after Efate.

Discovered in 1606 by the great Portuguese navigator, Pedro Fernandes de Queiros, who thought he had discovered the great southern continent, Australia. He was not that far off; had he continued in a westerly direction for another few days he would have arrived at what is now Noosa, in Queensland, and the world's history would be somewhat different.

The island has always had an independent streak, it was the main location of the Coconut Rebellion in 1980 when the charismatic Jimmy Stevens proclaimed it a separate country from the rest of the archipelago, just weeks before formal independence from Britain and France. Armed forces from Papua New Guinea quickly put a stop to that.

As an important World War II base, the island was home to thousands of US troops, including John F Kennedy briefly, and boasted at one stage over thirty cinemas. Not surprisingly, Santo has a lot of historical relics, from the dumping ground of Six Million Dollar Point, to the wreck of the *SS Coolidge*. With beautiful beaches, blue holes and caves, Santo has a lot to offer, and can easily take a week or more to explore.

Getting to Santo

The easiest destination to visit from Port Vila. Twice daily flights on the large Air Vanuatu ATR are combined with smaller aircraft travelling via Malekula and Pentecost to provide various options each day. The cost is approx 15,000 Vatu each way. Check out the travel section (page 23) to learn about ticket discounts using your international ticket.

The aircraft land at the island's only airport Pekoa International, just outside the main town, Luganville. Yes, Pekoa **International**, there is a weekly return flight from Brisbane in Australia on Air Vanuatu.

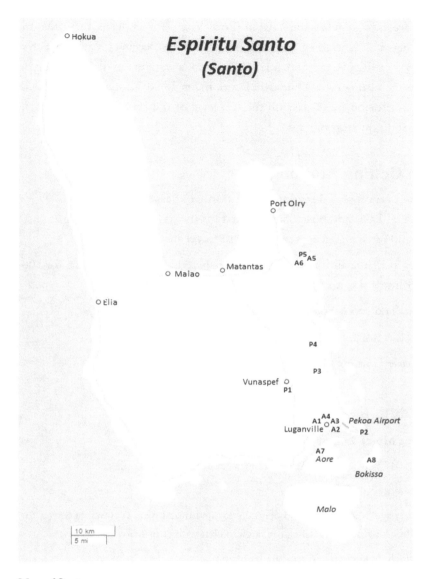

Map of Santo

Accommodation

A1 Hibiscus Motel

A2 Hotel Santo

A3 The Espiritu Hotel

A4 Deco Stop

A5 Friendly Beach Villas

A5 Towoc Bungalows

A6 Lonnoc Bungalows

A7 Aore Island Resort

A8 Bokissa Island Resort

Places

P1 Millennium Cave

P2 Million Dollar Point

P3 Matevulu Blue Hole

P4 Nanda Blue Hole

P5 Champagne Beach

169

There are also regular ships from Port Vila. If you have the time to experience a slow journey stopping off in Epi first, contact Vanuatu Ferry (26 999), or Big Sista (568 5225) who run a catamaran to Santo on a Monday, returning on a Thursday. Economy is 7,000 Vatu each way, 2,000 Vatu extra for business class on the top level of the boat with better seats, air con and non-stop movies.

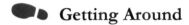 Getting Around

There is a now a sealed road up to the north and east coasts from Luganville. Taxis and buses can be hired for the day, but the roads are empty and hire cars are a great option to travel around the island.

Arriving at Pekoa airport you can catch a shared bus into Luganville for 500 Vatu or hire a taxi for approximately 1,000 Vatu.

Hire cars and scooters can be rented from:

Espiritu Car Rentals: 37 539

Deco Scooter Hire: 36 175

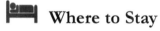 Where to Stay

Hibiscus Motel. Luganville (* FFP Recommended)

Contact: 547 1005   Price: 3,500 Vatu (per room, up to 3 people)

Email: lemotelhac@gmail.com

(**A1** map, page 169) A quiet and centrally located motel, very reasonably priced for Santo. Free wi-fi and a social central area to chat with your fellow travellers.

Rooms include kitchen and en suite bathroom.

Bokissa Island Resort. Bokissa (* FFP Recommended)

Contact: 36 913   Price: 40,000 Vatu + per room. (includes Breakfast)

Email: holiday@bokissa.vu

(**A8** map, page 169) A private island for your run of the mill film stars and those who want real luxury and are prepared to pay for it. 25 minutes from Santo, you will share with a maximum of 34 other guests.

No televisions, phones or fax machines (do they still exist?) but wi-fi and mobile reception should you wish to get in touch with the rest of the world in between swimming in the shallow waters and drinking cold beer overlooking the beach.

Deco Stop. Luganville

Contact: 36 175   Price: 14,000 Vatu + per room. (includes Breakfast)

Email: deco@vanuatu.com.vu

(**A4** map, page 169) A favourite with divers, it has a nice infinity pool. Comfortable and reasonably central, with great views over the harbour.

Rooms are fairly basic, but quiet. Family friendly.

Hotel Santo. Luganville

Contact: 36 250   Price: 15,000 Vatu + per room. (includes Breakfast)

Email: hotelsanto@vanuatu.com.vu

(**A2** map, page 169) The oldest hotel on Santo, and it does tend to show its age in its rooms. However it is centrally located and has a traditional British style bar to sup a Tusker beer after a heavy day's sightseeing.

Wi-fi in lobbies but does not reach all rooms.

Aore Island Resort. Aore

Contact: 36 705   Price: 18,000 Vatu + per room. (includes Breakfast)

Email: via website www.aoreislandresorts.com.

(**A2** map, page 169) A large resort on the island facing Santo. A fifteen-minute boat ride from Santo, with great pools and a beachfront location.

Not that Santo has much hustle and bustle, but Aore Island is a great place for getting away from it all. Five ferries a day connect to Santo.

Lonnoc Beach Bungalows. Lonnoc Beach

Contact: 36 141   Price: 5,000 Vatu + per bungalow (includes Breakfast)

Email: lonnocbungalows@gmail.com

(**A6** map, page 169) Thirteen bungalows, camping and dormitory accommodation close to Champagne beach on the east coast. Starve yourself before you go for the seaside buffet on Sundays for huge amounts of lobster, fish, crab, prawns and more. The restaurant is a highlight, even without the buffet!

You can also camp for 1,000 Vatu per person.

The Espiritu Hotel. Luganville

Contact: 37 539   Price: 12,000 Vatu + per bungalow (includes Breakfast)

Email: book@the-espiritu.com

(**A3** map, page 169) Another favourite for divers. On the main street, a boutique style hotel with in-ground pool and modern rooms.

Large portions of reasonably priced food, and the hotel also runs a small hire car business.

Towoc Bungalows. Champagne Beach

Contact: 563 6173   Price: 2,500 Vatu per person (includes Breakfast)

(**A5** map, page 169) Two bungalows beside Champagne beach. Vanuatu style rather than resort style. Basic, but so relaxing in lush green surroundings, no hot water or regular power but friendly local hosts who will cook tasty meals from local ingredients and show you the best places to snorkel and swim.

Gahena's Motel. Luganville

Contact: 544 8166, 777 7244   Price: 1,000 Vatu per person (Dormitory)

Lini Motel. Luganville

Contact: 37 152, 775 5152   Price: 1,500 Vatu per person

Belview Lodge. Luganville

Contact: 37 928, 774 650   Price: 2,500 Vatu per person.

Santo Vista Cottage. Luganville

Contact: 537 5152   Price: 12,000 Vatu + per room

Village de Santo Resort. Luganville

Contact: 36 123, 771 1706   Price: 12,000 Vatu + per room

Coral Quays Fish and DiveResort. Luganville

Contact: 36 257   Price: 15,000 Vatu + per room

Beachfront Resort. Luganville

Contact: 36 911, 773 3911   Price: 40,000 Vatu + per room

Two Canoes. Aore Island

Contact: +61 2 9091 1933   Price: 20,000 Vatu + per room

Oyster Island Resort. Oyster Island

Contact: 36 283, 778 2733   Price: 14,000 Vatu + per room

Barrier Beach House. Saraoutou

Contact: 710 5360   Price: 25,000 Vatu + per room

Lope Lope Lodge. Saraoutou

Contact: 36 066, 779 3065   Price: 30,000 Vatu + per room

Reef Resort. Turtle Bay

Contact: 37 627, 773 7627   Price: 12,000 Vatu + per room

Turtle Bay Lodge. Turtle Bay

Contact: 37 988   Price: 30,000 Vatu + per room

Bay of Illusion Guest House. Matantas (Vathe Conservation Area)

Contact: 535 7102   Price: 1,500 Vatu per person (includes Breakfast)

Muele Guest House. Malo Island

Contact: 536 0400   Price: 500 Vatu per person

Vanilla Guest House. Malo Island

Contact: 37 161, 536 0192   Price: 700 Vatu per person

Pantanas Guest House. Malo Island

Contact: 548 4390   Price: 1,500 Vatu per person. (includes Breakfast)

🍴 🍸 Where to Eat and Drink

Outside of Luganville you are going to be mostly reliant on your accommodation, but Luganville itself has some great choices.

The Curry House – located at the end of the main street, close to the dock for cruise ships. A Fijian couple have brought their skills to Luganville and serve the spiciest curries. We loved the Daal (450 Vatu) accompanied by a fresh roti, but the Lamb Curry for (550 Vatu) was a close runner up. Open for lunch and some evening dinners.

Natangaro Café – Middle of the main street. Japanese food at a reasonable price. Great sushi and Bento boxes as well as burgers and chips and normal café. Sit on the deck and look out to sea as you much away.

The Market Stalls – Behind the market are a number of small stalls cooking local food for approximately 500 Vatu per dish. The choice is usually beef, chicken or fish, but cannot be beaten for the large dishes piled high with root vegetables and rice. Bargain eating at lunch and early evening (closed on Sundays).

Tu Restaurant and Bar – Near the Natangaro Café. A refreshing pool in the middle of the restaurant provides a reason to visit on really hot days. Basic fare, but with fresh ingredients. Good selection of cocktails and draft beer.

Hotel Santo – Cold Tusker beer and bar snacks are the highlights in the traditional bar in the main street. Gets quite social in the evenings, and is a good place to meet sthe locals after work.

Santo Chinese Restaurant – Close to the cruise ship dock. Imaginatively named and with a building that looks like it has seen better days a few decades ago. But the food! Great Chinese food at reasonable prices, and packed out with all the local Chinese which is always a good sign.

🏃 Things to See and Do

SS President Coolidge

You need to be diver for this one. One of the best dives in the world, the *Coolidge* was a luxury ship converted to a troop carrier in the Second World War. Due to miscommunication it hit a mine protecting the harbour from Japanese submarines, and sank in shallow water. 5,340 men made it ashore before it sank, with only two deaths.

The Americans beached the ship, so virtually nothing was taken off it as it was believed salvage would be easy, and then it sank slowly into the harbour. Ammunition, personal goods, tanks, guns, plates and cutlery still remain in place, along with the coral that has grown all over it, attracting schools of tropical fish.

The ship lies between 29 and 72 metres depth making it fairly easy for recreational divers to explore, and it so large it can consume a whole week of diving with still much more left to investigate. The statue of 'The Lady' a woman riding a unicorn in the fireplace of the First Class ballroom has become an icon of the wreck, and is a must visit. As are the forward guns, library and swimming pool. You can enter via skylights and exit via the hole in the engine room where the ship hit the mine.

The water is warm, and clear (except after heavy rain). A rope runs from the shore to the bow, and decompression stops are required. It is a shore dive and these take place in the shallows surrounded by coral gardens. providing a fascinating view of fish and other creatures as you wait.

There are a few operators who dive on the *Coolidge*, but the original, and still the best, is Allan Power Diving , who have expert divers and an impeccable safety record.

Contact Allan Power Diving (+678 36822) or submit contact form via website www.allan-power-santo.com

Do not be tempted to souvenir ammunition. Travellers have been stopped boarding the plane with live ammunition from the wreck. Common sense should apply, as it is unstable and a great risk to the plane and its passengers.

There are other great military dive sites including a McDonald Douglas Dive bomber, and of course, Million Dollar Point.

Million Dollar Point

(**P2** map, page 169) You do not need to be a diver for this one. In fact it is great even for a family visit. Ten minutes by taxi from Luganville (approximately 1,000 Vatu, arrange to be picked up again as there is not much traffic on the road here). At the end of the Second World War the Americans wished to sell all their supplies to the local British and French government, but they refused to buy them, thinking they would get them for free. The Americans had a backup option, dump it in the sea.

Trucks, boxes of Coke bottles, clothes, cutlery, tyres, tools, medicines and more were bulldozed off a pier into the sea, followed by the bulldozers themselves.

An environmental catastrophe, but now you can snorkel over the coral encrusted remains, which has become a playground for tropical fish. Or you can wander the shore at low tide and pick up old Coke bottles or collect small pebbles of different coloured glass, smoothed over the years by the actions of the sea. Wear foot protection and take care as there are bits of rusted jagged metal also.

For more information read the story on page 257.

Entrance fee is 500 Vatu per person.

Champagne Beach

(P5 map, page 169) A long white beach on the east side of Santo, about one hour from Luganville. Now discovered by cruise ships, although they only visit a handful of times during the year, otherwise you will have the beach to yourself.

The aquamarine waters are warm and shallow, snorkeling is easy, and it is possibly the best beach in Vanuatu. The name comes from the water fizzing through volcanic rocks at low tide.

Entrance fee is 500 Vatu per person.

Luganville

The second largest urban centre in Vanuatu after Port Vila, it still resembles a frontier town. All the action is on the Main Street (also known as Boulevard Higginson), a street so wide you can drive four trucks along it side by side. It was built for this reason by the Americans during the war, and you can still see Quonset huts still in use.

A walk of one and half km from the port to the markets will see you pass by restaurants, banks, dive operators, tourist shops, hotels and supermarkets. The LCM store half way along is your best bet for loading up on provisions at a reasonable price. There are National, BSP and ANZ banks in the main street, as well as an Air Vanuatu office to book tickets at.

The market is worth a visit, whatever fruit and vegetables are in season will be sold for a very reasonable price and open 24 hours a day, except for Sundays. No haggling, all fixed price, and some great food stalls located next to it if you are hungry.

The Blue Holes

Half way between Luganville and Champagne Beach are the Blue Holes. Pure blue springs, with the deep water filtered through many layers of limestone and coral to give it its distinctive colour. There are two Blue Holes quite close together, **Matevulu** and **Nanda** (**P3 & P4** map, page 169), on the east coast.

You can swim, or use kayaks. Nanda now has a waterslide and bar.

Entrance fee to each is 500 Vatu per person.

Millennium Cave

(**P1** map, page 169) An adventure tour that takes you from Luganville into south central Santo by the Vunaspef village. Then you walk through rainforests, clamber down ladders and walk deep into the dark cave disturbing the bats. Canyoning and more rock clambering are followed by a swim under a waterfall.

An energetic day out, and requires at least moderate fitness. A lot of climbing up and down locally made ladders, which is quite tiring by the end of the day, makes for a good sleep that night. Life jackets and pick up from your hotel are included in the price.

Note that after heavy rain the tour does not operate for safety reasons. All profits go to the local village to support education for children.

Tour cost is 7,000 Vatu per person.

Contact: +678 547 0957 or email: bookings@milleniumcave.com

Paama

Paama Island is a small island south of Ambrym and north of Epi with a population of about 1,600. It is still largely untouched by tourism, and has few facilities.

It does have great snorkeling on the reef around it, and stunning views towards the volcanoes of Lopevi and Ambrym, and the opportunity for some decent trekking.

Getting to Paama

Air Vanuatu operates return flights to Tavue in the north on a Tuesday. Stopping off at Ambrym on the way travel time is one hour and a half cost is approx 9,000 Vatu each way.

Check out the travel section (page 23) to learn about ticket discounts using your international ticket.

You can also hire a speedboat from Lamen Bay on Epi for approximately 12,000 Vatu to take you to Tahal on the southern tip of Paama.

Getting Around

There is one road, on the west coast, although it can be impassable at times, particularly in wet weather.

You can share a ride on a truck (Ute) to travel at least part of the way between western villages, but the reality is you are going to have to walk almost everywhere if you want to explore the island.

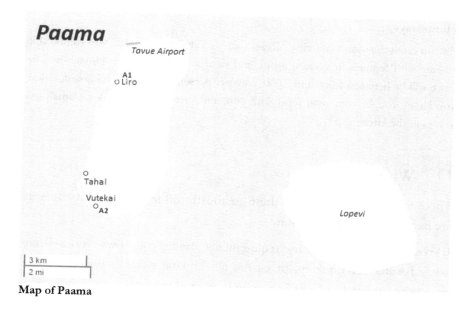

Paama

Tavue Airport

A1
o Liro

o
Tahal

Vutekai
o A2

Lopevi

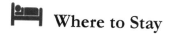
3 km
2 mi

Map of Paama

Accommodation

A1 Tavir Guesthouse
A2 Samson Bay Bungalow

Where to Stay

Tavir Guesthouse. Liro

Contact: 48 538   Price: 2,500 Vatu per person (includes Full Board)

(**A1** map, above) Basic bungalows with shared drop toilet in the centre of Liro.

Samson Bay Bungalow. Vutekai

Contact: 535 5435   Price: 2,500 Vatu per person (includes Breakfast) (**A2** map, above) Basic bungalows close to the beach and reef with a good view of Lopevi volcano. Extra meals 500 Vatu each.

Transfers by boat from Liro for 8,000 Vatu. Tours can be arranged to Lopevi, for deep sea fishing, snorkeling and for the local custom dance.

Homestays

As you cross the island and visit villages such as Tahal in the south, you will be able to stay with families in a spare room, and occasionally a separate bungalow. The price will be between 1,000 and 2,000 Vatu per person and will be full board, unless you have brought your own food with you, and then you can cook on small gas stoves in the kitchen.

⅋⅋ Where to Eat

There are very few shops, and these are mostly in Liro. The only restaurants are part of the accommodation.

If you have special dietary requirements, bring your own food. Bring bottled water for drinking, or ensure all drinking water is boiled. There have been outbreaks of giardia among locals and tourists.

🏃 Things to See and Do

Snorkeling

All along the coast are snorkeling spots by the reef, which is close to the shore. Turtles, dolphins and vast array of marine life can be viewed, and you will have it all to yourself. The south coast is renowned for shark attacks beyond the reef.

Lopevi Volcano

See page 166 for more details on Lopevi. Trips to Lopevi can be organised from Tahal and Vutekai for approximately 15,000 Vatu return, plus custom fees for visiting the island.

Trekking

The main walk is north to south, an 8 km trek, which can easily done in a day. A recommended itinerary would be to walk from the airport at Tavue to Liro, approximately 45 minutes, and stay the night there, before walking down to Tahal or onto Vutekai on the south coast. You can visit Lopevi or catch a speedboat to Lamen Bay (approximately 12,000 Vatu, unless you manage to share with others).

From both the north and south you can find spots easily to view the nearby volcanoes. Although Lopevi will not be spitting out lava, unless you are very lucky, the glows of the craters of Marum and Benbow in Ambrym are an unforgettable sight at night time. Low cloud, which is often present, increases the glow, giving off a wide orange halo around them.

Ambae

The island that inspired James Mitchener's paradise of Bali Hai in his best selling novel *Tales of the South Pacific*, on which the musical *South Pacific* was based. It can be seen from the east coast of Santo, usually early in the morning, before it fades into the sea haze and clouds.

Also known as Aoba Island, Ambae is home to the largest volcano in Vanuatu. Rising 3,000 metres from the sea floor and a further 1,500 metres from sea level, the Lombenben volcano is capped with the active Manaro crater, which had slumbered for four hundred years until 1991, erupting again in 2005-2006, and currently being observed very closely by vulcanologists.

✈ Getting to Ambae

Regular flights from Air Vanuatu to Walaha in the west depart from Santo on Monday, Wednesday and Saturday. Flights to Longana are on the same days, with an extra flight on Thursday. Redcliff airport in the south is currently not used.

The cost is approx 6,000 Vatu to Walaha and 7,000 Vatu to Longana, each way, check out the travel section (page 23) to learn about ticket discounts using your international ticket.

Ships depart regularly from Santo en route to the southern islands. A five or six hour trip will get you to the west coast, with the main stop being at Ndui Ndui. The ships are somewhat overcrowded and uncomfortable, but you may consider the 3,000 Vatu worthwhile for the experience.

Getting Around

There is no round island road on Ambae, although you can travel from the west to the northeast, from Walaha to Longana by truck. The last time we did this we managed to get thrown around a lot, and get a puncture, which was good to jump off for a break!

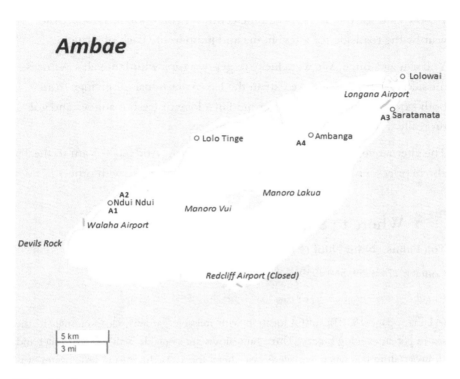

Map of Ambae

Accommodation

A1 Toa Palms

A2 Toa Lodge

A3 Tui Lodge

A4 Duviari Guesthouse

Tough road conditions make journeys quite expensive unless you share; 10,000 Vatu for the trip between the centres if you book it, 1,500 if you wait by the roadside for a few hours and jump in the back of a truck.

You can also hitch. We were lucky to get two trips with Jehovah's Witness missionaries from Salt Lake City in the US. After initial misgivings from both sides, we found common ground in a love of fresh mangoes and got on really well, which added to the experience.

The alternative, apart from walking, is speedboat. Add 5,000 Vatu to the above prices, unless again you can time it right and share with others.

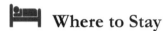 Where to Stay

Toa Palms. Ndui Ndui (* FFP Recommended)

Contact: 774 8259, 560 4959   2,000 Vatu per person (incl Breakfast).

Email: toa@vanuatu.com or toapalmsbungalows@gmail.com

(**A1** map, page 183) Beautiful location with massive gardens, close enough to the sea to get an evening breeze. Three bungalows are available with western toilet and shower (although when we were last there the drought meant little water was available).

Great to relax in the gardens after a hard day's trekking, and the food is superb, with large portions courtesy of the cook, Evelyne. 500 Vatu for lunch, 800 for Dinner

A short walk to the beach where there is great snorkeling inside the reef, and to the markets. Volcano climbing from the west side, transfers to Walaha (2000 Vatu each way) and other tours arranged.

Toa Lodge. Ndui Ndui

Contact: 540 1652   2,000 Vatu per person (incl Breakfast)

(**A2** map, page 183) A new addition to the Toa stable of accommodation in Ndui Ndui. Smaller than the Palms, but with nice rooms. A back up option in the very unlikely situation of Toa Palms being full. Located on the main road, although you are more likely to be woken by mangoes dropping from the trees rather than traffic. 500 Vatu for lunch, 800 for Dinner

Tui Lodge. Saratamata

Contact: 547 5509, 541 8209   2,000 Vatu per person (incl Breakfast).

(**A3** map, page 183) Modern guesthouse with six room and nice furnishings. Self-catering, but dinners are 1,000 Vatu a person. Volcano climbing and transfers (1500 Vatu each way) can be booked.

Duviari Guesthouse. Ambanga

Contact: 535 4571, 597 9945   1,500 Vatu per person (incl Breakfast).

(**A4** map, page 183) Basic but comfortable accommodation high up on the trail to the craters. Reached via truck from Lolowai (transfers 4000 Vatu each way) and then a short walk up from Ambanga village. No running water or electricity, but a real Vanuatu experience. Other meals 500 Vatu each.

A great water hole for swimming is nearby. Quite cool so bring warm clothes. A good base if you wish to climb to the craters from the east side.

Gamaliweu Bungalows. Gamaliweu (South Ambae)

Contact: 38 883, 540 9726   2,000 Vatu (Full Board)

Community Guest House. Luvunvilli

Contact: 544 0582   500 Vatu

Tarifarmer Guest House. Saratamata

Contact: 537 8595, 540 3040   2,000 Vatu (Full Board)

Penama Provincial Guest House. Saratamata

Contact: 38 348   1,000 Vatu

DJ Guest House. Saratamata

Contact: 537490, 777 3863   1,500 Vatu

Matereoh Lodge. Saratamata

Contact: 540 9169, 777 2383   1,500 Vatu

Japin Guest House. Lolowai

Contact: 537 8186, 779 3380   1,000 Vatu

Torgil Guest House. Torgil (East Ambae)

Contact: 54 2707   1,500 Vatu

Tatumba Guest House. Walaha

Contact: 534 8431, 534 6732   2,000 Vatu (Full Board)

Fanua Travel Lodge. Walaha

Contact: 547 5411, 538 8673   1,500 Vatu

Tua Guest House. Narako

Contact: 540 1652   2,000 Vatu (Full Board)

Narako Guest House. Narako

Contact: 54 13802   1,000 Vatu

Paradise Garden House. Navitora

Contact: 540 5417   1,500 Vatu, or 500 Vatu for camping.

Bue Guest House. Vilakalaka

Contact: 38 309, 544 1211   2,000 Vatu (Full Board)

♕ Where to Eat

In Ndui Ndui there is a market house with fresh seasonal produce, next to it is a bakery where you can get great fresh bread (dependant on when and what is baking). There is also a small market in Saratamata.

Apart from that, as in much of Vanuatu, the only place to get food is to bring it along for self-catering, or to eat at your accommodation where the meals are always filling and reasonably priced.

Depending on the season, fresh fruit is plentiful. So much so that the ground can be covered with fruit that is not eaten. Last time we were there in November, it was mango season, and you did not have to walk far to pick up fresh juicy mangoes off the ground. During the early parts of the trek up to the craters, we loaded up with mangoes, pineapples and bananas, which provided much of the food for the trip.

🏝 Things to See and Do

Manaro Vui

There are some nice walks and hidden beaches, as well as good snorkeling, but the reason most would visit the island is to climb the volcano and see the craters of Manaro Lakua and Manaro Vui.

The volcano is one of the most studied, and feared, in Vanuatu. With lakes only metres above lava an eruption could cause massive destruction, not only to Vanuatu, but also with tsunamis reaching the east coast of Australia. It has been increasingly active since 2005, when an Air Vanuatu pilot noticed smoke pouring from a crater. The explosions and eruptions that soon followed caused half the island to be evacuated to Santo. Minor activity has been ongoing since that time.

The craters can be approached by the east or west. Neither is easy! Some try to do the climb in a day, it will be a 14-16 hour exhausting day with not a lot of time to enjoy your time at the top. We recommend camping at the top and making it a two-day trip (bring your own camping gear, there is very little on the island).

Before you depart for Ambae, check out the Vanuatu Geohazards site www.geohazards.gov.vu to see the latest safety updates. In early 2016 the craters were placed off limits to tourists because of increased volcanic activity.

Guides are required as the volcano has parts which are to be avoided as they are sacred and are taboo. Your accommodation will be able to recommend one. They cost 2,000 to 3,000 Vatu per day, and they will come equipped with machetes to help clear the path. If you have camping equipment it would be worth considering a porter for another 1,000 Vatu per day. Climbing without a bag is so much easier as you reach the steep parts of the crater.

The weather is often wet, as the volcano has its own microclimate, even as the rest of the island is bathed in sunshine. Take wet weather gear and a walking stick to help you in muddy steep areas.

Climbing from the East

Approach from Ambanga, either starting early from Lolowai or Saratamata and getting a truck there, or by sleeping overnight at the Duviari Guesthouse nearby.

The walk takes 5-6 hours to both craters, and 4-5 hours return, and is mostly an easy climb until the crater walls where it can get steep and slippery with banks of mud to navigate.

Climbing from the West

Start early from your accommodation at Ndui Ndui and head north to Lolo Tinge village (about an hour's journey). The journey starts off easily, until you get close to the crater when the path gets very steep and slippery. Small rivers are crossed, which can become raging torrents after heavy rain falls.

The walk takes about 4-6 hours to the craters, and a slightly quicker time to return.

The Craters

Manara Lakua is the first crater you will visit. Unless hidden in clouds you will see a dark blue freshwater lake great for a refreshing swim after the climb, although the water can be very cold. Nearby is the campsite you can stay overnight.

Manara Vui is a further one-hour walk. As you get closer you will smell the sulphur, which drifts across the lake in the wind. A mask is recommended as the wind constantly changes direction and you cannot avoid breathing in the dangerous gas. Combined with the low cloud you may not actually much of the lake, which is another reason to camp, as the lake tends to be visible only in early morning.

The vegetation round the lake looks like a war zone, with dead trees jutting out of the mud. As you get close you may see gas bubbling in the lake. You would not want to swim in this crater.

A third overflow lake has been formed recently, **Manara Ngoru**, which only fills after heavy rain.

For more on climbing the volcano, read the story on page 274.

Devils Rock

Thirty minutes from Ndui Ndui, just beyond the Walaha airport is Devils Rock. One of the best spots to snorkel in Ambae due to its clear water and distant reef. The rock itself is an important part of local Custom beliefs, it houses the souls of the dead, but it was also a practice target for American fighter planes during the war. Bullets and bullet holes can be seen all over the rock.

Be careful of fast moving currents between the rock and the shore if you swim out to it. It is also one of the best anchorages for yachts on Ambae.

Ndui Ndui

A quiet and friendly village with a great market, a few shops and a National Bank of Vanuatu. If you are feeling hungry, and are not watching the calories, pick up one the fabulous home made cakes for sale at the market, alongside root vegetables and fish. There is not much fruit for sale, as so much can be picked up when wandering around.

Make your way down to the rocky beach for a spot of snorkeling by the reef, or watch the boats from Santo unload huge amounts of goods, and people, on their regular visits.

Behind the church are the remains of a US fighter plane which, damaged in action against the Japanese forces in the South Pacific, failed to make it home to its base on Santo.

Maewo

Harder to reach than Ambae, with only one flight a week and few ships calling, Maewo is a unique place, worth the effort to reach. With the highest recorded rainfall in Vanuatu, perhaps not surprisingly the island has some of the best waterfalls and cascades in the archipelago. The latest census has the population listed as 3,600.

En route to Espiritu Santo, the explorer De Quiros landed here in 1606. Claiming it for Spain, he named the island Aurora, and that was the last the islands saw of the Spanish until after independence.

Getting to Maewo

Air Vanuatu flies a return flight from Santo to Naone airport, in the north, on Thursday.

The cost is approx 9,000 Vatu each way, check out the travel section (page 23) to learn about ticket discounts using your international ticket.

Ships depart irregularly from Santo to Maewo. Enquire at the Vanuatu Tourist Office, or at the Santo wharf, to see if any ships are scheduled. Cost will be approximately 4,000 Vatu each way.

Speedboats to Laone in Pentecost from Asanvan will cost approximately 10,000 Vatu.

Getting Around

A truck meets the weekly plane; you can travel into the small local town of Naone for 500 Vatu. A west coast road connects the north and south of the island.

Shared trucks from Naone to Nasawa cost approximately 1,500 Vatu per person, hiring the whole vehicle will increase this to approximately 6,000 Vatu. The road ends at Sanasom, boats can be organised to take you to Asanvari at the southern tip.

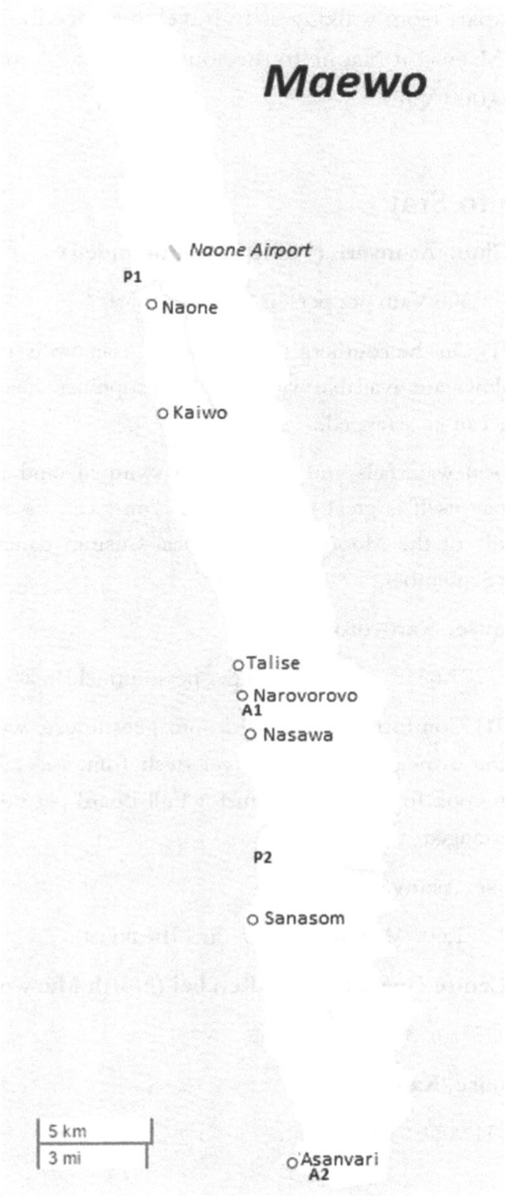

Maewo

\ *Naone Airport*

P1

○ Naone

○ Kaiwo

○ Talise
○ Narovorovo
A1
○ Nasawa

P2

○ Sanasom

| 5 km |
| 3 mi |

○ Asanvari
A2

Map of Maewo

Accommodation

A1 Aurora Guesthouse

A2 Asanvari Yacht Club

Places

P1 Big Wota

P2 Holes of the Moon Cave

The alternative, apart from walking, is to travel in a speedboat; a charter trip from the top of Maewo at Naone to the southern tip at Asanvari will cost approximately 10,000 Vatu.

 Where to Stay

Asanvari Yacht Club. Asanvari. (* FFP Recommended)

Contact: 38 239   1,500 Vatu per person (incl Breakfast)

(**A2** map, page 191) On the southern tip of Maewo Asanavri is a beautiful spot to relax. Two bungalows are available with 24 hr hydropower. Shared western style toilet. Other meals can be arranged.

Behind are the local waterfalls and cascades to swim in (and the hydro power source!) and the bay itself is great to snorkel in. Tours can be arranged by Chief Nelson to the Hole of the Moon cave, and local Custom dancing. Packed with yachties in May to September.

Aurora Guest House. Narovorovo

Contact: 535 6652, 777 6338   2,000 Vatu per person (incl Breakfast)

(**A1** map, page 191) Comfortable three-bedroom guesthouse, with self contained kitchen. Naomi, the owner, will help you get fresh fruit, vegetables and fish for your meals, or can cook for you (700 Vatu for Full Board per person). Tours and transport can be arranged.

Mule Guest House. Asanvari

Contact: 534 4489   1,600 Vatu per person (incl Breakfast).

Kerebei Health Centre Guest House. Kerebei (North Maewo)

Contact: 537 8410, 777 6338   1,000 Vatu.

Luaete Guest House. Kaiwo

Contact: 38 210, 534 9066   3,000 Vatu

¶¶ Where to Eat

Asanvari Yacht Club – Funded by NZ and Australian Aid, the yacht club cook lunches and dinners, try the tasty grilled freshwater prawns (1000

Vatu). Tusker beer is also available, except during peak yachting season in the middle of the year when the yachties tend to drink the place dry.

Lawai Sparkling Waters Bar – Contact 593 9196. At the far end of the bay from the Yacht club is this new bar. Again great seafood and cold beer can be had while watching the Lavoa cascades in front of you. On certain nights they have local dancers perform, check with the bar when.

You can also arrange at the bar to go on a tour with Barry, to visit the Waisale bat cave nearby, and to learn how to catch freshwater prawns.

Apart from that, well, it is self-catering over a gas ring, or you can ask your host to cook for you, for a nominal cost.

Things to See and Do

Hole of the Moon Cave

(**P2** map, page 191)) At Sanasom is the rarely visited but spectacular Moon Cave. Entering from the sea from one of three entrances in a small boat, the cave is impressively large.

Custom stories explain that Tagoro, a local spirit, lived here with his mother who was a weaver, but the cave was too dark for her to see to work, so Tagoro grabbed the moon, from the cave ceiling, and threw it out of the cave and into the sky to provide light. A large indentation, the size of a full moon can be seen in the roof.

The waters are clear and are great for a quick swim or snorkel, many fish live in the cave.

Malangauliuli

A short distance from the Hole of the Moon cave is a small beach, with a large rock wall. Engravings, some of Custom patterns, cover this, but many record the first contact with Europeans, with western style rigged boats pictured in a number of the engravings, reminiscent of the Aboriginal ochre drawings in Australia's northern Arnhem Land.

Big Wota

(**P1** map, page 191) Near Naone in the north are the waterfalls and cascades of the Big Wota. The locals love to come and swim here at weekends and late afternoon, else you will have the clear waters and stunning world class

falls to yourself.

Surrounded by lush green vegetation, the large waterfalls are impressive enough to relax in and swim below, but there are also caves to be explored behind them with stalactites and stalagmites (bring a waterproof torch).

A crocodile, swimming down from the Banks Islands, or maybe carried on a current from the Solomon Islands was found in a nearby river in 2003.

The Crocodile Hunter, the late Steve Irwin, was flown in from Australia to catch it, and move it to the Banks Islands. There are no crocodiles around the island today.

Big Wota is so good it even got featured in a stamp from the Vanuatu Post Office in 2013.

Pentecost

Renowned for the Nagol, where men and boys jump from land diving towers with only vines attached to their ankles to celebrate the beginning of the Yam harvest. Pentecost also offers treks, waterfalls and custom dancing.

At the last census the island had a population of just under 17,000.

Getting there

Air Vanuatu has return flights to Lonorore Airport in the southwest on Monday (from both Port Vila and Santo) and Thursday (Port Vila only), and to Sara Airport in the north on Wednesday (from both Port Vila and Santo) and Sunday (Port Vila only).

The cost is approx 12,500 Vatu each way from Port Vila, and 7,500 Vatu from Santo, check out the travel section (page 23) to learn about ticket discounts using your international ticket.

Ships do stop off on the west coast of Pentecost on the fairly busy Port Vila to Santo route. None run to a scheduled timetable so either ask at the Vanuatu Tourist Office, or at the wharf. Cost is approximately 5,000 Vatu from Port Vila, and 3,000 Vatu from Santo.

Ships depart irregularly from Santo to Pentecost. Enquire at the wharf to see if any ships are scheduled. The cost will be approximately 4,000 Vatu each way.

Speedboats to Asanvari in Maewo from Laone will cost approximately 10,000 Vatu.

Getting Around

There is a road connecting the island from north to south. However it is in poor condition and long journeys cost a lot of Vatu! For example if you wished to travel between the two airports you would be looking at 14,000 Vatu or more. Short shared journeys are more affordable such as Lonorore to Pangi for 1,000 Vatu shared, or 4,000 Vatu for a full charter.

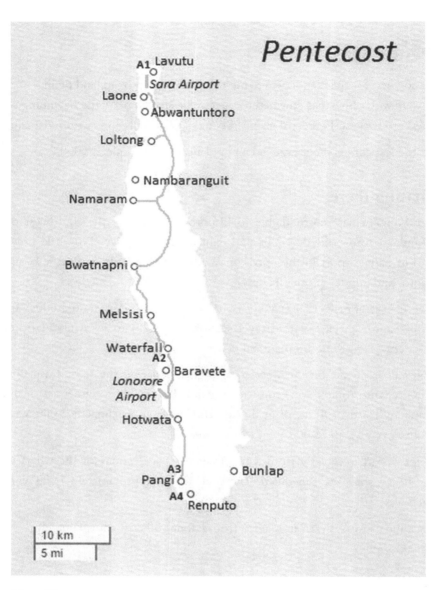

Map of Pentecost

Accommodation

A1 Walarua Guesthouse   **A4** Panlike Guesthouse

A2 Nonda Guesthouse

A3 Nak Bungalows

As with most islands the alternative is a speedboat, great if you can share, very expensive otherwise, or to walk. The trek from north to south will take you three to four days, with many options for accommodation. Stick to the west coast, where most of the villages are due to the rough weather on the east coast, and follow the example of the majority of the inhabitants of Pentecost Island, and walk.

 Where to Stay

Nonda Guesthouse. Waterfall (* FFP Recommended)

Contact: 547 3071, 548 5935 Email: nodaguesthousewaterfall@gmail.com

2,,500 Vatu per person (incl Breakfast). 500 Vatu for other meals.

(**A2** map, page 196) An idyllic spot, close to the huge waterfall, which is great for swimming, and to the beach where there is a small coral reef with schools of tropical fish. Friendly hosts, who love to cook and share their kava.

If there are a few people staying you may be lucky enough to have a roasted pig, else the plentiful seafood and root vegetables will more than fill you up.

Western toilets and a good shower.

Transfers are 2,000 Vatu from Lonorore, and tours can be booked to the waterfall cave, custom villages, and trekking, as well as land diving in season.

Nak Bungalows. Pangi

Contact: 381 02, 537 3761   3,000 Vatu per person (incl Full board).

(**A3** map, page 196) On the south coast, these bungalows are close to the black sandy beach and can sleep up to 14 people. Comfortable, albeit basic rooms, with western toilet and volleyball court!

The restaurant onsite opposite the beach cooks up fresh seafood for guests, which makes dinner a bargain, depending on the catch of the day.

At night sit on the beach opposite and watch the distant orange glow from the Ambrym volcanoes.

Transfers are 4,000 Vatu per vehicle from Lonorore, and tours can be booked, including land diving, trekking, snorkeling, and canoe trips. 500 Vatu for other meals.

Walarua Guesthouse. Lavutu

Contact: 543 2287   1,500 Vatu per person (Self-Catering)

(**A1** map, page 196) Ten minutes from Sara Airport, and five minutes to the beach. Fresh food can be purchased locally, and the owner can help order fish and other food for you, as well as organise tours. Pit toilet.

Panlike Guesthouse. Renputo

Contact: 543 5146, 543 4412   2,500 Vatu (Full Board)

(**A1** map, page 196) Close to the Nagol towers, and facing the beach. Basic rooms, with shared western toilet and shower.

Snorkeling and fishing tours, bird watching and trekking can all be organised, as well as land diving. Transfers are 5,000 Vatu from Lonorore.

Vanambil Guest House. Baravete

Contact: 38 308, 535 6178   3,000 Vatu

Londot Garden House. Londot

Contact: 535 5515   2,500 Vatu

Eddie Guest House. Pangi

Contact: 38 210, 534 9066   3,000 Vatu

Health Centre. Pangi

Contact: 38 852   1,500 Vatu.

Mansi Women's Club. Waterfall

Contact: 543 7417   1,200 Vatu.

Nog Guest House. Lalvise

Contact: 545 9145, 534 6058   2,000 Vatu (incl Breakfast)

Melsisi Catholic Mission Guesthouse. Melsisi

Contact: 38 328   1,000 Vatu.

Jobi Guest House. Nokobujuka

Contact: 542 2798   1,000 Vatu

Bangaware Bungalow. Nambaranguit

Contact: 543 3270, 560 6608   1,500 Vatu.

Dumi Guest House. Loltong

Contact: 547 8435   1,500 Vatu

Buloa Guest House. Loltong

Contact: 542 1090   1,000 Vatu.

Mauna Guest House. Pangi

Contact: 38 396, 535 6219   1,000 Vatu

Lango Guest House Centre. Abwatuntora

Contact: 543 9238   1,000 Vatu.

Adventist Guest House. Loltong

Contact: 534 3354   1,000 Vatu

Tamata Lodge. Arungwaratu

Contact: 544 3048   2,000 Vatu.

Tausala Guest House. Angavo

Contact: 543 6942   2,000 Vatu

Laone Beach Guest House. Laone

Contact: 536 3950   2,000 Vatu (Full Board)

❙❙ Where to Eat

Most guesthouses will give you the option of full board, with most meals fairly large with whatever is in season and has been caught by the local fisherman.

Some accommodation does offer the alternative or self-catering over a gas ring. If you do wish to cook for yourself. your hosts will be able to arrange the purchase of local fruit and vegetables, as well as fish and chicken.

There are few shops, so bring any particular dietary needs from Port Vila.

ᛏᛁ Things to See and Do

Nagol (Land Diving Festival)

Every Saturday between April and June in South Pentecost (fly into Lonorore). The event that does put Pentecost on the map and brings many tourists to the island on both cruise ships, which only dock at Pentecost during this time (and have private land diving festivals performed for the passengers), and charter planes from Port Vila (approx 40,000 Vatu per person, plus local fees).

Even so, except for the cruise ship days, you will still be one of a small crowd watching this ancient ceremony.

It inspired A J Hackett to launch the craze of Bungee jumping, with the men and boys climbing the rickety wooden towers, between twenty to thirty metres in height, and tying two flexible tree vines to their ankles before jumping off.

The towers have several platforms with only the most experienced land divers jumping from the top platform. The aim is to brush the shoulders lightly in the cleared ground below, to ensure a good yam harvest, which was vital to ward off famine in previous centuries.

Now it is more of a tourist spectacle than a ceremony for a good harvest, but it remains one of the most unusual and spectacular sights in Vanuatu.

The Guinness Book of World Records land diving has having the most g-force on a human body outside of aviation and space travel.

It can be dangerous, two divers have died, one in front of Queen Elizabeth II in 1974, when it was performed in a different time, during the wet season, and the vines were too elastic.

In case you were thinking of making this part of an activity holiday, tourists are not permitted to jump from the towers.

Expect to pay 12,000 Vatu to attend a Nagol. The event will include dancing, singing and the chance to purchase souvenirs.

There are two main sites for land diving:

Londot Village: Diving occurs on Wednesday, Friday and Saturday, by special arrangement. Contact: Luke on 535 5514

Waterfall Bay: Timed to meet Air Vanuatu arrivals, used by Air Vanuatu for their tours from Port Vila. Contact Silas on 772 7394 or 547 3071.

Trekking

Pentecost is becoming popular with trekkers who walk the island. Green and lush, with beautiful waterfalls and freshwater streams, with very tasty prawns for those with a net. The walk takes approximately five days, and can include a hike up Mt Vetmar (867 Metres) with great views across the island.

You can follow the main road on the west coast for part of the way, and then can continue on traditional walking tracks. Guides are not really necessary, as you can easily navigate from village to village, but can be hired from approximately 2,000 Vatu per day. Enquire at your accommodation for walks, and guides.

Custom Villages

Inland you can visit traditional custom villages. Traditional dances, food preparation, ancestor stories, and fire walking can be included as part of the tour, as well as kava tasting in the village nakamal.

Ratap, Bunlup and Lonlibili are the main villages that permit tours, others prefer not to encourage tourism. Your accommodation can arrange tours, expect to pay 5,000 Vatu, plus transport.

Melsisi

In northwest Pentecost is a rather strange juxtaposition of a western church and village emerging from the surrounding rainforest. Paved roads, French houses, shops, a guesthouse, and priests wandering the streets who would look more at home in Lourdes.

A Catholic mission since 1898, it has retained its French roots to this day, all the local schools only teach in French and baguettes are plentiful in the shops. A beautiful and rather unusual place

Laone

In the far north is Laone, where the founding Prime Minister of modern Vanuatu, Father Walter Lini, was born. He is commemorated with a statue outside of the local college.

The bay has great clear azure waters for snorkeling, a little way out in 18 metres is the well-preserved wreck of a US fighter plane that ran out of fuel during the war. Ask a local fisherman for the precise location.

The Banks and Torres Islands

The Banks and the far north Torres islands are the hardest islands to get to in Vanuatu. Irregular flights and rare ships make it an adventure to actually get there. In 2014 only 67 tourists made it to Gaua, the closest island to Santo.

Do not let that put you off, with a little time and patience you can make it to these small, untouched islands in the Pacific.

Beautiful beaches, where you can feel like a modern day castaway with no one in sight for miles, and incredible sights including treks to active volcanoes and waterfalls, unusual and colourful custom dances, and some great fresh food, with possibly the cheapest lobster in the world.

They are a destination that will reward you for your perseverance.

Getting to the Banks and Torres Islands

Air Vanuatu flies a return flight from Santo to the group, on Monday and Wednesday. This is the Banks and Torres 'bus' as it hops between all the islands with airports on this route.

It is not the most reliable Air Vanuatu service, departure times and even days may change, and if running behind schedule certain airports, particularly those furthest from Santo, may be missed out until the next trip.

See individual sections for ticket costs, but note that if you are travelling to other islands in the chain it is cheaper to buy a multi leg ticket and stop off and enjoy some of the other islands.

The planes used are small, De Havilland Twin Otters usually, with only 19 passengers, and sometimes much less depending on cargo for the islands. (We flew once with three rows removed and replaced with several pallets).

The airports are mainly grass, which means that after torrential rain the runway becomes waterlogged and the airport will be closed.

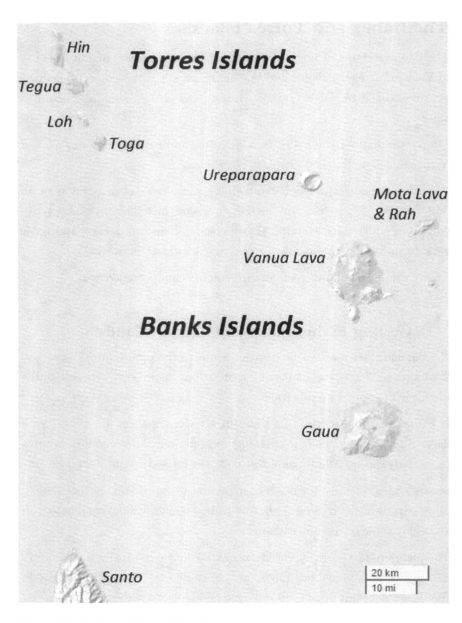

Map of the Banks and Torres Islands

The flights can sell out weeks, and even months, in advance. Do not despair if you have not got a ticket. Flight bookings are free and often cancellations occur when payment is actually required three days before the flight and then seats can become available. Put your name down on the waitlist at the Air Vanuatu office in Port Vila or Santo.

Note that the luggage limit is 10 Kg, plus a carry on bag, which sits in your lap, so pack as lightly as you can.

Sit near the front to get a great view into the cockpit, as there is no door.

Return flights can depart from the island at almost any time, ignore what your ticket says, as schedules change based on delays, loading, and weather, which makes staying close to the airport on the last day a sensible option where possible.

If you want to travel by ship, you may have to wait around in Santo for a long time, they are irregular at best. Enquire at the Vanuatu Tourist Office, or at the Santo wharf, to see if any ships are scheduled.

The islands are a favourite stopping off point for yachts, either cruising down from the Solomon Islands or up from Port Vila. The season runs from May to October. You may be lucky to get a working passage by asking around.

In Santo enquire at **Santo Hardware**, they have a dinghy dock for yachts and are the major supply store for yachting needs in town. They may let you put a notice up. In Port Vila head to the **Waterfront Bar**, it is the main place for yachties to drink and mingle, particularly during happy hour (16:00 – 18:00).

Gaua

The most populated, with 2,500 inhabitants, island in the Banks group. Home of the world famous Ladies Water Music, and the mighty Mt Garet volcano. A great place for trekking, seeing waterfalls, snorkeling, or just relaxing on a beach.

The island was discovered by Europeans on the voyage of Pedro Fernandez De Quiros in 1606, and was subsequently further charted and explored by William Bligh in the late eighteenth century, who named the group after his benefactor, Sir Joseph Banks; its original name was Santa Maria.

Getting to Gaua

Air Vanuatu flies a return flight from Santo to Gaua Airport, on the east coast, on Monday, Wednesday and Saturday.

The cost is approx 9,000 Vatu each way, check out the travel section (page 23) to learn about ticket discounts using your international ticket.

Getting Around

There are a couple of trucks that may meet the plane. Although if there has not been a ship for some time there will be no fuel on the island, and you have to walk, which is both easy and you get to see a lot more.

Trucks cost approximately 3,000 Vatu to Lembot, and 4,000 Vatu to Namasari from the airport. Walking to these villages will take you between forty minutes and one hour

Paths and tracks link all the main villages, although to get to the west side you will need to hire a speedboat. Cost, depending on fuel availability, will be between 6,000 to 15,000 Vatu depending on destination, considerably less if you manage to share the boat.

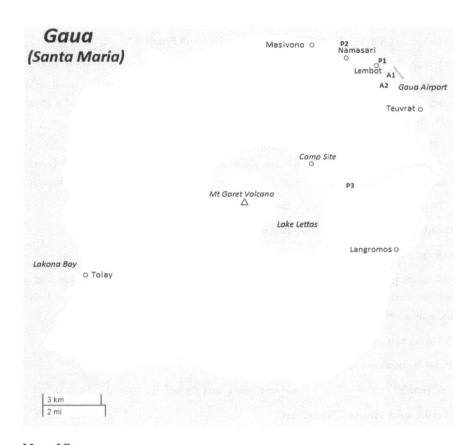

Map of Gaua

Accommodation

A1 Tammes Bungalows

A2 WonGrass Tracel Lodge

Places

P1 Lembot Water Music

P2 Liumoros Water Music

P3 Siri Waterfall

 Where to Stay

Tammes Bungalow. Gaua Airport (* FFP Recommended)

Contact: 541 3953   3,000 Vatu per person (incl Full Board)

(**A1** map, page 207) Located next to the runway. This would be a problem at JFK airport, but in Gaua, with so few flights, it is an advantage as it is only a small walk from the arrival hut, and a starting point for the trek to the volcano, and a short walk from Lembot village and the Ladies Water Music.

The bungalows are clean with comfy beds. A shared western toilet and shower are close by. The highlight is the incredible meals you get as part of the full board. Crab, lobster, fish and more vegetables than you can eat. You will not leave hungry.

All tours can be arranged, including volcano treks and Ladies Water Music.

WonGrass Travel Lodge. Gaua Airport (* FFP Recommended)

Contact: 539 1744, 771 2879   2,500 Vatu per person (incl Breakfast)

(**A2** map, page 207) Close to Tammes, with two comfortable bungalows and a garden area in which to sit and relax. Full board can be arranged, and the bungalows offer a laundry service.

All tours can be arranged.

Peba Bungalow. Lewuslat

Contact: 590 8971   2,500 Vatu per person (incl Breakfast)

Weul Guest House. Namasari

Contact: 539 7690, 5908971   2,500 Vatu.

Chez Maureen. Salomond

Contact: 595 6780, 778 9620   4,000 Vatu per person (incl Breakfast)

Lagoon View Bungalows. Lombot

Contact: 537 0939   2,500 Vatu.

⫙ Where to Eat

Your accommodation will provide you with meals, either as part of an inclusive deal or for approximately 500 Vatu per meal. Self-catering is possible, and there is a covered market with fresh vegetables, fruit and fish next to the airport.

Lobster and crab can be supplied on request to your host, basically they will contact a local fisherman who will go and catch it for you!

The recently opened **Kamsy Kamsy Kamsa** nakamal is a great place to partake of the local kava, fresh and as effective as any we have tasted. What makes this nakamal stand apart from the many others visited is that they serve small tapas dishes, fried fish and small vegetable dishes, which not only takes away the strong taste of the kava, but are tasty snacks in their own right. The nakamal can be found midway between Lembot and the airport on the main track.

Things to See and Do

Mt Garet Volcano

If the trip to the volcano is your reason for going to Gaua, do check out the Vanuatu Geohazards site www.geohazards.gov.vu to see the latest safety updates. The last major eruption was in 2013, but volcanic activity can place the crater off limits at any time.

The trek to Mt Garet is a highlight of any visit to Gaua. Bring your own small tent and sleeping bag. A guide and porter will be organised by your accommodation and the trip is a minimum of two days.

The first day will bring you from the coast up through coconut palm plantations to the lower levels of the caldera on fairly flat ground. Due to the fertile ground the path is overgrown and your guide will be hacking away with a machete for some of the way.

The climb up the side of the 500 metre caldera is a bit more energetic, but not too steep. The climb down is a little harder, very steep and slippery to the wet microclimate around the volcano. The local chief has thoughtfully placed wooden stakes into the ground to grab all the way down, making the climb down much easier.

You will overnight at the campsite there. If there is no one else there, and that is a very high probability, set your tent up inside the palm-roofed shelter, it is just big enough for two tents. This is a precaution against tropical downpours, which can happen at any time, but seem to prefer the hours around 2AM-3AM. Without the protection the rain will disturb your sleep and seep into most tents.

The camp site also has one of the best toilet views in Vanuatu, a traditional western toilet in a small coconut leaf thatched hut with a spectacular outlook if you can overcome any feelings of modesty and leave the door open.

Your guide will be likely to dive into the freshwater Lake Letas, which covers an older, but still active, crater, and catch some tasty and unique large local prawns which make for a great dinner.

Early morning you will cross on an outrigger canoe to Mt Garet (797 Metres above sea level), you will need to help paddle, before stopping off to look at bubbling mud pools near where the canoe comes ashore.

The actual climb up the volcano is fairly steep, but quick, taking thirty minutes to reach the top and gaze into the smoky interior, whilst trying to avoid the whirling sulphur gases. Only rarely can lava be seen at the bottom due to the amount of smoke pouring out of the crater. Dead trees surround the top, and some have fallen into the crater, adding to the unworldly landscape at the top.

Even if you linger for a while, the return journey across the lake and down to your accommodation will have you back in time for dinner.

For more on climbing the volcano, read the story on page 285.

The cost for a two-day trek, including custom land fees, meals and a porter, is 11,500 Vatu. Bring your own tent, sleeping bag and water (A 1.5 litre bottle is good, it can be refilled at mineral springs during the journey), and good walking shoes.

Book through your accommodation or contact the registered guides below:

John Atkins 537 8802

Paul Lazaros 536 7392

Larry Harish 530 7803

Siri Waterfall

(**P3** map, page 207) A spectacular 120-metre waterfall that drops from the caldera at Lake Letas. This can easily be combined with the two-day trip to the volcano.

After descending from Mt Garet your guide will navigate the outrigger canoe to a spot just above the waterfall. Here it is a thirty-minute walk to the top of the waterfall and a great viewpoint.

Climbing down at the side is the very difficult part, you can choose to go back via a much easier path which takes approximately two hours to reach the road, or on the steep thirty minute path to the pool and the bottom of the falls.

This path is hard with few handgrips and you are constantly walking over slippery rocks.

The cost is an additional 2,000 Vatu to the Volcano trek, or 6,000 Vatu for a separate day trip.

Women's Water Music

The Water Music is a world famous attraction. Few may get to Gaua to see the ladies perform on their home turf, but thousands see them every year when they are asked to perform at festivals across the world. In the last few years they have performed in Spain, Holland, Asia and Africa.

The twelve ladies, including young girls, enter the water and begin singing haunting custom stories about the sea, and then in a display of skilled synchronicity they create percussion by slapping the water and clapping.

It is quite astonishing to see, and the music created is beautiful and hypnotic.

The water music can be seen at two places on Gaua:

(**P1** map, page 207) **Lembot Water Music**: Lembot Village. Organise via your accommodation or contact Selina on 549 1392 or Catherine on 539 5315.

(**P2** map, page 207) **Liumoros Water Music**: Namasari Beach. Organise via your accommodation or contact Merilys on 536 7392 or Paul on 536 7392.

Cost is 2,000 Vatu per person (minimum of two people) per performance.

Qwat Dance

This is the Men's sacred dance, women are not permitted to see the preparations, and it is done in secret and only at certain times of the year, around the St Andrews Day Salav festival at the end of November.

The men dress in palm leaves and wear painted masks, using natural pigments found in the bush, while log drums provide the percussion for the dance.

The Qwat dance can be seen in the bush near Namasari during the festival. For details contact Paul on 536 7392.

Snorkeling

The reef on the edge of the island allows for great snorkeling; with some deep drop offs and colourful coral. Some of the best snorkeling, along with a beautiful sandy beach and safe swimming, can be found south of the airport at Paradise Beach in Bororig.

Either walk, or arrange boat transport if available for 5,000 Vatu return. There is also a campsite here.

Contact Tony on 539 3189. Access fees are 500 Vatu for a half day, or 1,000 Vatu for a full day. Camping is 1,500 Vatu per person, and Tony can prepare meals for 500 Vatu per person.

Vanua Lava

Just north of Gaua is Vanua Lava, with a population of 2,600. It hosts the main town and administrative centre for the Banks and Torres Islands, Sola.

The island offers great trekking, a climb on a volcano (the not so active Mt Sere Ama), snorkeling, and crocodiles. The two last activities do take place at different locations.

The island was again discovered by Europeans on the voyage of Pedro Fernandez De Quiros in 1606, and was first explored by an adventurous British Bishop, George Selwyn, in 1859.

Getting to Vanua Lava

Air Vanuatu runs a return flight from Santo to Sola Airport, on the east coast, on Monday, Wednesday and Saturday.

The cost is approx 11,000 Vatu each way, check out the travel section (page 23) to learn about ticket discounts using your international ticket.

Speedboats can be rented to take you across to nearby Mota Lava. This is dependant on the boats having fuel, being available, and on the weather. The channel between the islands can get very rough and you do not want to try and cross in stormy weather. The cost would be 15,000 Vatu for hire, or approximately 1,500 Vatu to share with others.

Ships depart irregularly from Santo to Sola and the Banks islands. Enquire at the Vanuatu Tourist Office, or at the Santo wharf, to see if any ships are scheduled. Cost will be approximately 5,000 Vatu each way.

Getting Around

The main road on Vanua Lava connects the airport to Sola Township. Trucks do meet the plane and you should be able to share a ride for 500 Vatu.

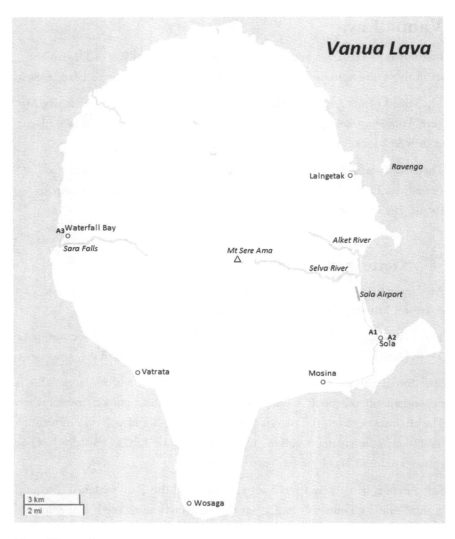

Map of Vanua Lava

Accommodation

A1 Leumerous Guest House

A2 Ulkel Guesthouse

A3 Malau Yacht Club

Speedboats can be hired from Sola to take you around the island, hiring costs 18,000 Vatu to Waterfall Bay, and 8,000 Vatu to Lalngetak.

Apart from that there are great walking tracks connecting Sola to Waterfall Bay and around the island.

 Where to Stay

Leumerous Guest House. Sola

Contact: 540 2806   3,000 Vatu per person (incl Full Board)

(**A1** map, page 214) Close to the beach. Five bungalows, with basic but filling meals provided.

Ulkel Guesthouse. Sola

Contact: 569 3858   2,000 Vatu per person

(**A2** map, page 214) Self-Catering bungalow, but meals can also be provided for 500 Vatu each.

Malau Yacht Club. Waterfall Bay

Contact: No phone   3,000 Vatu per person (incl Full Board).

Right on the beach by the waterfalls. Basic but comfortable bungalow.

(**A3** map, page 214) Enquire at Torba Tourism in Sola about availability, or turn up after a trek across the island.

Seina Bungalow. Sola

Contact: 534 8736, 5432771   3,000 Vatu per person (incl Full Board).

Elizier Travel Lodge. Sola

Contact: 598 0411   3,000 Vatu per person (incl Full Board).

⅋⅋ Where to Eat

Most accommodation is full board. There are shops in Sola, and a market for fresh vegetables, fruit and seafood for self-catering.

𝐏 Things to See and Do

Mt Sere Ama Volcano

If the trip to the volcano is your reason for going to Sola, do check out the Vanuatu Geohazards site www.geohazards.gov.vu to see the latest safety updates. It has not erupted since 1965, although there have been signs of increased activity, which you will see on your trip. Interestingly the last major eruption occurred at the same time as an eruption on Mt Garet on Gaua, which has been becoming very active in recent years.

The trek begins from Sola, with either a twenty minute on a speedboat (for 6,000 Vatu) to Lalngetak village, or two to three hour coastal walk with a guide (for 2,000 Vatu). This does require the crossing of both the Selva and Alket rivers, which have crocodiles. The locals seem unconcerned, as their belief is that crocodiles only attack bad people. Both rivers need to crossed at low tide.

You will need to pick up a guide and pay custom entry fees at Lalngetak village. The total cost is 1,000 Vatu per person and 1,000 Vatu per day per guide.

The trek will take you along, and in, the Selva River, before you reach the first fumaroles, or solfataras, that formed in the 1990s. They occur with increasing frequency the closer you get to the volcano.

The actual climb to the craters of Mt Sere Ama is rarely attempted, except by vulcanologists. It will require machetes to cut through the bush, which makes progress slow, and camping equipment as it will require at least one overnight stay below the volcano, and one by the lakes when you complete the steep climb.

Crocodile River

A trip up the Alket River to see the large crocodiles that inhabit this area. You travel in an outrigger canoe, but the crocs are quite shy and you may not see more than a splash in the water as they hide.

Contact Aton on 539 3964. Cost is 1,500 Vatu per person.

Waterfall Bay Trek

It takes a long day to trek from Solo across the island to Waterfall Bay. It is a fairly easy walk, although there are some steep climbs and river crossings. Homestays can be organised on arrival, you can stay at the Yacht club, or a local homestay, on arrival.

At the bay are the Sara Falls, twin thirty metre waterfalls that crash into the ocean from out of the rainforest.

The trek cost is 3,000 Vatu per person including custom entry fees and lunch (one way). Contact Kerelly on 539 9883.

Mota Lava and Rah Islands

Mota Lava and Rah are islands to visit to swim, trek, and forget about the rest of the world. Unspoilt is an overused term, but you will be unlikely to bump into any other travellers here.

With 1,600 inhabitants, solar power, and little in the way of modern 'conveniences' you can slip into a relaxed state very quickly. See the ancient Snake Dance, climb the Sleeping Mountain for 360-degree views around the Banks Islands, snorkel, fish, or just sit on the golden sandy beaches.

The islands were first discovered by Europeans on the voyage of Pedro Fernandez De Quiros in 1606, and explored by missionaries in the late nineteenth century.

Getting to Mota Lava

Air Vanuatu flies a return flight from Santo to Valua airport, on the east coast, on Monday, and Wednesday.

The cost is approx 12,500 Vatu each way, check out the travel section (page 23) to learn about ticket discounts using your international ticket.

Speedboats can be rented to take you across to Mota Lava. The cost would be 15-18,000 Vatu for hire, or approximately 1,500 Vatu to share with others.

Ships depart irregularly from Santo to Vanua Lava and the Banks islands. Enquire at the Vanuatu Tourist Office, or at the Santo wharf, to see if any ships are scheduled. Cost will be approximately 5,000 Vatu each way.

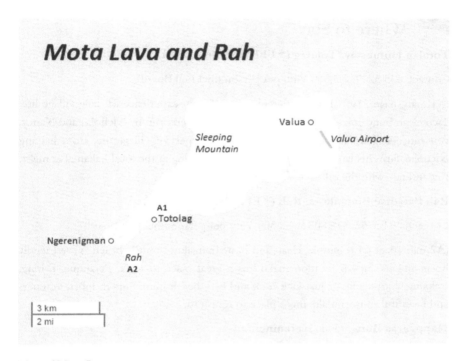

Mota Lava and Rah

Valua ○

Sleeping
Mountain

Valua Airport

A1
○ Totolag

Ngerenigman ○

Rah
A2

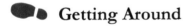
3 km
2 mi

Map of Mota Lava

Accommodation

A1 Totolag Homestay

A2 Rah Paradise

👣 Getting Around

The airport is close to Valua on the east coast. If you want to go to Ra you can share one of the trucks that come to meet the plane. The cost to travel on the 10km bumpy road to Nereningman will be 1,000 Vatu. Alternatively you can share a speedboat ride direct to Ra for 2,000 Vatu.

To get to Rah Island you can walk across at low tide from the mainland, or catch a taxi canoe from Nereningman for 500 Vatu per person.

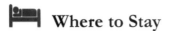 Where to Stay

Totolag Homestay. Totalag (* FFP Recommended)

Contact: 535 5209   3,500 Vatu per person (incl Full Board)

(**A1** map, page 219) Close to Nereningman, for an experience of daily village life. Two clean bungalows are located on the large property run by Nicholas and Nancy, you can take part in the daily activities and be part of village life, from helping Nicholas farm his land to joining in the kava drinking at the local nakamal at night. Eat and talk with the effusive and happy hosts.

Rah Paradise Bungalows. Rah (* FFP Recommended)

Contact: 594 5757, 537 8084   2,500 Vatu per person (incl Full Board)

(**A2** map, page 219) Simple, clean and basic bungalows on the beach. Very friendly hosts and its superb location make this a great place to relax. Petanque, fishing, trekking, snorkeling, or just kick back and be a beach bum. Superb lobster dinners and beautiful sunsets make this a place to return to.

Happyness Bungalows. Nereningman

Contact: 539 6697, 564 0420   2,500 Vatu per person (incl Full Board)

Mota Lava Gateway Lodge. Nerenuman

Contact: 569 0858   3,000 Vatu per person (incl Full Board)

Nisa Sunset Bungalows. Queremadge

Contact: 593 9777   3,500 Vatu per person (incl Full Board)

Dori Lagoon Bungalows. Rah

Contact: 534 8045   2,500 Vatu per person (incl Full Board)

Rah Beach Bungalows. Rah

Contact: 594 8835   4,500 Vatu per person (incl Full Board)

Where to Eat

All accommodation is full board.

🏚 Things to See and Do

Sleeping Mountain Tour

A bush trek to the highest point of the island with views across the Banks and Torres islands.

A fairly easy climb takes about two hours from Nereningman through the local gardens and the forest surrounding the base of Sleeping Mountain (293 metres above sea level). Coconut juice and seasonal fruits are served on the top.

Contact Charles on 566 7253. Cost is 2,000 Vatu (minimum of two people). Tours run subject to weather conditions.

Kwerumagte Custom Village tour

An insight into life in a traditional village. Dancing, magic, and money making - not counterfeiting Vatu notes, but a demonstration of how the original shell money was made which was currency on the island only thirty years ago.

Contact Parton on 594 8835. Cost is 3,000 Vatu (minimum of two people).

Rah Sea Snake Dance

An ancient custom dance performed by the men of Rah. The dancers are painted in white stripes to resemble Sea Snakes and perform with leaves in their mouths and vines in their hair, using their sticks for percussion, for thirty minutes on the white sandy beach.

Contact Noah on 539 6125. Cost is 2,500 Vatu (minimum of two people).

Vanua Lava Day

In the first week of September is Vanua Lava day, when Vanua Lava is full of islanders from throughout the Banks and Torres. Music and ancient custom dances from each of the islands are performed.

This is the only time accommodation maybe scarce and you will need to book ahead.

Contact the Torba Tourist Information Centre on 564 5440 for more details on the exact date.

The Reef Islands

Uninhabited since 1939 after a cyclone, these low lying reefs host a huge amount of tropical fish and bullets. They were used by the US Air force for target practice during the Second World War although what they were shooting at is not exactly clear.

You can camp on the sandy covered atolls and live life as a castaway, bring food and water, although if you are good at catching fish, food will not be a problem.

See the abandoned villages, and walk between the different islands at low tide, and swim in the shallow clear waters where manta rays, turtles and stingrays can be seen.

A speedboat will cost approximately 20,000 Vatu to take you there (including custom fees), make sure you arrange a time for a pickup for the return journey!

It takes about 45 minutes to reach the reef islands from Vanua Lava.

Ureparapara

A small collapse in the crater of an ancient extinct volcano gives the island a horse shoe shape. It is also the only way for boats to get to Ureparapara, even then the reef at the entrance makes for a hair raising and rough entrance into the calm waters of the crater and Lorup Bay.

Possibly the most far flung location in Vanuatu as there is no airport and a speedboat is going to cost a lot to get here. Budget on a minimum of 60,000 Vatu for a return journey, and stop off on the Reef Islands on the way.

If you have your own yacht, it is the perfect place to anchor a while before heading up north to the Solomon Islands.

There is accommodation available. **Titson Guest House** has two small bungalows available for 2,000 Vatu per night including all meals.

The locals will perform a colourful welcoming dance for the rare visitors who actually make it here. Clean and tasty mineral water is available for drinking, and food will be mainly from the sea with fresh fruit and vegetables from the fertile soil. A chicken may be sacrificed if you are lucky.

Ancient abandoned ceremonial stones can be visited in the interior, although all the 400 population live close to the crater shore now.

Tours can also be arranged to the top of the crater for impressive views, as well as nearby bat caves if you want to get up close to the flying mammals.

The snorkeling here is a highlight, the sea life is very much undisturbed and flourishes in the warm waters of the crater. Bring your own snorkeling gear.

The Torres Islands

At the far north of the Vanuatu archipelago lie the Torres islands, only 170 km south of the Solomon Islands.

Seven small islands, with a population of 1,000, make up the Torres group. They are hard and expensive to get to, and this results in very few tourists making it this far north. White sandy beaches surround each of the low lying islands, and they are a place to snorkel, fish, east cheap lobster, and relax.

The islands were not even seen by De Quiros on his northerly Pacific voyage in the early seventeenth century, yet over time gained the name of his navigator on that voyage, Luis Vaz de Torres. They were first explored by European missionaries in the early Eighteenth century.

✈ Getting to the Torres Islands

Air Vanuatu flies a return flight from Santo to Linua airport on the east coast on Monday and Saturday.

The cost is approx 16,000 Vatu each way, check out the travel section (page 23) to learn about ticket discounts using your international ticket.

The return flights are rarely on time, but the plane can be seen, and heard, arriving and since you will probably be staying on the small island with the airport, you can easily get to the tin shed terminal if your bags are packed.

Getting Around

The airport is on Linua Island, with no villages, and you can wade across to Loh Island at low tide, or catch a canoe. There are speedboats to access the different islands, but a lack of fuel often means they are not running, and when they are, can be expensive due to the high fuel cost.

Canoes are usually the only means of transport between the islands.

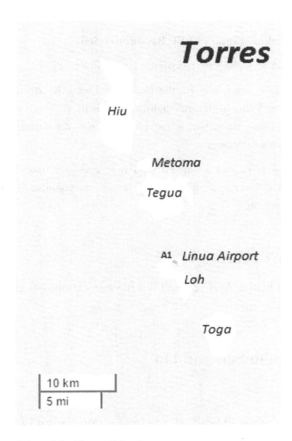

Map of the Torres Islands

Accommodation

A1 Kamillisa Bungalow

 # Where to Stay

Kamillisa Bungalow. Linau (* FFP Recommended)

Contact: 711 4506   3,000 Vatu per person (incl Full Board)

(**A1** map, page 225) Four huts by the beach on Linau, handy for catching that unannounced Air Vanuatu return flight! The island is quiet with a beautiful protected beach, honeymoon bay, a few minutes across the island. The bungalows are clean and have solar power.

The food here is tasty and a bargain, you may even get tired of eating whole lobsters for dinner. Your host, Whitely, will be able to organise canoes and guides to see the caves at Loh.

Where to Eat

Kamillisa is full board. And you will not have any room left after their beautifully cooked meals.

Things to See and Do

Snorkeling

Bring your own gear and head out to Honeymoon Bay on Linau. Alternatively cross over to Loh Island and walk to Rinuhe, where there is a sparkling bay with many turtles.

Loh Island

You can walk around the island in about an hour, there are ancient caves to explore, Lienwet and Maraohi, and custom dances can be arranged (contact Whitely to book).

Be Robinson Crusoe

Swim, drink rainwater, eat lobster, relax on the white sand, and read those books you never had time to until now. There is no Internet and poor mobile reception, so you really can get away from modern life.

A Quick Guide to Bislama

The national language of Vanuatu is Bislama, an English based pidgin language. In Port Vila and Luganville you can easily survive without any knowledge of it, as most city dwellers speak English, and a fair bit of French, thanks to the colonial history of the country, but it is still good to know and use a few words of Bislama.

If you are heading to the outer islands a smattering of Bislama will prove to be even more useful there. Bislama dictionaries can be purchased in Port Vila, try the **Stop Press** book shop at the **Au Bon Marche** supermarket in Nambatu

Online, head to www.bislama.org a comprehensive resource on the language, including dictionaries, an online translator, and recorded examples of Bislama pronunciation to play back.

A good introduction to learning basic Bislama is provided by Andrew Gray at www.pentecostisland.net/languages/bislama/guide

If you really want to go into depth and learn to speak competent Bislama, go to the US Peace Corps website (Vanuatu has many Peace Corps volunteers, often in the most unlikeliest of places) where not only do they have many language tools, but you can download mp3 lessons as well. Head to vanuatu.peacecorps.gov/content/resources-language-tools.

There are some great words and phrases out there, as the language is often both phonetic and literal, so that breaking down in a car is *bagarap* (say it out loud) and a bra is *basket blong titi*. Here is our list of common, and useful words and phrases, in Bislama and their English translation.

Halo	*Hello*
Olsem wanem? I gud?	*How are you? Are you Ok?*
I stret nomo! **(or)** stret!	*Everything is good*
Tata **(or)** Ale	*Goodbye*
Lukim yu	*See you later*
Tankyu tumas	*Thank you very much*

Gudmoning	*Good Morning*
Gudnaet	*Good Night*
Plis	*Please*
Pikinini	*Children*
Toti	*Rubbish*
Nambawan	*Great* **(or)** *The very best*
Nem blong mi	*My name is*
Wanem nem blong yu?	*What is your name?*
Mi save	*I understand*
Mi wantem pem	*I want to buy*
Mi toktok smol Bislama	*I speak only a little Bislama*
Mi blong Osrelia	*I come from Australia*
Mi go fastaem	*I have to go now*
Tumoro	*Tomorrow*
Long aftenun	*In the afternoon*
Tedei long naet	*This evening*
Wanem taem plis?	*What is the time please?*
Bae stop I stop wea?	*Where is the bus stop?*
Stop ia plis	*Stop here please*
Hamas long?	*How much is?*
Hamas long taxu fea?	*How much is the taxi fare?*
Sip i kam tumoro long morning	*The ship comes tomorrow morning*
Wanem taem bae plen I kasem?	*What time does the plane come?*
Kakae	*Food*
Mi laekem	*I like*
Mi no laekem	*I don't like*
Mi sik tumus	*I feel very sick*

NOTIS

PLIS NO SAKEM TOTI OLBAOT LONG ERIA
ARAON SARALANA STAGE. PLES IA I NO
PLES BLONG DRINK ALKOHOL O KAVA
SO PLIS RESPEKTEM ERIA IA.
TAKIU TUMAS LONG COPERESEN BLONG
YUFALA.

With your new found Bislama skills, see if you can translate this sign from Port Vila. The translation is on page 310.

Vanuatu: The Stories

A Captain in the John Frum Army

A Cargo Cult meets Kanye West. Tanna

The John Frum Army marching to Sulphur Bay on John Frum Day

The ash plains beneath the continually erupting Mt Yasur in Tanna are usually an empty black expanse devoid of colour and life. Today it was different, the vibrant clothing of groups of people, often numbering twenty people or more, were slowly converging from all directions to the village beside the volcano, Sulphur Bay, for today, February 15th, is John Frum day.

This is the holiest of days for those who believe in John Frum, an American messiah who will return one day bringing gifts of cars, boats, televisions, DVD players and Coca Cola. This is one of the last remaining cargo cults, surviving on a remote island in the Pacific Ocean.

The John Frum cult had its roots in the early twentieth century. Missionaries were swarming across Tanna, telling the locals to forget their ancient kastom belief system and turn to Christianity. Locals were told their old ways were sinful, particularly polygamy and the worshipping of spirits, and they were forced to endure no dancing or kava drinking on the Sabbath.

Not surprisingly, not all welcomed this new order, with open protests and a gathering of villages opposed to Christianity and wanting to return to their traditional kastom (custom) ways. This culminated in the 1930s in bonfires of western clothes and bibles, and the throwing of the colonial money into the sea.

The British and French rulers responded to this perceived unrest with the arrests and the imprisonment of the village leaders. The protestors moved further into the bush and isolation, getting as far away as possible from both the missionaries and the government.

In prison in Port Vila, the nation's capital, the leaders of those opposed to the new religion, Chiefs Nikiau, Nampas, Meles and Nakomaha met and described a joint vision of a spirit 'John' who would come from America to help them return to their traditional ways. They sent this message back to their villages, and the idea was widely accepted.

With the beginning of the Second World War, the kastom believers hiding out in the bush had an abrupt ending to their isolation, as Tanna became an important base for the American air force and navy preparing to fight back against Japan. The island began to swarm with troops building airports and bases.

Huge amounts of equipment arrived in silver planes from the sky, vehicles, clothes, cutlery, canned food, and Coca Cola became common place, and the Americans, unlike the colonial rulers, accepted the Tanna communities, paid them real wages and shared their goods. The local communities learnt that the aeroplanes delivered all these wondrous goods, which the servicemen called 'Cargo'.

This is when the John Frum cult really started to gain strength. As the noted Australian anthropologist and one of the founding members of the Vanuatu Cultural Centre, Kirk Huffman, notes: "You get cargo cults when the outside world, with all its material wealth, suddenly descends on remote indigenous tribes". The black soldiers who were part of the US army were sharing the white man's wealth and goods. It was believed that they were ancestors of the John Frum believers.

The barefoot army parading in Sulphur Bay

The soldiers and the cargo disappeared equally as abruptly as they had arrived and traditional kastom life returned for the John Frum villages.

With their leaders released from prison, the worship of Cargo took on more ceremony with the first procession and raising of the American flag on February 15th 1957 in Sulphur Bay. Other John Frum villages went to more extreme lengths, building makeshift landing strips in the jungle onto which the planes could land their cargo.

With the death of the original leaders, the son of Chief Nikiau, Issac Wan, took over to become the sole uniting leader, dressing in General's uniform for John Frum days and special occasions, and ensuring the Friday was kept as a Sabbath for John Frum when dances and festivities are held in Sulphur Bay to this day.

Chief Issac Wan observing the ceremony with other dignitaries

Life is never simple, even in a Cargo cult, and Chief Issac was challenged for the leadership by Prophet Fred. He was a Sulphur Bay local who worked on Taiwanese fishing factory ships before returning home and warning of the danger of the large lake Siwi, sitting on the lava plain beneath Yasur, breaching its banks and Sulphur Bay being washed away.

After an earthquake in 2000 this is exactly what happened, destroying a few houses but luckily with no loss of life.

Prophet Fred wanted his followers to believe that John Frum was Jesus, and that they should be waiting for his return. American flags and talk of cargo were banned. This resulted in a massive schism, which included the burning down of houses and mass battles with axes and bows and arrows resulting in 25 serious injuries in April 2004.

Despite Prophet Fred's recent death, his beliefs are followed by those closer to the sea at Sulphur Bay, totally at odds with the John Frum followers living in the same village but closer to the volcano. It is situation a little like East and West Berlin before the wall came down, although in Sulphur Bay there is no wall, and outside of John Frum day all live fairly peacefully together.

I arrived at Sulphur Bay early; flowers were still being affixed to bamboo poles on the road into the village from the ash plain. The few non-John Frum followers there, myself, a couple of American tourists, and a photographer from the *New York Times*, were herded into a shelter in the middle of the parade ground made of compacted ash. I quickly wandered off as I heard the sound of military commands being barked out, to watch and capture the sight of the John Frum army marching barefoot down the mud road towards the parade ground.

The army were looking smart with their real Second World War US uniforms, discovered a few years ago in a container in the Solomon Islands (before this they marched bare-chested with the words USA painted on their skin), and carrying bamboo rifles with red tips. The soldiers marched in perfect time, and with a very vocal sergeant major cajoling them, moved onto the parade ground in front of a coconut thatched dais of dignitaries.

These included a resplendent Issac Wan, his son and associated senior John Frum members in military uniform, one of whom looked disconcertingly like a young Idi Amin. Behind the leaders was the ever-active Yasur volcano, belching its clouds of fumes, along with the occasional eruption, to make a spectacular backdrop to the parade.

The volcano is part of the John Frum religion; the literal translation in the local dialect for it is 'God'. Before the ceremony began I wandered inside the headquarters, a breezeblock building next to the ceremonial dais. The soldier on duty waved me in, apparently only the most senior John Frum members may enter here, and the occasional foreigner.

Eyes straight ahead

The first thing that confronts you is a large wall painting of Yasur, with a door clearly marked on the side of the volcano. Behind this door, it is believed, John Frum lives and will emerge one day to bestow cargo on his followers. He moves between the volcano and the US along special pathways under the sea.

I walked further into the headquarters, alongside rooms of spare bamboo rifles and the discarded clothes of the soldiers. On the wall are photographs of Isaac in uniform in the USA, he was taken there on an all expenses-paid trip in 1995 by a wealthy American benefactor, alongside American flags, both real and also images cut awkwardly out of magazines and then taped to the wall.

Alongside artillery abandoned by the US Army as they left Tanna, and ceremonial swords, which actually looked Japanese, there is a large and curious poster of cats and lions by the artist Carol Lawson who I learn later produces art for fairy tale books and specialises in schmaltzy teddy bear images. This confused me somewhat as it is clear that the poster is in an important position, and is venerated.

Dancers from a John Frum village perform in front of the US flag

I asked a soldier who was following me around what was the meaning of it? The gist I gathered was that John Frum's ancestors were cats, which then later became lions, before assuming human form. This left me slightly confused as it had not been mentioned before, but showed the complexity behind the followers' beliefs, if nothing else.

I wandered back to the parade ground and, after a long drill, looked upon in awed silence by the large crowd of John Frum followers, the US flag was slowly and solemnly raised. The crowd had been silent up to this point, now they let loose with shouts and applause, and the entertainment began.

Every John Frum village, and there are quite a few across Tanna, had its own troupe of entertainers, and they varied from traditional kastom dancers, to plays with heavily made up monsters fighting against tribesmen with bows and arrows, with the crowd shouting gleefully the Vanuatuan words for "look behind you" as the monsters crept up behind the warriors.

After about ten of these performances I walked downhill towards the sea and into the other part of Sulphur Bay, a small settlement of houses known as Ipikil, where the Prophet Fred believers lived. Not to be outdone by the John Frum celebrations closer to the volcano there was a celebration taking place on a football field.

No tribal dancing for the Prophet Fred followers, but dancing to the latest pirated songs of Miley Cyrus, Taylor Swift and Kanye West. It was a very modern celebration, and seemed somewhat out of place when compared to what was occurring only fifteen minutes' walk up the hill.

The crowd was decidedly much smaller and more uninterested than those singing and taking part in the celebrations on the John Frum parade ground, and after a quick dip into the sea, which being boiling hot in places and smelling like rotten eggs helped totally justify the nomenclature of the village, made my way back up to the main event.

The dancing and entertainment would continue until close to dusk, when as solemnly as it had been raised, the US flag was slowly taken down, folded, and removed back to the John Frum headquarters.

The John Frum believers began their long walks back to their villages across the island of Tanna, some taking advantage of their proximity to

Yasur to climb it and look down into the fiery depths of the volcano, from which, one day, John Frum will emerge and dispense wealth to all.

The door to the volcano from a painting inside the John Frum Headquarters

The Easiest Volcano Climb in the World. Tanna

Yasur Volcano taken from Volcano Island Paradise Bungalows on a clear day

The mighty Yasur volcano was not visible from the hut I was staying in. It should have been, as the Volcano Island Paradise bungalows were situated just below the volcano, but the rain had come, and when the rain arrives in Tanna it comes down in torrents and blocks out anything in front of you. The rain water did help encourage Yasur to be extremely noisy, producing a noise sounding a little like a sonic boom every ten minutes. With a few minor earthquakes also occurring I did not sleep well, but at least I was comfy and dry.

I was lucky to actually make it through to the bungalows. Ours was the last car that risked crossing the rising river that snaked through the ash plains. Other tourists heading for their accommodation, or hoping to see Yasur on a day trip, were all turned back and had to return on the rather bumpy unpaved road two hours back to the other side of the island.

The glowing crater of Yasur tempted Captain Cook to Tanna in 1774, and he landed at Port Resolution but none of his party made it to the top of the volcano, not least because the Tanna locals were rather unhappy at his incursion, throwing rocks and firing arrows at any opportunity.

Not all volcanoes demand a multi-day hike, camping at the base and are accompanied with an arduous climb to the top. Most do, but not Yasur. At 361 metres and with a relatively easy 4WD road to a car park just below the crater, it is one of the most accessible volcanoes in the world, and is a huge draw for tourists to fly in to Tanna for a holiday.

Day trips are sold widely in Port Vila, but beware and check both the weather for the island, it is one of the wettest islands of the archipelago, and the volcano alert status to ensure you can actually get close to it. If you do have limited time an overnight trip would be much better than just flying in and out in the daytime. To see the volcano at night is when it is at its most impressive, with the flying lava standing out in the darkness (this also makes it safer as it is easier to see). The more days you have the better, as you have a much higher chance of seeing Yasur on a clear day.

After three days, and on my very last day, the rains finally cleared. The volcano was clearly visible and seemed quite angry, smoke was pouring into the air and was accompanied by the sound of thunderous explosions.

I had planned to walk to the top but the roads were still flooded and the ground had turned to mud, so I hired a smol truck (Utility vehicle in the English language) for 2,000 Vatu (US$20) to take me up. We stopped at a small booth, where the local kastom owners collected their 7,500 Vatu (US$75) fee. If you visit more than once, your subsequent visits are at half price. Some tourists, notoriously backpackers, try to avoid this fee by taking routes avoiding the toll booth. This is easy to do but strongly inadvisable because:

A) They are the traditional owners of the land and the volcano, which plays an important part in their belief system, and has done for centuries. If the owners allow visitors to climb, and ask for a fee in return, that is their prerogative. Charges such as this fee are common throughout the islands of Vanuatu.

B) You will get caught. Everybody knows everyone else, and a new (particularly if you are white) face tends to stick out like a sore thumb. You will be noticed and will face an angry and possibly violent confrontation as has happened on several occasions.

So do the right thing. Fees have increased for the first time in over ten years on April 1, 2016, making Yasur a little more expensive to visit.. Their argument, which is not unreasonable, is that the majority of the money from tourists goes to expat hotel owners on the east coast, where resorts (over)charge tourists up to US$200 for the trip.

Of course, the hotel owners will just increase the fees charged to tourists. This will provide another reason to stay at the local bungalows near the volcano; it may not be as luxurious, but the experience is totally unforgettable.

A timely reminder as you climb the last thirty metres from the car park

The small road, with concrete in places to help with the grip for the tyres, wound its way up to the small car park. The weather had put paid to most tourists and only a handful had made it up to the top of the crater.

Yasur did not disappoint, within minutes of making my way to the edge of the crater a huge explosion sent massive lumps of red hot lava way up in to the air above us, before tumbling slowly back into the crater.

The heavy rains had raised the ground water level, coming into contact with the magma chamber, causing larger explosions than usual. I have been to the top of Yasur three times, but this was the most impressive I had seen it.

The moisture still remaining in the air meant that shock waves were visible a second before the actual eruption of lava. You can watch the small sea of lava, as it moves backwards and forwards before ferociously erupting, ejecting material in all directions.

The small pieces of lava thrown highest hang in the air and gracefully fall like raindrops onto the sides of the crater to cool and slowly change colour to black. Eruptions vary, but there will usually be one large eruption every 15 – 20 minutes, with smaller eruptions every few minutes. Yet this is Yasur, and he can be totally unpredictable.

Your position is vital for your safety. Do not stand on the crater edge downwind so that material comes your way. Having said that, this is a live volcano, and it is dangerous from any position.

Five minutes after I had moved to view the explosions from a new angle, a huge lump of lava sailed over where I had been standing, to land some twenty metres behind.

The local advice is to not wear a cap, and not watch the volcano through a camera lens, you need the perspective to see where the bright orange pieces of lava are going.

The reality is that taking photos of the amazing eruptions is impossible to ignore, but do always take a local guide who will be watching closely and can warn you if lava is heading your way.

Yasur can be closed on occasions; the Vanuatu Geohazards Observatory defines the alert status. At level 2 and above, a fairly major eruption, it will be closed. This can, and does, happen at any time. The alert statuses are:

Level 0: - Low activity. Access to the crater is allowed.

Level 1: - Normal activity. Access to the crater is allowed.

Level 2: - Moderate to high activity. Lava bombs and other material may be ejected beyond the crater. Access to the crater is closed.

Level 3: - Severe activity. Lava bombs are ejected beyond the crater rim, and ash clouds will obscure the crater. Access to the crater is closed.

Level 4: - Major eruption affecting both the local area and other parts of Tanna. Access to the crater is closed.

Mt Yasur explodes at sunset

Do not ignore this alert status. You may have travelled half way around the world to see Yasur, but it is better to return home again to tell the tale.

The last significant group death occurred when two Japanese tourists ignored the high alert status, and cajoled and bribed a guide from Sulphur Bay to take them up when the volcano was officially closed.

Tourists, with a guide, wait on the crater rim for an eruption

In an earlier trip to Tanna I had met one of the rescue party who went up to retrieve the bodies. Lava bombs had dismembered them, and what was left was brought back in three small wicker baskets.

Reluctantly, after three hours on top of Yasur, I made my way down to the car park, and then a quick trip back to the bungalows. With clear skies it was captivating to watch the orange glow and frequent eruptions lighting up the sky from the safety of my hut.

Yasur is truly one of the world's great experiences.

What to take

- A torch. The most important requirement. It is pitch black on top of the crater when you finish your visit, and to descend safely you need a good torch.

- A jacket. It can be freezing up on the crater when the winds are blowing, even if it is 35C at ground level.

- A guide. Included in hotel organised trips, but if you are staying locally organise a guide for approximately 1,500 Vatu (US $15). He will know the best spots for views, and be your eyes in case you are taking photos and chunks of lava are heading your way.

- A tripod. If you can fit it into your bag. Keeping your camera steady is an art otherwise.

A large eruption hurls lava skywards

Surfing on a Volcano. Tanna

Keeping his balance. The next Olympic hopeful from Vanuatu.

If climbing up and seeing an active erupting volcano is not enough of an adrenalin rush for you, then there is now the opportunity to surf, or rather ashboard, down the sides of the crater (and this is the outer sides, obviously, to avoid the rider having a sudden and violent early cremation).

I had heard talk of this occurring in Central America, but when I was offered the chance to try it for myself in Tanna I could not refuse. It all starts with a walk, or a ride in a smol truk, to the ash plains. These themselves are worthy of an extended visit, no living thing exists here, and all that can be seen for miles around is black ash, with the occasional large lava bomb to remind you of where you are.

Boards can be rented from a local living nearby for between 1000 and 2000 Vatu (US $10 to $20) for two hours, but you do need to book ahead. This is easier if you are staying in a local bungalow, but somewhat harder if you are staying in a beach resort on the other side of the island (you will need to ask around at the resort or arrange a day trip to the ash plains).

The surfboards have seen better days, probably because of the abrasive ash, but the experience of riding on them is one you will not forget in a long time. You start off practising on the small slopes near the bottom of the volcano until you get the hang of it.

Falling off is, well, just like falling into thick muddy sand. It does not hurt you and it also really cushions your fall and slows you down quickly if you can push out your hands or feet into the ash. Once you gain in confidence you then take the surfboards higher up the flanks of the volcano. This is the only really hard part as the trek up seems to take three steps forward and then two steps back, as you sink into the ash without seemingly any real progress.

Making it look easy, Tanna locals show how it is done

Once you reach a point halfway up the volcano the fun really begins. The view down to the ash plain makes you wish you wish you had brought your camera (unwise unless it is waterproof and can keep the ash out of it).

I climbed gingerly onto the board, kicked back, and it started to gain speed rapidly.

If you can keep your balance the ride would be even more exhilarating. I tried this several times and lasted only 10 metres or so before flying head first into the ash and rolling down most of the way to the bottom. My only real success came when I decided to sit on the board and use my hands to dig into the ash to give me a flying start. Even then I did not make it quite to the bottom before over turning the board and skidding into deep ash.

Watching the locals speed with ease on the boards was the real spectacle. Few in Tanna would have ever seen snow, but you get the feeling that in the next winter Olympics the ashboarders here could be a lot more successful in snowboarding than the Jamaicans were at bobsleighing.

The major downside to ashboarding is, of course, the ash. It does not hurt you if you fall off, even at speed, but it does gets everywhere. I was picking particles of black ash out of my ears weeks later despite many showers trying to rid myself of the pervasive black particles.

Even so, it is totally recommended if you do visit Tanna, as how often do you get the chance to say you have surfed down an active volcano?

Carving out a living. Ambrym

Abel carving a mask

Ambrym is one of the most unusual islands I have traveled to in Vanuatu. It is dominated by the active volcanoes of Marum and Benbow, the centre surrounded by a huge ash plain and caldera where nothing lives, with the population inhabiting the coastal fringes.

The island is steeped in ancient beliefs and black magic, and has a very distinct culture apart from the other islands of Vanuatu.

The island has some very skilled wood carvers, creating the large Tam Tam figures (or Slit Gong drums) to communicate between villages on the island, and for ceremonial purposes. You can see Tam Tams throughout Port Vila these days as well, popping up outside restaurants, banks and Air Vanuatu's headquarters. They have become a symbol of Vanuatu as recognisable as its colourful flag.

I met one of the best carvers from Ambrym, Abel Sailas, and talked to him while he was hard at work creating a mask for an upcoming art exhibition in Noumea, New Caledonia. The interview was conducted mainly in Bislama, and fast Bislama at that, so apologies for any translation errors that may have crept in.

Where did you learn to carve?
As a young man I watched the elders in my village Ranuetlam (on the North coast of Ambrym) carve large Tam Tams and ceremonial sculptures.

After they had finished for the day I would practise on some discarded wood using their tools, and I found this was something I could do well and really enjoyed.

I learnt from watching the best carvers on Ambrym, but a lot of my skills now have been self taught.

The designs belong to the Chief of the village, not anyone can carve them. I first had to ask permission to carve designs such as this Lengnagulong mask I am working on now. This was only approved after the Chief saw my skill and I also contributed several pigs to him.

To carve Tam Tam faces you need to be skilled and pay more pigs as tribute to the Chief. Currently I have given enough pigs and yams to be able to carve two faces on a Tam Tam. I only use traditional Ambrym methods and tools to carve, all is done by hand.

A Tam Tam may take me two day or more days to carve and even this carving will take me all today to carve and then polish.

What would happen if you carved a three face Tam Tam statue?

I could not. I do not have the right. It has happened that men without permission have carved Ambrym statues. Not so long ago these people could have been hunted down and killed, but now their work would be destroyed and the carver fined.

Only man Ambrym (men from Ambrym) are able to carve these in the first place and you must have the right from the Chief to do so.

Where has your work been exhibited?

All over Vanuatu, and now New Caledonia. My work has sold to galleries in France and Australia too.

How do you choose your wood?

A truck comes around once a month with local soft wood. I choose which pieces I want by visualising my carving in them, and store them until I can carve them. I look carefully at the grains in the wood, they are important in deciding the type of carving and where I begin to carve.

This is your full time job?

It is. I work 7 to 5 every day except Sunday. I have been able to take on an apprentice. I sell my work at a Hibernian market stall (opposite the Bank South Pacific branch, and next to Centre Point in Port Villa) and at the new Vanuatu Handicraft Market on Wharf Road as well as at exhibitions in the French Cultural Centre and overseas.

Tell me the Custom story behind the Lengnagulong mask you are carving

This is one of the most famous Kastom (custom) stories from Ambrym. Lengnagulong lived in a wood near the top of the volcano. But the local villagers were jealous of him because he was famous throughout Ambrym for his intelligence and beauty.

He told them: "You cannot kill me. I will survive wood, stone, metal, even a bow and arrow. The only thing I fear you cannot control, a storm of thunder and lightning".

The villagers used Kastom practices to call a severe storm. The storm destroyed the wood that Lengnagulong lived in and the water washed him and the trees through the villages of Konkon, Olal and Magam where the villagers tried to save him but the waters were too strong and he was washed into the sea to drown.

He was washed up on the shore of the village Melvat where an old carver found him and took him back to his hut as he was so beautiful. He then carved the first mask of Lengnagulong.

The mask is still powerful. You can ask Lengnagulong to send his spirit to get things you need, and you will get them. The mask was too good for me to let it go to the exhibition in New Caledonia and I purchased it from Abel. It is a thing of beauty, the wood grain accentuates the detailed carving. I have yet to ask Lengnagulong for anything, until I need to.

WW II Madness. Six Million Dollar Point. Santo

The remains of a US Army vehicle uncovered by the tide

Like most of Vanuatu, Espiritu Santo in the northern chain of islands was occupied by the Americans during WWII to launch their attacks on the Japanese in the Pacific. On their departure from the island they left behind infrastructure like roads and runways and their buildings, with army built Quonset huts still standing around Santo.

The biggest legacy is Million Dollar Point, both historically fascinating, but environmentally destructive and a monument to greed and stupidity.

The Condominium of the New Hebrides (as Vanuatu was then called), run by Britain and France, thought they had the Americans over a barrel as the time for their departure neared at the end of the war. The American bases were full of vehicles, furniture, clothing, food, drink and all that had been required to sustain the troops.

A decision had been taken that this was not going to be repatriated, and that the Condominium could buy it all at rock bottom prices. Unfortunately the British and French got extremely greedy, refusing an offer from the Americans to pay only 6 cents in the dollar for everything,. They thought by waiting they would eventually get it all for nothing.

The Americans were none too impressed with this, and came up with another option in a moment of madness. They took all the vehicles, food, clothing and other equipment to a wharf on the south side of the island.

The army then drove the vehicles into the sea, and used bulldozers to dump the rest over the end of the wharf, before they also were driven into the sea. Millions of dollars of goods were destroyed over a period of two days, contaminating the sea with fuel, rubber, metal and Coca Cola.

What the locals would have thought watching this wasteful destruction would be hard to understand, although quite rightly they looted what they could get when the Americans had left.

Today you can take a 10 minute taxi from Luganville to Million Dollar Point and snorkel over entire rusting vehicles, which have become home for vast arrays of tropical fish. You can see the remains of tanks, bulldozers and cranes.

Go at low tide and pick your way over the remains moved by the water over a large area around the wharf. Steering wheels remain embedded in the reef, unbroken coke bottles lie on the sea bed, alongside cutlery, plates and a huge amount of twisted rusted metal. We had a great time scavenging for souvenirs, although you have to take care to not get cut as you walked though the historical junkyard.

There are now discussions, sixty years later, about the American military returning to clean up the area. It is quite likely this may happen in the next few years, obviously a good thing for the environment, but Million Dollar Point is one of the most amazing places I have been to, a memorial to political madness, but now a historical treasure trove.

An old bottle of Coke adding life to the seabed

Life and death in a Vanuatu village. Tanna

Returning from the market garden with the ever present bush knife (machete)

Chickens. You have to love chickens, and pigs. And then there are the dogs getting under your feet. And of course, the children, small toddlers wandering everywhere without a worried parent in sight. Welcome to village life, Tanna style.

I am staying with Lionel and Elen and their two children. It is communal living, everything is shared from food to parenting, and it is very social. Two hundred and thirty two people live here. The families are all intertwined over the ages, so that everybody is in someway related.

The small houses are quite spacious, with rooms separated by coconut matting walls, and with overlaid woven palm fronds used for the roof to ensure it remains dry. Not a drop gets in when the torrential downpour hits us, unfortunately the pathways of ash and hardened mud outside turn into small streams, but they are lower than the houses, so no flooding occurs.

There is no electricity here. Food is cooked over wood burning stoves, and the few lights are powered by solar panels. These are also used to power up mobile phones, which have had a huge impact on communications in the village and increased the income of the few who have decided to become Digicell phone credit resellers.

You adapt to local ways, and that means you go to bed really early, when it gets dark, and wake up really early, thanks to the chickens in particular.

The village is located 3 kms from the main road, a smol truk (utility vehicle) can and does make it here occasionally, bringing back large purchases from the market. The lack of traffic does mean that animals and children are not corralled into a small area and wander freely. It also means to get anywhere here you have to walk.

Distances are measured in hours, although this is not a very reliable measurement. Walking to Port Resolution one day, I was told the distance varied between 30 minutes, two hours and five hours. Logic made me ignore the first one, too much kava had obviously been imbibed by the individual, but neither of the other measurements were true; for my walking pace, it turned out to be closer to four hours.

The market gardens located a short walk from the village are the one of the key secrets behind the country's high happiness ratio. People just do not go hungry. The soil is good over most of Vanuatu due to the volcanic nature of most of the islands, although here the volcano Yasur can hurt crop growing on occasions when a large amount of ash falls, or acid rain kills some crops.

Yam, taro island cabbage, carrots and very tasty small potatoes are grown here, along with plentiful, and often wild, bananas, pineapples, oranges and passion fruit. A larger area behind the market garden has been planted with tobacco and coffee beans.

The coffee beans are bought by a small company on the island and exported as *Tanna Coffee*, which is developing a cult following in Australia and the UK. It is not drunk on the island though, the locals prefer juices, Liptons tea, and of course kava.

Kava is the reward for a hard days work in the market garden. Still segregated by sex, the males drink in one bar and the females in another. I sit with the chief and the men folk and drink the mud coloured murky concoction. Few actually likes the taste, spitting after drinking it is the way many try to remove the bitter earthy bite that kava has, it is the effect that the drinker craves, a feeling of relaxation and happiness.

I get dinner at the kava bar, as Elen brings the meal to her husband who is with me there. She cannot stay, as that is taboo, and quickly leaves us with a plate piled high with very fresh chicken, killed earlier that day, the ubiquitous staple of white rice, and cabbage and taro.

Maggi noodles, which all of Vanuatu seems addicted to, unfortunately, are usually served on the same plate, but I had protested the day before that rice was healthier and tastier, and these did not surface again for me again. Breakfasts are less exciting, usually dry breakfast crackers, with imported Australian jam, unless someone has journeyed early in the morning to the village a few km away, which has a baker, but even then he does not bake bread every day.

Unlike western bars, the kava bar is a very quiet place, the kava, unlike alcohol, does not promote conversation. One or two shells are enough for me, and although I do not smoke normally, I toke on fresh tobacco rolled in a ripped page from a school book. This does take away the taste of the kava, and the chemical free cigarette is actually a pleasure to smoke. I try to make some small talk, but English and even Bislama is not spoken much here, with the local language dominating.

Lionel's grandfather died while I was staying with them, this caused a lot of commotion in the village, but not too much grief. He was old, in his eighties, which is still rare in Tanna, and he had been ill for a long time.

Simple graves, tended regularly by the family.

The family prepared for a massive feast, as relatives walked to the village from across the island. The body was wrapped in calico and then coconut matting, and then was buried on the day of death as is the tradition. With no mortuaries and hot tropical temperatures, this makes perfect sense.

A huge feast was prepared and a fairly sombre party began, the Vanuatu version of an Irish wake. A cow was purchased at an expensive price for the family and was then sacrificed and cooked with a variety of vegetables and rice. The women stayed around the burial site, cooking more food, while the men went off to drink kava. The whole ceremony would last 24 hours, until all the food and kava had been consumed and then the official mourning began.

What this actually meant was, out of respect for the dead man, his direct family (such as brothers and sons) was not allowed to work or play sport for two weeks. Indirect family (such as nephews) had to withdraw from these activities for one week.

Respect for elders and family members is an important facet of life here, something that we have lost in the west.

Confusion at the Stadium. Port Vila

Tafea in dark shirts take on Ifira at the Port Vila Stadium

A Saturday afternoon in Port Vila and what to do. Picking up the *Vanuatu Daily* I read that the TVL Football Cup Final is on at Port Vila Stadium. That sounds like a must see, so I grab my camera and walk towards the stadium. The first thing I notice is how many people have gained vantage points on the hill outside the ground to watch the action for free. Admittedly binoculars would make it easier to see, but through the branches you can glimpse almost two thirds of the ground.

I actually wanted to get bit more of the atmosphere, and get closer to the action, so I paid 200 Vatu (US$2) to get in and wandered around the ground looking for a good position. Having turned up just before kick off the ground was packed, and all terrace seats had gone. I managed to get a position beneath the scoreboard as the two teams came out to massive roars from their fans. The team was Tafea, made up of players from Tanna Island and Ifira, the island in the middle of Port Villa harbour.

The standard of football was pretty high but neither team could convert their attacking play into actual goals, and after 90 minutes the score was still 0 - 0. This meant another thirty minutes of extra time, but yet again neither team could score. The match had not started on time, as you travel around the islands you realise this happens with many things in Vanuatu, but this was now causing big problems as dusk descended.

The best view of the match is from the scoreboard

The floodlights at the ground, which was also used as the international stadium, had not worked properly for many years. This meant that the penalty shoot out began in very poor light. This would not have been an issue if either team had successfully gained a goal advantage over the other but the team matched each other goal for goal and miss for miss. I have never seen anything like it in all the matches I have ever watched anywhere!

It came down to the eleventh penalty kick, with the score on 4-4. It was the goalkeeper's turn. I took a long exposure shot which makes it appear much lighter than it was, the brightness of the lights outside the ground gives you some idea. It was night time now.

The Tafea goalkeeper took a shot at goal and the Ifira goalkeeper saved it to roars from the Ifira supporters. Reversing their positions, the Ifira goalkeeper took a couple of steps back, walked forward and the ball went into the net. Exactly where it went in the net was not clear from where I was standing and I was on the edge of the pitch. The Ifira crowd went wild, invading the pitch and partying to celebrate their cup final win.

Unknown to the fans, the referee had decided that from his position by the goal even he could not see where that last ball had been kicked, and after conferring with his linesmen, decided to abandon the match. The strange thing about this was that this had been the same for the previous 4 or 5 penalty kicks taken in the darkness.

The non-result only became clear on the Monday morning when the abandonment of the match made front page headlines, so for the rest of Saturday night the Ifira fans could be heard celebrating their win with honking car horns, shouts and loud singing all across Port Vila.

The distant lights pierce the darkness as the goalkeeper shout out begins

The match was replayed the following Saturday, and Tafea won 3-0 in normal time. Ifira fans could with some honesty say "We were robbed".

Dancing while the Rain Pours. Port Vila

A sea of umbrellas in Sarafina Park

One of the biggest annual music festivals in the Pacific Islands happens in Port Vila, Vanuatu every October. The Fest Napuan showcases the best in Pacific music and dance, attracting bands from New Zealand, Australia, New Caledonia, Papua New Guinea and the Solomon Islands as well as from the many small islands of Vanuatu. We were there to experience a festival that shared one major thing in common with the legendary Glastonbury music festival, apart from great music: huge amounts of rain and mud.

Located at Sarafina Park just outside the CBD there are already traffic jams of local buses and road closures on the opening night. Even the torrential rain, which is bouncing off the road in its ferocity, does not prevent a huge turnout. Looking from my vantage point on the side of the stage all that is visible is a sea of umbrellas

Due to travel issues a number of bands from other island nations have not been able to make the 19th Fest Napuan, which has resulted in the local bands headlining on each day. The crowd reaction is noticeably calm, rarely more than engaging in modest clapping. That is until the Friday headliners take the stage, 'Stan and the Earth force'. Stan risks electrocution as he gets off the stage and dances with his microphone on the tarpaulin covered platform in front, which is now acting as a paddling pool as the rain

The Brian Eno of Hora Mona

continues. Even a French film crew making a film about the culture of the islands, is forced to give up and retreat to the safety of the sheltered stage. Meanwhile Stan interacts with the crowd, throwing out t-shirts and beckoning people to dance with him. The small number of security out front have a hard time restraining the crowd and cannot prevent numerous stage invaders dancing with the lead singer as the band belt out their Vanuatu reggae songs.

One thing that does differentiate Fest Napuan from the other festivals I have attended around the world was the vast array of food and drink options available from the palm and coconut leaf covered stores, which surrounded the park on all sides. Chicken wings and rice dishes, a staple of Vanuatu, could be bought for 250 Vatu ($2.50), or a whole fish and rice for 300 Vatu ($3.00). British festival goers would be overwhelmed with the choices and prices. Cold local Tusker beer could be had for 250 Vatu ($2.50), or you could risk the effects of the local throat numbing and sedating drink of choice, Kava, for 50 Vatu ($0.50C) a cup.

The rain continued to pour on each of the three days, soaking the crowd, but not reducing its numbers. Reggae beats constantly vibrated around the park as families picnicked under umbrellas on the grass. The Rasta way of life has a strong following here, and special mention should be made of sets by 'Smol Fyah', 'Young Life' and a band from the Solomon Islands called 'Solomon Group' in the descriptive and helpful program. All played great songs to an increasingly appreciative crowd.

Fresh fried fish. The festival food is also a huge attraction

The highlight was 'Hora Mona' a band from the Northern island of Espiritu Santo with a Maori lead singer. Dressed in traditional clothes they played mainly Vanuatu custom (tribal) music. The band's percussion instruments were traditional slit log drums and they played with such enthusiasm that they kept breaking the drum sticks that were being used to create an echoing powerful sound.

Backstage with the Hora Mona dancers from Espiritu Santo

A conch shell was produced creating a noise not that dissimilar to wailing guitar feedback. The crowd stood amazed as the Maori singer did a 'Hakka' dance at the end of their set, complete with much shouting and violent rolling of the tongue. The response, in a typical shy Melanesian way, was small bouts of giggling along with a smattering of polite applause.

The festival was very well organized; as soon as a band finished a local dance troupe would come onto the platform in front of the stage and mime and dance to recent hits, while the next band set up. Despite the terrible weather it all went incredibly smoothly and the crowd melted away at just after midnight as the last act finished. The tiny nation of Vanuatu has won the title of 'Happiest place on Earth' twice in recent years and with festivals as good as this one you can see why.

Black Magic and Sand Drawings. Ambrym

A traditional Ambrym sand drawing of the Leaf Man

Ambrym Island in Vanuatu is still relatively untouched by western thoughts and values and traditional custom beliefs remain very strong, particularly in the North East and North West villages, maybe not coincidentally the furthest settlements from the two small airports here.

The volcano Mt Benbow is the focus for much of the beliefs (and also for the surrounding islands like Malekula and Epi, where its glowing orange lava lakes can be seen eerily in the night sky). It is dangerous, destroying a village in 1913, and its eruptions have caused evacuations on several occasions, yet it provides life through rich farming soil. Certain clans or groups are believed to be custodians of the volcano, and use it to their benefit to threaten to cause it to erupt unless they get their way in village disagreements. Conversely, when it does erupt unexpectedly they get blamed and can be forced to escape to other islands for their safety.

Certain parts of the volcano are reserved for the islander's spirits after they die, each village has their special area. Not knowing this, the early Christian missionaries who visited the island failed dismally in their attempt to convert the local populace, their threats of a fiery end for their souls if they did not convert was not really going to provoke much fear and immediate conversion when locals believed that was their traditional destiny anyway.

My guide, from North Ambrym, was a firm believer in the traditional custom ways. The lava bombs he eagerly collected that had landed both recently and overnight close to our flimsy tents could be buried around his land to provide protection against those families who control the eruptions of the volcano. They could also be carved into faces and placed in other people's homes to control them and cause "problems". These exact problems were not specified, but I could guess.

He was also an expert in sand drawings, a beautiful and unique way of telling ancient stories and beliefs by tracing a finger through the ash to produce intricate artwork, in an amazingly quick time. These are given as gifts to people; he kindly gave me a few drawings after I gave him my solar torch (he really needed it a lot more than I did).

This beautiful drawing is called 'The Leaf Man' and it represents the story of a local villager who went exploring and was about to be attacked by a group from a rival village. He placed a leaf on his head, and vegetation on his body for camouflage, and was able to move through the villagers without being seen. It took about thirty seconds to draw the symmetric and complex patterns, and after viewing it (and letting me quickly take one photograph) he destroyed it so others could not see it.

Mangoes Under the Volcano. Ambae

Looking into the Vui crater, resembling a vision from the First World War

This island could just be mango heaven. I had barely grabbed my luggage and walked out of the small hut which acts as the Air Vanuatu terminal at Walaha on Ambae Island, before I encountered the sweet smell of fermenting fruit. Mangoes were everywhere, crushed into the road, lying beside it, even on the roof of the terminal building. I picked one up to eat, and one of my fellow passengers quickly told me it was not ripe enough, so I stuffed it in my bag for later. As I jumped on the back of the Ute the same passenger returned with his arms full of ripe mangoes, "These you can eat!!" he told me happily.

I had travelled to Ambae, also known as the island of Aoba, to visit the volcanic crater Monaro Vui. The whole island is in fact a volcano, rising 4000 metres from the seabed. On its peak the crater has three lakes filling old craters, they had been fairly inactive until recently. Previous eruptions had occurred long ago in 1670 and 1870 which had resulted in Ambae receiving scant attention in recent years compared to the more active volcanoes in Vanuatu.

This all changed in 2005 when an Air Vanuatu pilot noticed smoke and a new crater forming inside Lake Monaro Vui, and then later a sudden change in water colour from blue to bright red. Small eruptions and earthquakes followed with plumes of ash visible from nearby Santo. Villages began to be evacuated, and almost half of the island's population was moved away from the danger zone. And then the volcano returned to slumber.

The Grass strip at Walaha airport

Monaro Vui still remains one of the most dangerous volcanoes in the world. In vulcanology terms it is a Surtseyan type, one that will explode with tremendous power when magma contacts water. With pools of lava sitting just underneath the large lakes the threat of a catastrophic explosion is great, with the risk of tsunamis that would not only affect the whole of Vanuatu, but could also impact the east coast of Australia. A smaller eruption could create lahars, combinations of volcanic material, water, trees and mud, which also would potentially wipe out many of Ambae's villages located at sea level.

Why would you live on such an island? Well, there are previously mentioned mangoes. The earth is incredibly fertile due to its volcanic origins; you would never starve on Ambae. Pineapples, watermelon, bananas, mandarins, passion fruit and pamplemousse can be picked from the side of the road. There is an abundance of fish both inside and outside of the reef. And the locals are very relaxed and happy with life on this little paradise with little need to go across to neighbouring Santo or to the fearful noise and hustle and bustle of Port Vila.

Sitting beneath a mango tree in the small village of Ndui Ndui on the west coast of the island I began to understand this. I had just bought some delicious fresh banana cake from a stall at the market for 20 Vatu. For dessert I reached down to grab a mango, and sucked the fruity juice out of it, before discarding it and picking up another. This was a place I could stay a long time in. Unfortunately, I was only here for a long weekend and had to prepare to climb up to the top of volcano the next day.

A Ndui Ndui local relaxes under the mango tree

Setting off at 4:00AM I clambered aboard the back of a small truck with a motley crew of locals who were coming with me to visit the crater. Most were climbing up because opportunities were rare due to the lack of visitors to Ambae, while Stuart, a local student who was studying geology at the USP in Fiji wanted to visit his first volcano. All considered it a special occasion as the craters are considered a very sacred place in Ambae, due to it being the resting place for human spirits after death.

We bounced around on the single track road (there are very few cars and you are unlikely to meet them, particularly so at this time of the morning), crossing dry river beds at speed and then going slowly up alarmingly angled inclines with the tyres losing their grip on the polished rock surface. After an hour we reached the village of Lolo Tinge, and made our way to the hut of David Maga Tao, the guide for our climb to the volcano.

Only a few guides are allowed to take visitors to the crater, and you cannot travel alone, not that you would want to as you would easily get lost. The guides are the custodians of the crater and pick the best route up to avoid the sacred places that are taboo. David was thin and wiry, and extremely fit. He had just finished helping build a village home by lugging bags of cement up from the beach, a thousand metre journey on a small muddy path. In his early forties he was easily able to out climb the younger members of our party. He told us he could do the climb in two hours. Looking up at the crater high above us I was dubious I could do it in ten.

The climb was David's 38th trip to the crater. This was over a period of sixteen years, which shows how few people actually make it to Ambae and attempt the walk up to the top of the volcano. We set off, with an additional member of our team, John, David's son, who he was teaching to become a guide. The route up took us past long abandoned homes with terrific views out to the sea with the island of Santo just visible in the far distance. Even here mangoes were lying on the ground, being grabbed for a quick juice hit as we travelled ever higher.

The path was slippery in places. Ambae was suffering from a drought on the coast, but up here the volcano has its own weather system and decided to unleash a tropical rainstorm accompanied by scarily loud thunder and lightning around us, which made the going slow. The dry creek beds we crossed on the way up later became raging torrents when we descended that evening.

A young fruit bat clings to a branch

As we got closer to the top the foliage became rainforest and the path had grown over, requiring considerable hacking from our guides with their machetes, which slowed us down further. Going at a slower pace meant I had more time to look at the wildlife around me. I was admiring a large spider in the middle of a glistening web, when I looked up saw a beautiful baby flying fox (fruit bat) hanging from a branch. With flying fox being a local delicacy I was certain that it might have ended up as the evening meal had I not paid it so much attention with my camera.

Up and over the crater edge we saw Lake Monaro Lakua or rather glimpsed it as the clouds began to cover the entire crater. On a dry day, with more time, you can swim in its fresh water and recuperate from the climb. As we were already behind schedule we pushed on to the volcanic crater lake of Monaro Vui.

The closer we got to Monaro Vui, the more ghostly our surroundings became. The weather was closing in with the mist descending and rain lashing down, accompanied by waves of sulphur being blown towards us from the crater lake. Nothing lives here as the sulphur kills everything in its path. It reminded me of a photograph of a World War I battlefield in Northern France, with mud, mist and the skeletons of trees. The sulphur made it hard to breathe as we walked through the dead forest, the branches breaking as they were grabbed for support while walking over the uneven muddy ground. The gas, mist and rain prevented us from actually seeing into the actual crater, but the smell made it clear it was still very active.

We rested for a while before deciding to start the climb back to the village. It was already late, and only a few hours of daylight remained. For those who want to visit the volcano I would strongly recommend an overnight camp; you would have more time to explore and would be able to take advantage of the clouds being usually much higher first thing in the morning than in the afternoon. The descent was quicker and more slippery than the journey up and we arrived back in darkness for our return trip to Ndui Ndui. We were slightly delayed, and bounced round a bit more than on our earlier journey, when we suffered a tyre blow out on the rough road.

I was still in time for a late dinner. The meal was fresh reef fish, taro, cabbage and rice. Even though I was ravenously hungry, I was concerned about the possibility of getting ciguatera, the nasty and painful fish poisoning that can occur by eating reef fish. Evelyne, the cook at Toa Palms Bungalows where I was staying, told me that the Ambae fisherman have developed a method for beating ciguatera by weeding out the poison fish. After catching the fish they return to land and lay them on the ground, near an ants' nest. The ants will clamber over all the good fish, and will leave the poisoned fish well alone, which are then buried. How scientific this method is has yet to be proven, but it seemed reasonable to me, and the fried fish I ate that night was delicious and I had no ill effects.

I reluctantly left Ambae the following day. The island was described by James Mitchener in his book *Tales of the South Pacific* as a mystical, magical island, and known to his readers as Bali Ha'i. He wrote that it was a remote place of great happiness but impossible to reach. These days you can get there fairly easily from Santo (depending on Air Vanuatu or cargo boat schedules, that is), but it still remains a magical and happy place to visit. I look forward to returning and exploring more of the island, lingering under the trees, and eating more mangoes.

The Monaro Vui crater from the air on a rare clear and dry day

The X-Ray Art of Kiki Kautonga. Futana

Kiki Kautonga displays a half finished x-ray artwork

I was in Port Vila for the opening of the annual Nawita Contemporary art exhibition, showing off the best works by young Vanuatu artists. The opening night was held in the Alliance Francaise gallery on Rue Mercet and was packed with dignitaries including the Prime Minister, respective diplomatic representatives and all the artists.

With typical French flair extremely tasty, and highly alcoholic, punch was served alongside the ubiquitous massive tub of kava to the crowds admiring the work of Vanuatu's top artists.

The theme of the exhibition this year was 'recycling'. The first exhibit was a sculpture of a totem, similar to a Tam-Tam statue from Ambrym, but made from soft drinks cans. The tables of jewellery were equally clever, with glass ear rings and necklaces recycled from old coke bottles discarded by the US navy in Havannah Harbour during the war. Even old satellite dishes had been converted into both wall hanging fish and large silver striped ear rings.

My favourite exhibit was the intricately cut x-ray art showing Vanuatu custom stories. We are talking about actual medical x-rays being used for art, and not the ancient aboriginal rock paintings from Arnhem Land in Australia.

What made this artwork particularly special, and each piece unique, was that there were still signs of the original broken bones and twisted backs that caused the x-ray to be originally taken, amongst the designs of Spirits, Gods and Ceremonies intricately cut out by knife. The art was a focus for many of the visitors, and all the work was marked by a blue spot (meaning it had been sold) by the night's end. I wanted to know more, so I decided to come back the next day when the artist Kiki Kautonga was going to be there for an hour to show how he created his artwork.

Kiki was working hard on a new artwork when I arrived the next morning. A class of Ni-Vanuatu school students was surrounding him and looking on with awe as, only using a sharp box cutter knife, he cut out precise designs on an old x-ray on the table in front of him. I started talking to him, while he focused on his cutting.

He is from Futana, a small island off the east coast of Tanna, but has been brought up and lived most of his thirty four years in Port Vila. He started out cutting paper and discovered he had a knack for creating intricate designs by hand.

Kiki discovered that paper was not the best medium for his work, easily getting spoiled and damaged, and discovered an old x-ray at home. This required a sharper knife to cut through the plastic, yet it was easy to work with and more robust than paper.

The best place to pick up old x-rays was the Port Vila General Hospital in Seaside. Kiki spent half a day trying to find the right person to talk to, and then finally found an administrator who pointed him to the storeroom where all the old x-rays were kept.

Doing a deal, Kiki arranged to buy all the x-rays that were old and uncollected for 100 Vatu (US $1) each, and he now has a ready supply which will keep him going for a few years. Even though the rest of the world is turning to digital online x-rays, Vanuatu has older medical facilities, often given as aid by hospitals upgrading to the latest technology.

His supplies will not be in any danger of drying up soon.

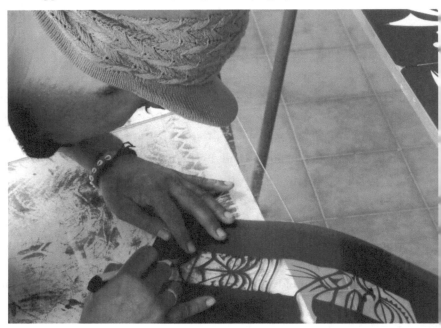

The artist works on the x-ray with a box cutter knife

Kiki uses Kastom (Custom) traditional stories for his designs, tales that were taught to him by his parents and grandparents about the life of his ancestors on the small island of Futana.

What makes them so impressive is that they are each done free hand and not copied from a previous design. It takes him between two to five hours to make each one, and he rarely has to throw away one because of a mistake.

Kiki Kautonga's work is gradually being recognised as a unique art form and has been collected by galleries in Vanuatu, France and New Caledonia. Recently the Jean-Marie Tjibaou Cultural Centre in Noumea bought one of his works, and this is now on display in the Pacific art gallery there.

The finished artwork, telling a Custom tale from Futana

Fresh Prawns from the Volcano. Gaua

Freshwater prawns just caught in the volcanic lake

Feasting on an early morning breakfast of pamplemousse, pineapple and freshly squeezed lemon juice, the conversation turned towards the dinner menu. Would I like lobster, yet again, or would I perhaps celebrate the end of my stay in Gaua with the more expensive option of a fresh local chicken?

This was not a hard decision to make, thinking back to my last meal of a huge lobster caught fresh off the beach behind the bungalows, served with local vegetables and a tasty sauce and accompanied by a few glasses of Bordeaux wine (which I had remembered to bring with me from Port Vila).

I had come to Gaua to climb the volcano, but the trip was fast turning into the gourmet food holiday.

Gaua, situated in the Banks and Torres islands in Vanuatu, is rarely visited. Only 67 visitors made it to the northerly island in 2014. I was visitor number 2 this year and I really did not think I was going to make it.

There are not many flights a week, and they are often fully booked, so you need to book well in advance. I had done this, yet I was stuck at Santo airport. The engineer had been working on the small Twin Otter plane for a couple of hours before there was an announcement:

"The plane is out of service. We are going to put you in hotels in Santo and maybe fly you out later in the week".

I like Santo, but the Banks and Torres was where I wanted to be. There was a general disappointed shuffling to the outside of the terminal before the engineer walked out amongst us and told us that we should board the plane. He had fixed the problem. And we were off!

Forty minutes later we were flying low over coral reefs into the grass strip airport at Gaua. I was met by Amelia from the Tammes Guesthouse, who walked me the 100 metres to my hut, basic but comfortable, with a view overlooking the runway. Perfect for plane spotters, although with only a few flights a week they might get a bit bored. Which would not be the case for everyone else, for although rarely visited, there is still a huge amount to see and do on the island.

Walking is the best way to see everything, although during my visit I did not actually have much of a choice. The smol trak (Ute) for transport was not running, as there had not been a shipment of fuel for a while. It was easy walking, and I had the bonus of not having to worry about being run over as I slowly meandered down the rutted pathway, looking through the tall grass at scenes of village life, until I reached the *Kamsy Kamsy Kamsa* kava bar.

I like the occasional shell of kava, but this was one of the best bars I had visited in Vanuatu. Less than a year old, the bar had comfortable seats backing onto the bush, and the kava was as relaxing and throat numbing as ever, but with no after effects.

What made the place even more special was that they served a local form of tapas with the kava shells. Tiny dishes of tasty small fried fish and vegetables kept appearing from the kitchen, and complemented, or rather overcame, the pungent taste of the kava. It set me up for a really good night's sleep, because the next day I was trekking to the Mount Garet Volcano.

Early in the morning, John Atkins, my guide, knocked on my bungalow door. He was strong and wiry, carrying a huge backpack, tent and a long bush knife, and he was accompanied by Fudi, my porter. Normally I would carry my own tent and gear (well, to be honest, only if there was no other option!) but the trekking price actually included a porter and it really made the journey both more enjoyable and faster.

The trail needs severe hacking with bush knives to trek through

We walked passed market gardens full of root vegetables and trees bursting with pamplemousse, pausing to knock down some for later meals. The going was fairly easy, the biggest problem being the long grass that often reached above our heads and required liberal hacking using bush knives to travel through. As we got close to the crater the path started to wind upwards and we encountered rain, so often associated with volcanoes that have their own, often wet, weather systems.

After five hours walking we stopped and John pointed out a small path to the left, which we followed, bringing us to a clearing where spring water was spurting out from the rocks. We filled our bottles with the slightly effervescent water; it tasted so much better than any of the mineral water I had brought with me. If this could be commercially bottled it would be a big seller, then again maybe it is best to leave it as a reward to the few who climb up to the volcano.

Reaching the top of the caldera we gazed down at Lake Letas and the smoking cone of Mt Garet in the distance. This was the difficult part of the trek, clambering down a steep path holding onto poles the local chief had helpfully placed a few metres apart, we rapidly descended to the lake. We pitched our tents inside a thatched hut on the shore.

I thought that this may be slightly excessive, my tent was more than able to withstand rain, but during the night as the torrential downpours hit, I was glad for the extra protection it gave me. Perhaps the best feature of the lakeside camp is the toilet. A basic coconut palm construction but with one of the best throne views in the world, looking through the rainforest and out to the lake and volcano beyond.

John and Fudi picked up a snorkel, face mask and spear and within twenty minutes had returned with a huge bowl of Lake Letas freshwater prawns. With no predators these grow to enormous sizes.

Cooked quickly over a wood fire they tasted as good as any I have ever eaten, more like lobster crossed with banana prawn, absolutely delicious, and a perfect way to end the day as we sat and talked beneath the stars and the ever smoking Mt Garet.

What you can see or achieve at the lake is in the hands of the weather gods. Sometimes the volcano is obscured in mist and cloud, and you do not even get to see it. The lake itself can misbehave; with the water becoming so rough you cannot cross. Not all tourists listen to their guide as John recounted the fate of two Germans who ignored his advice and set out to cross the water in rough conditions and were promptly swamped, sinking the canoe, only losing their cameras and luckily not their lives.

The volcano was visible and the lake was calm for us, the actual walk up Mt Garet is relatively easy and takes about an hour. The smoke plume and gases do obscure any lava visibility when you do get to the top of the cone, unless you are very lucky, but it is still an imposing sight, with the overwhelming smell of sulphur, and the ghostly trunks of dead trees lying on and inside the craters.

Mt Garet Volcano

Mt Garet erupts fairly often, with the last major eruption in 2013. The reality of an active volcano with lava lakes sitting next to and under the largest lake in Vanuatu has resulted in extensive evacuation plans being drawn up for the entire island should the alert level reach Three (which would be a major eruption).

Not surprisingly the volcano also plays a significant role in the islanders' belief systems, particularly in the relationship with birth and death. John was at the volcano when his uncle died recently, and at the exact moment of death, the volcano let out a huge bang as his spirit returned there.

After the trek up and back from the volcano I relaxed, swam at the beach, and enjoyed the fresh fish and lobster meals at the Tammes

Bungalows before going to see perhaps Gaua's best known attraction, the women's water music at Lambot village.

Walking down a muddy path, past pig pens and small orchards I reached a few huts on the sea shore. I was greeted by the ladies, already looking slightly damp in their pandanus and coconut leaf matted costumes from an earlier morning practice. I learnt later that they had actually been practising for three days once they had learnt they had a visitor to perform to. Their last performance had been six months ago and they wanted to ensure they put on a good show. And they did.

Damp but poised, the Water women of Gaua line up to perform

Water flew in the air as the women hit the sea water hard with their hands creating a hypnotic beat. The songs are passed down from generation to generation, custom stories about life living near the sea and the creatures that live in it.

The women and young girls stood waist deep as they slapped, splashed and hit the water creating amazing percussion, accompanied by their singing. They may not get that many visitors to see them in Gaua but that does not stop the world from experiencing their unique music. In the last few years the ladies had travelled to Mozambique, Spain and Thailand, and they were preparing for another European visit later this year.

The Water women of Gaua in action

Walking back to my bungalow in the darkness, as the fruit bats flew low overhead, I reflected on my time on the island. There was still more to see, the Siri waterfall, a 120 metre drop from Lake Letas that I had only viewed from the air but wanted to trek to, and the Qwat Dance, the men's answer to the women's water music, performed in secret spots in the bush in elaborate costumes and headdresses.

That could only mean one thing, I have to return to Gaua to spend more time there, even if I only come again for the food. How can you not fall in love with an island where lobster is cheaper than chicken.

(Abridged versions of this article appeared in Issue 21 of *Island Life Magazine* in 2015, and in issue 72 of *Island Spirit Magazine* in 2015)

Prince Philip is a God. Tanna

Being chased as we leave Yakel village

Hidden deep in the bush in central Tanna are many villages that are closed to outsiders and follow traditional (Kastom) ways, despite the ever encroaching technology of mobile phones and DVD players. As with most villages they are self sufficient in food and only rarely pop into Lenakel for the odd luxury. Although to call Lenakel a town may be something of a stretch. It has only one street, a very active market, a number of small shops, a post office and a small Air Vanuatu office.

Down a rutted and difficult to drive bush track about 20 kms from Lenakel lie the villages of Yaohnanen and Yakel. They are most famous for regarding Prince Philip, the consort of the British monarch Queen Elizabeth II, as a god. Just like the Cargo Cult believers in southern Tanna, these villagers have a totally different, and fascinating belief system. How did this come about?

Anthropologists believe that it was a marriage of several beliefs, both traditional from kastom life, and from new experiences from the missionaries in the eighteenth and nineteenth centuries, and the colonial powers that followed. The ancient belief is that a powerful spirit figure would leave Tanna and marry a powerful women far, far away, before returning and helping the villagers. With the arrival of the missionaries on the island, at least the ones that avoided being eaten, preaching of a return to earth by a messiah, and then the locals seeing the veneration shown by the British colonial government for the Queen and her husband, the powerful spirit figure became represented by Prince Philip.

The villagers of Yaohanenen like to keep themselves to themselves, but the neighbouring village of Yakel welcomes visitors. In the main hut which also serves as a retreat for the men to drink kava when it is raining, is a dusty and faded photograph of the Prince in a broken frame. He, or rather his office, has been in regular communication with his supporters on the island and has sent several photographs, including one where he is pictured with a club for killing pigs that the villagers sent as a present.

The villagers are extremely friendly and put on regular dances for tourists beneath a dominating banyan tree in the centre, and sell wooden statues of the ancient spirits after the show (sadly none look like the Prince). They live a very traditional life, with no electricity (although solar panels are encroaching nearby), and banana leaves for carpet and kapok for mattresses. They looked extremely comfortable and replacing them was easy from the forest around, with no need for washing machines to clean sheets. And those that I talked to were very content, again proving money and possessions do not necessarily increase happiness.

Despite their beliefs being challenged in a somewhat tabloid manner by a UK television show, which brought some of the Tannaese to London to try to get an audience with the Prince (not surprisingly, and maybe thankfully, this did not happen), they strongly believe that the Prince is spirit of their ancient god and that he will return. Despite the occasional royal visit –Princess Anne came on a private trip in 2014 but did not visit the villages – he has yet to come. The Prince is getting on in years, but there is still time for him to visit his believers. Whether he would stay and lead them, as is their fervent wish, is more debatable.

Living by Solar Power and Bartering. Ambrym

The tribal Tam Tam gong in the centre of the village

Alarm clocks are unnecessary on Ambrym. If it was not the cockerels sensing 4AM was a good time to test their lungs, then the pigs scrabbling and fighting beneath my hut ensured sleep was over.

Smoke from fires for boiling kettles and cooking breakfast was already hanging over the small settlement as I wandered sleepily looking for a pig to remonstrate with. Behind my hut was a beautifully carved Tam Tam (aka a Slit Gong), an Ambrym statue that was there to ward off evil and was used as a communication device, being hit with sticks to communicate from settlement to settlement both news and warnings.

There is no electricity at Craig Cove, apart from what is produced by solar, resulting in houses having many large batteries to provide power for TV and DVD players. The local Telecom company, Digicel, has cleverly provided solar powered mobile phones, which you see charging in rows in the bright sunshine wherever you walk.

Breakfast was tasty free range eggs and freshly baked bread. Perfect for getting me ready for the climb tomorrow. I had come to Ambrym to climb Mt Benbow, one of the most destructive volcanos in the world.

A huge Plinian explosion 2000 years ago resulted in a massive caldera, which occupies much of the centre of the island, and it is active, with its last major eruption in 1913 causing the evacuation of the whole island to Efate.

The village of Mele, 5kms from Port Villa is still a transplanted Ambrym village, populated by those who decided not to return to the dangers of villages built around the edge of a volcano.

Walking around the small settlement I was followed by dogs and small children. Vegetable crops and fruit were planted everywhere, the fertile soil being the devil's bargain of living on an active volcano. Barter was the major currency for food, as locals swapped yams for bread. Fruit was everywhere and plentiful, ripe bananas often lying on the ground providing useful dog snacks for my followers.

Services were also bartered in the community without any Vatu (the local currency of Vanuatu) changing hands. If you needed help building or repairing a house there was always someone to help. With the understanding that help would be returned when it was needed. This was a very traditional, close knit society, where people would not be poor or hungry.

Those that did have money would travel to Port Vila and buy luxuries, but these were shared on their return, with many families joining together to watch DVDs.

The one shop on the edge of the village did not seem to be that busy, only selling a few luxuries like canned tuna and cheap plastic cooking implements. Chinese run, like so many shops in obscure outposts of the Pacific, the owner looked lonely. Sadly, the only thing I wanted was not available, Vanuatu Tusker beer was not available on the island I was told. Although Ambrym is not a dry island: this being Vanuatu, there is always plenty of kava.

Solar chargers for mobile phones at midday

Small Nambas and Big Statues. Wala

The Small Nambas of Wala perform a ceremonial dance

Wala is a small island, a short ferry ride off the north eastern tip of Malekula, its much larger neighbour. The island is a curious mix of Malekula and Ambrym, with Tam Tam statues making an appearance in most villages, while the islanders themselves wear a small Namba leaf penis sheath. Namba in Bislama means Number, an oblique reference to the penis, and their traditional costume proudly shows off their small Nambas, albeit surrounded by a healthy amount of flowers from a native tree.

In northern Malekula the locals wear big Nambas, and there is great rivalry between the two groups, which in the past resulted in fighting and the eating of the vanquished, as cannibalism was rife. The small Nambas celebration of a smaller male organ size is a welcome antithesis to current western cultural obsessions.

The custom dances are both colorful and noisy, with Tam Tams being used as drums, and fire, and the island itself is a great place to explore. Wandering into the hilly interior I was warmly welcomed by the locals, as I stumbled along tiny paths into their small villages. Each time I was offered bananas, which seemed to grow everywhere, and the ubiquitous kava to drink.

Wala has largely been undisturbed by tourism, until P&O Cruises, part of the global Carnival Corporation, started visiting a couple of years ago. Cruises only arrive four times a year, which has boosted the local economy, and also those of Malekula and Ambrym, as stall holders descend on Wala from the surrounding islands on cruise days. Tourists are seen as somewhat strange, with most wanting to only paddle and swim in the warm water where the tenders drop them off, with many not even leaving the ship, but the money they bring has helped pay school fees for some families.

Not all have benefited from this sudden influx of money. As the Australian TV network SBS reported in 2013 in the program 'Vanuatu's Broken Dreams', the large cruise landing fees seem to have disappeared, and ended up in Port Vila bank accounts, and there are now land disputes over who should get what percentage of the cruise fees at the landing stage. This has resulted in an, at least temporary, end to cruise ship visits to Wala.

Perhaps the most bizarre story to emerge from the sudden and occasional influx of tourists is the construction of the modern amenity building near the beach. This has fresh clean water, and warm showers, and also uses a significant amount of the available water on the island. The building was funded entirely by Australian Aid, and was initially seen as a great gift and a major improvement to the lives of the locals where easy access to pumped clean water is difficult, and warm showers are unknown. Unfortunately, the building is locked for most of the year, and only opens when a cruise ship arrives, which does not even happen at this current time.

The lack of cruise ship passengers does return Wala to a beautiful and serene island. As all the locals live inland you feel like a modern day Robinson Crusoe as you walk around the beautiful beaches, and sip on the coconuts that litter the ground.

Making fire as part of a Harvest ceremony on Wala

Thunder from the Earth. Ambrym

The route taken to climb to the crater. Note the bare foot of the guide

My host booked the car for 5:00AM, the local pigs removed any need for my alarm clock. When I say the car, I mean literally "The Car". West Ambrym had only one small truck operating. This could make for a problem if it ever broke down, but that was not something I thought of at this time.

The Blue Ute arrived on time, and drove me from Craig Cove to Yaotille, an even smaller village about 8km away. The roads were wonderful, muddy, rutted, and criss-crossed by streams coming down from the volcanoes, but surrounded on both sides by lush vegetation.

I was glad I was in the cabin, as this afforded a little more comfort via the seat and stabilizers. In the open back of the Ute, where we had already gathered 2 locals off to other villages, the bouncing would have made life quite difficult.

I got out at Yaotille, grabbing my one man tent and backpack, and waited by a Tam Tam as the driver went off to find Bae Willpen. Bae was a local guide who would take tourists to climb Mt Benbow, if they were mad enough.

A tall, thin man emerged from a hut and shook my hand. We quickly agreed a price (12,000 Vatu, about $120 US) and then went to a small hut near the centre of the village. This was the community shop, packed full of bananas, yams and various other root vegetables. We loaded up on supplies and jumped back in the Ute for a short 4km drive to a black volcanic stream.

Grabbing our bags and tents we jumped out and started to walk on the volcanic ash river, created by flash floods coming down from the volcano. The fine black ash of the dry river bed contrasted vividly with the lush green vegetation all around. Apart from ash getting blown everywhere, the walk was straightforward. I was already thinking this was easier than I expected.

Walking on black volcanic ash is not as easy as it looks. Initially it was hard and compacted and like walking on a footpath, but soon it became loose and feet could disappear to above the ankle. The ground was still flat, but after about an hour we started to climb and the ash ended, being replaced by lava and mud.

The weather also changed, Mt Benbow had its own weather system, which seemed to vary between torrential rain and burning sun. I would get soaked to the skin and then dry out in minutes. Thunder and lightning could be seen above the distant rim of the volcano, and the white billowing smoke from its heart could be seen blowing out to sea to the west.

Walking into the muddycanyons

The climb became harder, the ground was slippery and we had to climb and descend old lava flows and canyons created by floods. There was little or no vegetation any more, and bird life had ceased. I focused on the music on my mp3 player to motivate me to climb, the more aggressive songs the better, songs by the band 'The Damned' in particular helped me keep one foot in front of the other. By mid-day the heat from the tropical sun was intense, and the sudden thunder and downpours were a relief, although there was no shelter. We stopped every half an hour, drank water and talked.

Bae was an experienced guide, telling me he did this trip maybe once or twice a month, and his last group had been filming for National Geographic. He had to carry his own pack, and heavy camera equipment, as the team struggled to climb the trail. He had not lost anyone, yet, although had come close when a tourist had lost his footing climbing the crater and had slipped sixty metres over sharp lava and rocks, resulting in a broken leg and many abrasions. Bae carried him on his back the 12 kms to the road, and an air ambulance was organised. I now paid more attention to my foot placement.

We reached the camp site and began to erect our tents. Bae suddenly cried out with joy. He had a found a fresh lava bomb (a piece of lava that has solidified in the shape of a tear as it was flung out of the volcano). I was told these were extremely useful for black magic ceremonies. As happy as I was for him, I was more concerned about one or more of these landing on my tent in the night.

Sleeping on a ridge next to an active volcano was an experience I will never forget. Mt Benbow in Ambrym was noisy all night long. There would be a period of silence, and then it would make a rumbling noise like thunder, which shook the ground, before subsiding to silence again.

It was the ground shaking I was not used to. I have experienced a few earthquakes in both Tokyo, and Port Vila in Vanuatu, but these were one-off events, and the shaking lasted for less than 30 seconds. But this was continuous. Mt Benbow was displaying its power, and also its beauty, as the warm orange glow of its lava lake lit up the sky above us.

In the early morning, the volcanic rumblings were overshadowed by an intense tropical thunderstorm, which flooded the single man tents we were in. I could not tell which was thunder and which was the volcano rumbling.

It was 4AM, sleep was now impossible. We decided to collapse the tents and store them to be picked up on our return journey, as we walked to the rim of the volcano. Fresh lava bombs lay on the path to the top, a constant reminder to stay alert and watch the volcano and sky at all times.

The climb to the crater was hard. Climbing canyons and lava flows are one thing, clambering up a crater with nothing to grab onto (oh, how I missed those tree roots) on a slippery ash based surface is another.

I had walked up mountain sides with scree before, but scree is made up of small rocks and gives your feet more grip than the tiny particles of ash.

The scenery was bleak, volcanic acid rain had removed all vegetation, and it was 15C colder than the coast.

I was struck with that awful panic feeling, with butterflies in the stomach as I crouched, pushing my back almost to a horizontal position, placing each foot carefully one in front of the other as we did some serious climbing. One slip would mean serious injury with massive drops on either side.

The winds felt gale force and the torrential rain was returning which all added to my instability. The grip on my Aussie Blundstone boots gave me some confidence, until I saw that Bae had taken off his old flip flops, stuffed them in his bag, and was climbing over this surface bare foot. He was also traveling at twice my speed.

Looking into the Mt Benbow crater

There was a strange feeling of emptiness. There was no animal or visible insect life. It was just black ash on rock, with a lingering smell of sulphur. In this huge caldera we were the only people climbing. It was not peak season, when maybe 5 people or more a day might attempt the ascent.

The bellowing smoke obscured the lava lake in the inner crater, with only occasional glimpses of the lava being possible. The noise was tremendous, the sound was similar to massive waves breaking on the shore, and then being sucked back out to sea again, as the lava moved backwards and forwards in its crater.

We stayed up there watching, listening and enjoying the activity and noise, before reluctantly starting the walk back out of the caldera. The volcano had one last surprise for us, as we left the rim a huge explosion occurred, the ground shaking, and smoke and lava being thrust high into the air. We watched the arc of the lava bombs as they cooled, moving as if in slow motion, before they succumbed to gravity and hit the side of the outer crater.

Recommended Reading

Crispin Howarth, Kirk Huffman – Kastom, Arts of Vanuatu. *(NGA, 2013)*

A coffee table sized tome, full of wonderful pictures from the Vanuatu art collections in the National Gallery of Australia, focusing mainly on Ambrym and Malekula.

Sethy John Regenvanu - Laef blong Mi: From Village to Nation *(USP, 2004)*

The father of the current high profile politician, and possible future leader, Ralph Regenvanu, details the change from colonial backwater to independent nation, with great insights into life under the colonial powers. He does get a little bit technical when discussing the details of creating the institutions for the new government, but overall it provides one of the best Ni-Vanuatu sources for the relatively recent history of the birth of the nation of Vanuatu.

Richard Shears – The Coconut War: Vanuatu and the struggle for Independence. *(Kindle 2014)*

Entertaining introduction to the period of island conflict prior to independence. The author, an Australian journalist, arrives in a Pacific paradise, and looks hard to find any sign of trouble. Eventually he meets with Jimmy Stevens and, ever so briefly, finds himself in a war zone. Both humorous and also provides a good western overview of the crisis prior to the formation of Vanuatu.

Paul Theroux – The Happy Isles of Oceania *(Putnam 1992)*

Theroux spends most time on Tanna on his Pacific Island paddling adventure, encountering John Frum followers and fishermen from Futana. Written in typical Theroux acerbic style, he realises early on how civilised Vanuatu is today, as "multiple copies of my books (are) displayed in Port Vila Public Library".

Darrell Tryon – Let's Talk Bislama – Evri samting yu wantem save long Bislama be yu fraet tumas blong askem. *(Media Masters, 1982)*

An amusing book and it provides easy lessons on learning Bislama, the title in English is; 'Everything you wanted to know about Bislama but were afraid to ask'. Hard to get outside of Vanuatu, but copies can be found in Port Vila.

Martin Johnson – Cannibal Land, Adventures with a camera in the New Hebrides. *(Houghton Mifflin, 1922)*

Fascinating insight into life in what was then the New Hebrides from the pen, and lens, of an American adventurer. Obviously, of its time before political correctness was invented, and somewhat exaggerated in the dangers he faced, but the photographs beautifully record life in the islands a hundred years ago. Can be read online at The Open Library.

Translation from the Quick Guide to Bislama Chapter.

Please do not throw rubbish all around the Saralan Stage area. Alcohol and kava are prohibited, please respect this area. Thank you so much for all your co-operation.

Useful Links

Vanuatu Tourist Office: http://vanuatutravel.info/

Air Vanuatu: http://www.airvanuatu.com/

Vanuatu Weather and Tides: http://www.meteo.gov.vu/

Volcanic Activity and Warnings: http://www.geohazards.gov.vu/

Vanuatu Government: https://governmentofvanuatu.gov.vu/

Positive Earth Guide to Vanuatu: http://www.positiveearth.org/bungalows/explorer.htm

Shefa Province Tourism: https://www.facebook.com/ShefaTourism/

Malampa Province Tourism: http://www.malampa.travel/

CIA Factbook Vanuatu: https://www.cia.gov/library/publications/the-world-factbook/geos/nh.html

Yachting guide to Vanuata: https://issuu.com/vanuatucruising.info/docs/all_ports_lead_to_vanuatu

Vanuatu Cultural Centre in Port Vila: http://vanuatuculturalcentre.vu/

Vanuatu Daily Post: http://dailypost.vu/

Yu Mi Toktok Stret News: http://www.yumitoktokstret.com/

Island Life Magazine: http://www.islandlifemag.com/

ACTIV Fair Trade in Vanuatu: http://www.activassociation.org/

A study of kava: http://www.liveibiza.com/ibiza_anthropology/champagne_ibiza_1.htm

A journey to the volcanoes in Ambrym: https://vimeo.com/78180243

Webcams in Port Vila: https://www.telsatbb.vu/Public_Cams.aspx

(you can even watch live cricket or rugby on the Independence Park stream in season!)

V

W

Y

About the Author

Simon first visited Vanuatu in 1998. The uniqueness of the islands and of the people who live there acted like a magnet, and he has been back many times since then, including living there with his family.

He has a travel addiction, loves history, active volcanoes, punk music and local food and home brewed beer. A bottle of wine and fresh bread & cheese on a beach is some of the best luxury travel out there, although he will never say no to hanging out in a five star resort.

When not travelling, he lives in the Northern Beaches of Sydney, Australia, with a similar travel addicted son, who wants to get back to the Amazon rainforests and see more monkeys, and an adventurous wife who enjoys swimming with whales as often as she can.

No pets, but various wildlife roams through his garden, from blue tongued lizards to ring tailed possums and bandicoots.

He writes for various publications including News Corp, *Island Life*, *Island Spirit*, and Louder than War, the UK music site. He contributes photographs to Getty Images, and some of his Vanuatu collection can be seen on the walls of resorts in Port Vila.

His first book, *Adventures on the Silk Road, a Guide to Turkmenistan* has become the number one travel guide to Turkmenistan on Amazon.com.

Updates on his latest travels can be found at www.farflungplaces.net and he can be contacted at simon@farflungplaces.net

Acknowledgements

This book would not have been possible without the encouragement, knowledge and tireless help of Dianne Hambrook in tropical Port Vila, and the patience and skills of my editor, Joyce Woolridge, in the colder climes of Bristol in England. Lea Dorrian in Sydney was always there for me when needed, and was supportive as ever, particularly during my long travels in Vanuatu. Tank yu tumus to all of you!!

Many other wonderful people helped me during my travels and research in Vanuatu. A big thank you goes out to the following. If I have forgotten to include your name, sori tumas.

Capt. Jan Bochenski, Pascal Guillet, Keith Hambrook, Claire Davis (Numbatu), Olivet Dorony, Anne and Eric Simmons, Daniel Ringiau, Vanuatu Tourist Office, Shefa Tourism Office, Torba Tourism Office, Malampa Tourism Office, Tafea Tourism Office, Sanma Tourist Office, Poita Morris, Elly Van Vliet, Positive Earth, Aus Aid, Babera Kaltongga, Lionel Tavunwo, Norman Taso, Charlie Tapawa, McGlen Trevor, Capt. Yan Nicholls and all at Air Vanuatu, Patricia Gil and all at Island Life Magazine, Sarah Doyle, Thomas Dick, FurtherArts, George Borugu, Almonique Wells, Ian Bani, Pulpe Waiwo, George Thompson, Janet Samuel, Adela Issachar, Jane Wright, Lucy Battaglene, TVET for Tourism, Edna Paolo, Tiffany Carroll , Sylvie Lemaire, Nikki Marshall, Susan Schulman, Des Ross, Island Spirit Magazine, Karin Ohlhauser, Kirk Huffman, Elinda Taleo, Becky Last, Lou Cochrane, Wycliff Bakeo, John Nibtick, all at Shefa Nakamal, Claire Jackson, David Jackson, Tom Robb, Christina Goulding-Robb, Jillian Greenhalgh, Emma Coll, Sarai (NumbaSeven), Alcina Charlie, Denny Stephens, Sarah Lay, Pacific Aviation Safety Office, Getty Images, Paul Lennis, Lengkon Tokan, The Guardian Newspaper, Thisara Lakshitha and Ryan Jones.

Thank you for reading, please share your comments on Amazon and GoodReads.

After Vanuatu, why not try Turkmenistan?

Review

Caravanistan (The Silk Road Travel Guide) Book Review

Published in 2014, here is finally an update to Paul Brummell's seminal effort. Based on 1 long trip through Turkmenistan, this guidebook gives good practical advice about what's important: how to visit Merv, where to find wi-fi in Ashgabat or a vegetarian meal in Mary.

The writing style is pleasant and humorous, and Proudman does not forget to add some entertaining and inspiring storytelling into the book. All in all, an excellent guidebook anyone traveling to Turkmenistan will find very useful, for an unbeatable price.